VOID

Library of
Davidson College

PATRONS AND PERFORMANCE

PATRONS AND PERFORMANCE

Early Tudor Household Revels

Suzanne R. Westfall

CLARENDON PRESS · OXFORD
1990

Oxford University Press, Walton Street, Oxford OX2 6DP
Oxford New York Toronto
Delhi Bombay Calcutta Madras Karachi
Petaling Jaya Singapore Hong Kong Tokyo
Nairobi Dar es Salaam Cape Town
Melbourne Auckland
and associated companiees in
Berlin Ibadan

Oxford is a trade mark of Oxford University Press

Published in the United States
by Oxford University Press, New York

© Suzanne R. Westfall 1990

All rights reserved. No part of this publication may be reproduced,
stored in a retrieval system, or transmitted, in any form or by any means,
electronic, mechanical, photocopying, recording, or otherwise, without
the prior permission of Oxford University Press

British Library Cataloguing in Publication Data
Westfall, Suzanne R.
Patrons and performance: early Tudor household
revels.
1. Drama in English, 1400–1558, Critical studies
I. Title   822'.2'09
ISBN 0–19–812880–0

Library of Congress Cataloging in Publication Data
Westfall, Suzanne R.
Patrons and performance: early Tudor household revels/Suzanne
R. Westfall. p. cm.
Includes bibliographical references.
1. Theater—England—History—16th century. 2. Amateur theater—
England—History—16th century. 3. Authors and patrons—England.
4. England—Nobility—History—16th century. 5. Aristocracy in
literature. I. Title.
PN2590.C66W48 1990
792'.0941'09031—dc20   89-22920
ISBN 0–19–812880–0

Typeset by Cambrian Typesetters, Frimley, Surrey
Printed and bound in
Great Britain by Bookcraft Ltd,
Midsomer Norton. Bath

To Irene and Charles Westfall
and
To Steven Putzel

For some of us it is performance, for others, patronage. They are two sides of the same coin, or, let us say, being as there are so many of us, the same side of two coins. Don't clap too loudly—it's a very old world.

> *Rosencrantz and Guildenstern Are Dead*,
> Tom Stoppard

Acknowledgements

Many people assisted me in the research and writing of this study. For their assistance both in person and by post, I would like to thank Mr D. H. G. Bourke of the British Library, Ms J. Rose of the National Register of Archives, Ms Ann Morton of the Public Record Office, Ms Patricia Gill of the West Sussex Record Office, and the staff of the London Institute for Historical Research. I am grateful to Lord Egremont for permission to reprint ground-plans of Wressle.

My work would have been considerably more difficult were it not for the extensive materials and supportive researchers at the University of Toronto's Records of Early English Drama project. Credit, or blame, should also be extended to Dr Ian Lancashire, who first encouraged my interest in court revels, then became a patient and painstaking taskmaster for the first draft of the study.

My debt to the many scholars and critics of early English drama is reflected in the select bibliography rather than in lengthy footnotes, which might inconvenience the reader. I have tried to compress the footnotes, relying on surnames for sources and appendices for extended explanations. Those who desire more or more detailed information on the various topics I raise here will find important works listed at the end of the study. Because it is selective, the bibliography is but a pale reflection of many years, many pages, and many minds. Although I do not include extended footnotes each time I begin a discussion, I am aware of, and grateful to, those who have blazed the trails before me.

Thanks are also due to various programmes and people at Lafayette College. The Committee on Advanced Study and Research generously provided funds for research, travel, and illustration collection; the Skillman Library staff has been tremendously efficient in persuading other libraries to lend rare sources; my colleagues have been unflagging in their interest and assistance, particularly Dr James Woolley and

Dr James Lusardi, who will find various of their suggestions incorporated here.

Finally, my family has threatened, proof-read, criticized, edited, and encouraged me at the appropriate moments. Without Steven, master of my revels, the fabric of this vision might, like the substantial pageants themselves, have melted into thin air.

S. W.

Contents

	ILLUSTRATIONS	xiii
	ABBREVIATIONS	xiv
	INTRODUCTION	1
1.	THE CHAPEL	13
	Administration and Facilities	14
	Performance: Plays, Pageants, and Disguisings	28
	Play Texts	49
2.	THE MINSTRELS	63
	Heraldic Minstrels	64
	Soloists	74
	Consorts: Resident and Travelling	81
	Minstrels in Performance	94
3.	PLAYWRIGHTS AND PLAYERS	108
	Playwrights	114
	Players: Duties and Privileges	122
	Players and Household Administration	128
	The Advantages of Patronage	134
	Touring	140
4.	PLAYS	152
	Characterizations	157
	Structures	170
	Ideologies	180

CONCLUSION   200

APPENDICES
A. Size of Itinerant Player Troupes   210
B. Solo Instrumentalists   213
C. Recorded Movements of Patronized Troupes   216
D. Biographical Notes   220

SELECT BIBLIOGRAPHY   243

INDEX   259

Illustrations

1. Ground-plan of Wressle (*c*.1600)	19
2. Second storey of Wressle	20
3. Third storey of Wressle	21
4. (a) Plan of Smithills Hall, Lancashire	24
(b) Plan of Agecroft Hall, Lancashire	25
(c) Plan of Woodlands Manor, Wiltshire	25
5. Plan of Haddon House, Derbyshire	26
6. 'The Martyrdom of St Apollonia' by Jean Fouquet	29
7. Ivory carving of 'The Siege of the Castle of Love'	40
8. Minstrels at table	82
9. John of Gaunt and the King of Portugal at dinner	90
10. Map of Conjectural Touring Routes	146–7
11. Title-page of *Roman Comique* by William Haithorne	148
12. 'Sir Henry Unton's Wedding'	204

Abbreviations

Arch.	*Archaeologia*
BJRL	*Bulletin of the John Rylands Library*
BL	British Library
Bodl.	Bodleian Library
Collier	Collier, *The Household Book of John, Duke of Norfolk and Thomas, Earl of Surrey*
EDC	Murray, *English Dramatic Companies*
EES 1/2/3	Wickham, *Early English Stages*, 3 vols.
EETS	Early English Text Society
Eg.	Egerton
EHR	*English History Review*
ELN	*English Language Notes*
ELR	*English Literary Renaissance*
EM	*Early Music*
ES	Extra Series
Hall	Hall, *The Vnion of the Two Noble and Illustre Famelies of Lancastre and Yorke*
Harl.	Harleian
HMC	Historical Manuscripts Commission
HMSO	Her Majesty's Stationery Office
JEGP	*Journal of English and German Philology*
Lans.	Lansdowne
L & P HVIII	Brewer et al., *Letters and Papers, Foreign and Domestic, of the Reign of Henry VIII*
MLN	*Modern Language Notes*
MM	Bullock-Davies, *Menestrellorum Multitudo*
MS 1/2	Chambers, *The Mediaeval Stage*, 2 vols.
NHB	Grose, 'The Earl of Northumberland's Household Book'
NQ	*Notes and Queries*
NS	New Series
OS	Old Series

PMLA	Publications of the Modern Language Association
PQ	Philological Quarterly
PRO	Public Records Office
REEDN	Records of Early English Drama Newsletter
Register	Bullock-Davies, Register of Royal and Baronial Domestic Minstrels, 1272–1327
RES	Review of English Studies
Revels	Sanders et al., The Revels History of Drama in English: Vol. ii
RORD	Research Opportunities in Renaissance Drama
RR	Renaissance and Reformation
SOR	Great Britain Records Commission, The Statutes of the Realm
Sp.	Speculum
SP	Studies in Philology
Spain	Bergenroth and Gayangos, Calendar of Letters, Dispatches and State Papers Relating to the Negotiations between England and Spain
SS	Shakespeare Survey
Stevens	Stevens, Music and Poetry in the Early Tudor Court
The Black Book	Myers, The Household Book of Edward IV
TRP	Hughes and Larkin, Tudor Royal Proclamations
Venice	Brown and Cavendish-Bentinck, State Papers and Manuscripts Relating to English Affairs, Existing in the Archives and Collections of Venice
WANHM	The Wiltshire Archaeological and Natural History Magazine

Introduction

> And in a stage play all the people know right wel, that he that playeth the sowdayne is percase a sowter. Yet if one should can so lyttle good, to shewe out of seasonne what acquaintance he hath with him, and calle him by his owne name whyle he standeth in his magestie, one of his tormenters might hap to break his head, and worthy for marring of the play. And so they said that these matters bee Kynges games, as it were stage plays, and for the more part plaied vpon scafoldes. In which pore men be but ye lokers on. And thei yt wise be, wil medle no farther. For they that sometyme step vp and play with them, when they cannot play their partes, they disorder the play & do themself no good.
>
> Sir Thomas More, *The History of Richard III*, 80–1

Eighty-five years before Shakespeare wrote 'All the world's a stage', Sir Thomas More, with uncanny foreshadowing, pointed out the conventions and dangers of participating, as an actor or a spectator, in the 'Kynges games'; 'the more part' would indeed be 'plaied vpon scafoldes' when he diverged from the script that Henry VIII had composed. While noblemen were acting roles in the complex play of early Tudor politics, produced and directed by Henry VII and his descendants, they were also acting as patrons to players, minstrels, and a myriad of vaudeville entertainers such as bearwards, tumblers, and jugglers. The artistic splendour of the Tudor royal court has been on record since Hall composed his chronicle, yet only recently have scholars begun to explore the relationship between the patron and his theatrical productions, to examine the social, political, and aesthetic motivations that inspired such extravagant entertainments.

Sydney Anglo, in the vanguard of such studies, has meticulously analysed Tudor ceremonialia, and determined that the spectacles produced by the royal court were designed specifically to present images and themes that reinforced particular aspects of Henrican political policy. David Bevington, T. W. Craik, and Ian Lancashire, among others, have made valiant forays into the dangerous territory of political allegory, stressing the role of noble patrons in the creation and production of entertainments that reflected the aristocratic point of view. Glynne Wickham notes the remarkable homogeneity of early Tudor audiences, and examines the social and political context of later Renaissance entertainments to confirm my premiss that the propagandistic influence of patrons increased over the years. Recent scholarship is making it increasingly clear that noble patrons did not simply foot the bill for theatrical performances; rather, they influenced the form and the content of the performances offered within their households.

Consequently, when I speak of the entertainment of a noble patron, I intend a double meaning, one that can be interpreted in both the genitive and the dative sense. The patron exercised ownership over his revels, in that he ordered them and paid for them. At the same time, however, he was also the object of the revels, which were designed to glorify him by representing his ideas, his wealth, and his artistic tastes. The patron's dual role as producer and spectator formed an elaborate fugue, unarticulated in the dramatic theory of the period but omnipresent, resonating below the surface. The earliest explication of this complex contrapuntal role was suggested not by theatrical or even by musical theory, but by Serlio's theory of perspective in *Architettura* (1545), a work that influenced Inigo Jones and consequently virtually all Stuart masque. Serlio's scenery was designed to be in perfect perspective when viewed from one and only one point: the seat of the patron. In the Stuart masque, therefore, the quintessential but invisible role of the patron is concretely manifested; the bass, descant, and plainsong unite in harmony.

Just as the king staged elaborate entertainments to impress his visitors, his immediate retainers, and his subjects at large, noblemen also produced, to the best of their financial and artistic means, performances that would entertain and influence their allies and subject populations. Within the great households, Tudor noblemen exploited a number of different types of entertainers to attain these goals. They commissioned plays and disguisings that could delight the eye and ear while selectively educating the mind and soul. They welcomed travelling performers, who brought news and novelties from other lands and other households. They also sent forth their own artistic emissaries as player and minstrel troupes. Since the great household was the genesis of these various activities, it is surprising that early Tudor theatre has never been considered from the perspective of these unique sources of information. This study will begin an exploration long overdue, considering the performers involved in household revels, as well as the form and content of their performances, in order to emphasize the artistic and theoretical sophistication of early Tudor drama.

The noble court drama is here examined within its sociological context, to demonstrate that the structures and styles of these theatrical forms were influenced by the social and political concerns of the select audiences for whom they were intended. These influences encouraged a complex blending of multimedia effects, including music, dance, allegory, and visual spectacle, which challenges the notion, too common among modern readers, that pre-Shakespearian theatre was simplistic and crudely didactic. Since we no longer share a common *Weltanschauung* with our Renaissance forebears, it is often easy to overlook structures and ideas that were significant to them, but seem trivial or even bewildering to us. This ever-increasing chasm between the entertainments' two historicities (the context at the time of composition and the context at the time of reception) has consistently impeded critical understanding of the revels. While theatre historians have been energetic in tracing changes in conventions and theatrical styles, we have neglected to consider the more subtle implications of changes in expectation horizons, perhaps because reception theory is still in relative infancy, because we have only meagre snippets of documentation to support our conjectures, and because audience response is notoriously difficult to measure at any time or place. Nevertheless, if we hope to appreciate the complex purposes and aesthetics of early Tudor revels, we must gather what evidence we can and make an effort to adjust our own horizons to theirs.

The lack of contextual understanding has been particularly damaging to our appreciation of the disguising or masque, an exceedingly popular form which appears to have died out (albeit in a blaze of Jonsonian and Jonesian glory), after the seventeenth century. Perhaps theatre historians have neglected this form because it appears to have found refuge in the ballet or opera. It is more likely, however, that the disguising has been given short shrift because it is ephemeral, a performance text without a dramatic text that often leaves critics searching madly for tools with which to interpret non-linguistic signs. In addition, the disguising was an élite, occasional form of drama that did not find frequent expression in the public theatre. Consequently, the theoretical influence of the masque upon the evolution of English drama can be easily, but mistakenly, dismissed.

In order to explore these ideas, this study is divided into four chapters. Each of the first three considers a particular kind of performing group retained by the patron of a great household, tracing the evolution of the group, its relationship to the household it served, and its function within that household. Different groups were expected to produce different types of entertainments, usually determined, of course, by the specific talents and expertise of the groups, but also affected by such factors as the ages of the entertainers, their availability, and their status within the household structure.

Chapter 1 is concerned with the Chapel Gentlemen and Children, who, during the reign of Elizabeth I, proved to be worthy competitors of the adult companies. These clerk-players performed both scriptural and secular plays, as well as elaborate disguisings for their patrons. Examination of the particular theatrical talents of the Chapel, and analysis of the entertainments it was known to have performed, indicate that some techniques of great household Chapel performance were absorbed into the interlude structure.

Chapter 2 concentrates upon the minstrels within the great households, showing how ceremonial and incidental music was integrated with visual and rhetorical elements to produce plays and disguisings. Ambiguous terminology in the extant records has long blurred the distinction between minstrel and player; yet while we blithely assume that all Tudor actors sang and danced, we rarely consider Tudor minstrels as actors in entertainments. Although it is accepted that their music was necessary—but tangential—to the theatrical performance, period accounts indicate that minstrels were visually and thematically integrated within the performances, and that they may have produced independent entertainments.

Chapter 3 begins by discussing the authors of some extant early Tudor texts. Playwrights such as Bale, Skelton, Medwall, Heywood, and many whose names are now lost were closely associated with one, and sometimes more than one, noble patron. As should be expected, the scripts these men composed reflected not only their own philosophies, but also the ideas of the aristocrats with whom they were associated. In addition, these men also served as schoolmasters (as John Skelton did for Prince Henry), enabling them to study and adapt classical structures used for school exercises, to influence students who would be assuming positions in churches and noble households throughout the land, and to experiment with new styles and themes with relative impunity behind school walls.

The men who actually communicated these texts, the players, are, in almost all cases, impossible to identify. Although their identities were not important enough to record, at least in the minds of medieval and early Renaissance scribes, the player troupe's connection with a noble patron was generally considered important information. Chapter 3 continues by examining the relationship between aristocratic courts and the players they retained, presuming that understanding the motivation behind such retention may indicate why the nobleman's name was considered so crucial.

My last chapter concerns the texts of early Tudor interludes, analysing their characters, structures, and themes from the perspective of the private auspices (including great households, ecclesiastical households, schools, and Inns of Court) under which they were performed. Almost without exception, the early Tudor interludes portray noble characters involved in struggles and expressing dialectics of specific interest to élite audiences. As Wickham notes, such audiences were more able and more inclined to experiment, both by education and security, than were their counterparts in the public theatres.[1] Furthermore, the dramatic structures of the interludes, considered by many modernists and post-modernists to be boringly simplistic and didactically predictable, were actually part of a conscious plan to inculcate a firm acceptance for the ideology of social concepts of hierarchy, retention, and ceremony, by using these very things as patterns for dramatic development. My focus here is on the early Tudor interludes current from 1485 to 1558, though I do make reference to plays from before and after this period. I do not intend this study to be another 'roots of Shakespeare' exercise; rather I make reference to plays more familiar to the general reader in order to illustrate the continuity of early Tudor aesthetics, events, and experiments.

Reconstruction of these great household performances is difficult because of the nature of the source materials. When sorted, compiled, and fused, the financial accounts of the aristocratic households form a skeletal system. Just as fossilized bones provide fundamental clues to the palaeontologist about the external attributes of extinct beasts, so household accounts provide basic details about the existence and day-to-day lives of retained performers. These details, pieced together and compared with other noble and royal household accounts, suggest typical structures for household entertainments, which can then be examined systematically. Unfortunately, these accounts are scattered throughout the country, buried in local repositories, hibernating in private archives, and perhaps hidden away in unknown hoards; some have been collected in the Public Record Office and in local Record Offices, and a few have found refuge in the British Library, but even these are perfunctorily catalogued and poorly, if at all, edited. Many are damaged or have deteriorated, and most are unindexed, forcing the researcher to pore through countless listings of expenditures for 'pane' and 'vino' to extract the rare morsels that refer to performers

[1] Wickham, *EES 3*, 223.

or performances. This search may seem tedious, but it rewards the persevering reader with a unique view of the daily operations of the complex corporations known as great households, and shows how integral a part of the households the entertainers were.

Prescriptive accounts, or household books of ordinances and regulations, provide the viscera and musculature for theatrical reconstruction. *The Black Book* of Edward IV and the *Second Northumberland Household Book*[2] delineate the privileges and duties of various household members, including theatrical performers. These books also dictate the administrative details that accompany the theatrical events, such as the organization of the household for the occasion, the sequence of events, and the placement of the physical 'set' and properties in the performance space. Since these orders were designed to be guidelines for the household's servants, to be followed when the occasion arose, they are general in nature, omitting specific details of any particular occasion in order to be generally useful, preserving the form and structure but not the content of household revels.

The external façade, the dermis and dress of the recreated event is provided by the more vivid descriptive accounts in chronicles and in letters. Hall's *Chronicle* and Leland's *Collectanea* preserve eyewitness accounts of many entertainments, but also have many drawbacks. Since they are subjective accounts, they often concentrate on details of interest to the chronicler, such as the identities of the audience members, while omitting details of interest to the theatre historian, such as the title, theme, or nature of the play. Descriptions of theatrical events by audience members, preserved in the letters and papers of foreign diplomats and in the letters and papers of Henry VII and Henry VIII,[3] are similarly subjective, and often politically biased; nevertheless, these accounts provide visual and auditory details that financial accounts and ordinances lack. Unfortunately, these descriptive accounts are generally restricted to observations

---

[2] Hereafter referred to as NHB and *The Black Book*.
[3] Hereafter cited as *L & P HVIII*; *The Calendar of Letters, Dispatches and State Papers Relating to the Negotiations between England and Spain* is hereafter cited as *Spain* and the *State Papers and Manuscripts Relating to English Affairs, Existing in the Archives and Collections of Venice* is hereafter cited as *Venice*.

of entertainments at the royal court—for very few descriptions of noble household revels survive for the early Tudor period. These royal court performances, however, provide models for similar revels conducted in smaller courts.

When assembled, all these historical source materials contribute to the recreation of the dramatic form. Yet the body cannot be truly resurrected without a soul; this is formed by literary allusions, the most interesting, yet the most elusive and tenuous, observations about great household performers and their techniques. Many playwrights such as Medwall, Shakespeare, and Jonson include imaginative examples of great household performances within their dramatic texts, often indulging in comments, both caustic and complimentary, about early Renaissance performers. These comments flesh out the information preserved in financial accounts, descriptions, and ordinances, providing the emotional, philosophical, and theoretical details which conjure up the human qualities that other records neglect. In addition, characters and stage directions in the interludes show how performers such as minstrels and Chapel Children participated in plays. Since no objective, analytic, or critical accounts of these practices survive, the literary references and analogues are rare and valuable indications of early Renaissance theatrical conventions.

No study of early Tudor drama can ignore the contributions of the many scholars and critics who have examined these materials. Edmund K. Chambers, Glynne Wickham, Sydney Anglo, John Payne Collier, the Malone Society, and the Records of Early English Drama project have collected and edited valuable primary source references to performers. Countless critics have analysed the records, the plays, and the historical materials to weave individual threads together into a vivid tapestry that grows more colourful and more detailed each year. David Bevington, T. W. Craik, Alan Nelson, Richard Southern, and many others have examined Tudor theatre from various aspects and each has influenced my thoughts about early Tudor theatre.

Although this study makes reference to many great households of the medieval and Renaissance eras, it concentrates primarily on five early Tudor families: the royal households of Henry VII and Henry VIII; the northern household of Henry Algernon Percy, fifth Earl of Northumberland; the East Anglian households of the Howards, dukes of Norfolk; the Gloucestershire household of Edward Stafford, third Duke of Buckingham; and the households of the de Veres, earls of Oxford. These households were selected for various reasons, including geographic location, availability of primary source materials, and social and political prominence. The revels within the royal households are, naturally, the most extensively documented and also serve as models for other aristocratic households, since the king set the fashion of the day. Household accounts for the Percys, Howards, Staffords, and de Veres have been printed,[4] whereas household accounts for many other aristocratic households have been destroyed, or have not been properly collected. The Percys, Howards, Staffords, and de Veres also represent four of the wealthiest and most influential families under the Tudor monarchy, so their household activities are not only better documented than most, but are also more extensive than those of other great households, who could perhaps not afford such frequent or expensive entertainments. In addition, these families represent various regions of England. All had close connections with the king and responsibilities to him, and consequently spent a great deal of time at the royal court, performing their duties and observing royal household revels. Yet they all headed independent households of their own, and retained various entertainers to produce performances that reflected the individual tastes and ideologies of the patrons.

A great household was not a specific architectural structure; it was not a place. Rather, a great household was a collection of people assembled to serve an aristocrat in the maintenance of his person and his property. Since most Tudor noblemen owned a number of properties scattered over many miles, both he and his relatives were constrained to travel. Thus, the aristocrat formed an epicentre for a semi-itinerant company of family, bureaucrats, officers, and servants.

[4] NHB; Collier, *The Household Book of John, Duke of Norfolk and Thomas, Earl of Surrey*, hereafter cited as Collier; Rawcliffe, *The Staffords, Earls of Stafford and Dukes of Buckingham*.

The number of persons within a great household varied both from time to time and from patron to patron. For example, Henry Algernon Percy, fifth Earl of Northumberland (1478–1527), retained 166 domestic servants on a permanent basis at a cost of £1000 per annum, one-quarter of his yearly income. This number included Percy's chief household officials, such as the Chamberlain, Treasurer, and Steward, as well as henchmen (noble youths), scores of gentlemen, yeomen, grooms, clerks, chaplains, Chapel Children, minstrels, and various domestic servants. At times, the entire household would move from one property to another, for the *Northumberland Household Book* records that 17 carriages were required for transportation of personnel and 'movable stuff', such as furniture, beds, carpets, and cooking and eating utensils.[5] More often, however, the Earl travelled with an itinerant or 'riding' household numbering only 57, including his chief officers, one chaplain, and servants and clerks to care for them. When Percy travelled to collect rents and administer his various estates, or to visit other great households such as the royal court, he had no need for his entire household to accompany him, for the huge group would slow down his travel and create an incredible burden on the resources of another household with retainers of its own to support.

Other noblemen kept similarly large households. At the time of his arrest in 1546, the staff of Thomas Howard, third Duke of Norfolk, was listed as 147, including 16 gentlemen, 6 chaplains, 12 'servants of the chapel', 52 yeomen, and 61 grooms.[6] This list omits mention of clerks and domestic servants, so the full great household probably

---

[5] NHB 12, 55–6, 179, 289; Bean, *The Estates of the Percy Family*, 140. Edward IV's *Black Book* outlines the duties of the major household officials. The Chamberlain was the chief administrator, responsible for supervising all household functions, including economic and political matters as well as general housekeeping (104). The Steward acted as a sergeant-at-arms, responsible for discipline and order (142). The Treasurer or Comptroller was the chief economic official, keeping the accounts of his patron's estates and households: 'the grete charge of polycy and husbandry of all this household growth and stondyth most party by hys sad and dylygent purueyaunce . . .' (144). Another chief official, the Surveyor, was a purchasing agent, responsible for seeing that the household was provided with its necessities (113), an awesome responsibility considering the size and complexity of a noble patron's retinue. See Van Brun Jones.

[6] Williams, 15.

numbered at least 50 more. Edward Stafford, third Duke of Buckingham (1478–1521), kept a staff of 225 on his payroll, including 86 to attend his duchess, Eleanor Percy, the sister of the Earl of Northumberland. Not all these were in attendance at once; in 1521, his permanent following numbered only 148.[7]

Not all aristocrats could maintain such large households, but, as these figures indicate, many of the chief nobles of early Tudor England retained approximately 150 servants of various social degrees. The patron was responsible for providing clothes (usually in the form of livery), food, and shelter for servants while they were resident in his household. He was also expected to keep this small army under control, and to keep them loyal to himself and to his household. This was accomplished primarily through wages, but patrons also inspired loyalty through largess, by rewarding attentive servants with gifts, properties, privileges, money, feasts, and entertainment.

Thus theatre became, for the Tudor nobleman, a means to secure the loyalty of his domestic army, a loyalty that both reflected and reinforced the patron's political and economic power. Social and theatrical conventions were crucial to a society that was attempting to redefine itself, to consciously forge an identity in marked contrast to the medieval Plantagenet War of the Roses era that had preceded it. Multimedia displays were as common to public life as they were to private theatre; as Stephen Greenblatt puts it, 'Henry's [VIII] taste for lavish dress, ceremonial banquets, pageantry, masque, and festivity astonished his contemporaries and profoundly affected their conception of power.'[8] In this context, More's observations on 'Kynges Games' articulate a complex theory of performance and performance reception, a theory that will begin to close the gap between fifteenth- and twentieth-century historicities.

Tudor performers and performances were inextricably woven into the fabric of this theatre of power, but they were not ignorant of the power of theatre. Like all rituals, early Tudor household theatre provided a mythology that assisted

---

[7] Rawcliffe, 88.   [8] Greenblatt, 28.

in the social construction of a desired reality. In order to delight a household and to teach it to subscribe to particular philosophies and virtues, however, household theatre also had to appeal to the hearts and minds of its audience. Regardless of its motives and themes, drama must entertain. The entertainments of Tudor noblemen exploited any and every means at their disposal to do just that.

I
The Chapel

> What, are they children? Who maintains 'em? How are they escoted? Will they pursue the quality no longer than they can sing? Will they not say afterwards, if they should grow themselves to common players (as it is most like, if their means are no better), their writers do them wrong to make them exclaim against their own succession?
>
> *Hamlet*, II. ii. 337–44

Hamlet's barrage of questions reveals how bitterly common players felt toward the privileged child actors who, for hundreds of years, had been performing under the aegis of school, parish, and private Chapel. Together with the priests, clerks, and adult choristers, the children formed a rigidly structured, professionally trained group, responsible within noble households primarily for the religious welfare of the lord, his family, and his retainers. The Chapel was also a performing coterie, however; during the early Tudor period, household Chapels were staging sacred and secular plays, providing concerts within the context of great household banquets and religious festivals, and blending their unique talents with those of other household performers to produce disguisings. Although many scholars have examined the tradition of the child players, particularly the professional troupes of the Elizabethan period, few have concerned themselves with the role of the entire Chapel within the noble household.[1]

Eyewitness accounts of Chapel performances within these aristocratic households are virtually non-existent, although Hall provides indispensable descriptions of such activities at

---

[1] Portions of this chapter first appeared in my article 'The Chapel: Theatrical Performance in Early Tudor Great Households', *ELR* 18/2 (1988), 171–93.

the royal household. Play texts which actually stipulate Chapel performance are rare, so external evidence must be carefully considered in order to reconstruct these performances. For example, household accounts and ordinances do not describe performances, but they do delineate the composition, duties, and privileges of the Chapel, factors which determined what types of entertainment the Chapel was able and expected to perform. Also, chronicles, civic accounts, and household accounts provide some fragmentary evidence about the activities of Chapels attached to royal and ecclesiastical households, as well as to parish churches and cathedrals. Since the noble Chapels were microcosms of these organizations, such evidence also helps us understand analogous private Chapel performances. Finally, many extant Tudor play texts either bear evidence of Chapel involvement or can be positively identified as Chapel plays. Analysis of these texts reveals that the Chapel's influence upon the structure and aesthetics of early Renaissance drama has been significantly underestimated.

ADMINISTRATION AND FACILITIES

Certain distinctive characteristics of Chapel personnel, such as their rhetorical and musical expertise, their privileged position within the household hierarchy, and their liturgical responsibilities, influenced their art. Household accounts and ordinances show that keeping a resident Chapel was expensive, which was not a prohibitive factor for most ecclesiastical households, priories, or churches, where Chapels were part of the *raison d'être*, or for Tudor royal households, which could afford the expenditure. Cost did, however, concern the noble households, for although all aristocratic households retained at least one priest, not all could afford to keep a full Chapel. The Percy earls of Northumberland, the Howard dukes of Norfolk, the de Vere earls of Oxford, and the Stafford dukes of Buckingham all kept Chapels, but these men were among the most affluent and influential of the aristocracy.[2] Others, such as Sir Thomas Lovell and the Earl

---

[2] Since the Chapel did not usually tour or go on progress with its patron, a manor or castle had to be kept open to house it, even when the patron and his staff were not

of Rutland, retained a few adult clerics, but their records indicate no choristers.[3] Indeed, we have positive evidence that many wealthy nobles and gentry felt the need of their own Chapel but did not retain one. Edward Seymour, later Lord Protector, employed a professional troupe, Paul's Boys, as New Year's Day performers;[4] Paul's Boys also performed for the wedding of Sir William Petre's daughter in 1560. Lord Clinton imported an external troupe, the boys of Maxstoke Priory, at Candlemas as early as 1430.[5] Since the accounts of noblemen who retained their own Chapels do not list expenditures for external choristers, any nobleman who hired choristers on an occasional basis, or who travelled to churches or households that staged their own Chapel performances, would be unlikely to have possessed a full Chapel.

The number of men and boys employed in a resident Chapel varied, depending upon the interests and resources of the noble patron. According to *The Black Book*, Edward IV employed thirty-seven persons, eight of whom were children.[6] The fifth Earl of Northumberland's Chapel was almost as large at twenty-eight, including six children.[7] The records of

in residence. This expense, combined with expenses for room, board, and wages for the Chapel, was high, thus effectively limiting resident Chapels to the richer households. Expenditures for these Chapels are scattered throughout the household accounts of various families. For Northumberland, see NHB; for the Howards, Collier. The accounts Collier attributed to Surrey are actually de Vere's: see Tucker, 468–74. For Buckingham's accounts see Gage, 311–41, and Rawcliffe.

[3] The list of Sir Thomas Lovell's servants in 1522 includes three priests and an organ player. Rutland's in 1539 specifies four chaplains and a schoolmaster, presumably for his and his retainers' children; no Children of the Chapel are mentioned. 'Manuscripts of the Duke of Rutland', *Reports of the Historical Manuscripts Commission*, 4 (London: HMSO, 1874), 260–2; 296 ff.

[4] Jackson, 174.

[5] Petre's entertainment appears to have been a disguising. Two men were rewarded for transporting 'the chests wherein their playing garments were and instruments . . .'. Emmison, 76. Chambers suggests that Clinton's entertainment was a religious play: *MS* 2, 184.

[6] *The Black Book*, 133–6.

[7] NHB 322–3; 27. The adult members of Northumberland's Chapel included a dean, subdean, gospeller, Lady Mass priest, master of grammar, riding chaplain, almoner, six additional chaplains, and nine gentlemen. The nine gentlemen were further specified as a choirmaster, a 'pistoler', an organist, four counter-tenors, and two tenors. Later Northumberland hired two more counter-tenors because the original six adult choristers could not fulfil their duties to his satisfaction: NHB 163.

the thirteenth Earl of Oxford and the first Howard Duke of Norfolk mention payments to resident Chapels, but it is difficult to ascertain from them the exact number of Chapel employees. Oxford apparently retained twelve children, but he must have employed more than the two adults mentioned in his accounts.[8] Norfolk's Chapel included seven adults, and five to seven children. In 1526, the number of children in the Chapel Royal was fixed at twelve. Generally then, the number of children employed in the noble Chapels ranged from six to twelve. The number of adult members of the Chapel varied more considerably, since their responsibilities increased with the size of the household.[9]

The number of choristers affected the style of their performances in several ways. Primarily, the Chapel could create a more extravagant display than could the players, simply by mustering numbers. In addition, the Chapel could utilize the particular talents of both children and adults to perform entertainments that required several women (boys dressed as women) and children. Aesthetically, they could

---

[8] Collier, 510–11. Oxford's records are confusing about the number of children his Chapel employed. His will records 'xxx surples corse w^t iiij albys for children for the chapell': Hope, 300. Thirty children seems excessive; not even the Chapel Royal supported such a number. Oxford's household accounts mention a payment for 'shoryng and dyeing of ix gounnys for the chylderyn off the chapell', yet list twelve names (Collier, 510–11). The accounts mention only two adult members of the Chapel by name: Sir John Mechelson, 'mastir of the chylderyn of the chappell', and John Sergeaunt, 'on of the Chappell', (Collier, 509, 505). The reference to Sergeant as *one* of the Chapel implies that Oxford employed other adults; a Chapel with eleven or twelve children could not function properly with only two adults. A large household certainly required more than two adults to handle religious duties and the complex harmonies common to Chapel services: see Stevens, 297.

[9] Like Oxford's, Norfolk's records are imprecise about the number of Chapel personnel. In 1482/3 when the records begin, clothing for four children was bought. In July of the same year, five children were rewarded. A comparison of names listed reveals seven in total; expenditures during the following year for seven 'bonettes for chyldryn of the chappell' confirms this number; 1489/90 accounts also specify 'vij tany gowns [Norfolk's livery] for the chyldreen of the chappell . . .': Collier, 196, 344, 379, 465. The fact that Oxford's child choristers rivalled the royal household in number indicates an early interest in child players among the de Veres, an interest that is clearly demonstrated by the eighteenth Earl's extensive involvement with the Children of Blackfriars. Chapels provided four services daily: High Mass, Lady Mass, Matins, and Evensong (NHB, 367–9). It was also responsible for special services on holy days, of which the NHB specifies sixteen (198). Besides preparing and rehearsing for the services, the priests were responsible for the religious welfare of the entire household. They were empowered to dock wages and issue punishment for misbehaviour. (*The Black Book*, 135; Van Brun Jones, 184–7.)

exploit the humour inherent in the idea of a child portraying an authoritative adult figure, a folkloric tradition of overturned order that the election of the 'Boy Bishop' had been celebrating for centuries.

The Chapel had another advantage over the players: it did not have to tour in order to survive, since it was completely supported as part of the ordinary household.[10] A nobleman did not require the continuous service of a troupe of players, but early Renaissance religion and social position dictated daily service by his Chapel. Further, in order to make a tour profitable, players needed texts that had general appeal, that could be performed for any occasion, that did not depend upon a specific audience, extensive sets, or costumes. In marked contrast, the play texts of Chapel performers had none of these limitations, allowing the Chapel to perform occasional pieces, and to make specific allusions to visitors, household residents, places, or events. Since no one had to fetch the Chapel from unknown parts when an unexpected need arose, it was available to perform on short notice. All these qualities enabled the Chapel to participate extensively in disguisings.

The Chapel's musical and rhetorical training contributed significantly to the quality of its art. *The Black Book* stipulates that the King's Chapel members be 'in descant clene voysed, well relysed and pronouncyng', in addition to being 'eloquent in reding' both English and Latin. The number of antiphons and prick-song books with which the aristocracy supplied their Chapels indicates that they could read music as well, and household accounts reveal that many Chapel members could also play the organ that each Chapel possessed. Wickham believes that '... it is evident that the plays which make the fullest use of songs and music are those, as we would expect, which were composed for

---

[10] *The Black Book* clearly sets out the expenses, servants, and privileges to which the Chapel was entitled. Both *The Black Book* and NHB stipulate that the Chapel was allowed a table at dinner, a significant privilege extended only to noble members of the household and to guests. Constant references occur in household accounts to wages and livery for the Chapel, and to educational expenses for the children during and after their tenure within the household. None of these advantages was extended to players or minstrels. (NHB 322–3, 247; Van Brun Jones, 43–4; *The Black Book*, 135–7.)

occasional performance by schoolboys or students where the play-maker could anticipate easy access to trained voices and skilled instrumentalists at no extra cost.' Clearly, household performers, including Chapel men and boys, should be added to this list.[11]

Musical and rhetorical training was primarily undertaken to enhance religious services, but it was obviously an asset for household entertainments as well. The number of playwrights who were members of Chapels or closely involved with Chapel performances shows that the great households understood this relationship. Within the Earl of Northumberland's household, the almoner was a 'maker of interludes', and a chaplain, Peres or Pyers, apparently wrote for the Chapel. The subalmoner at Westminster was paid in 1526 for 'wryttyng of a play for the children'. Henry VII's Chapel Gentleman, William Cornish, senior, provided pageants for the 1501 wedding of Prince Arthur. Later playwrights, such as Redford, Heywood, Udall, and Hunnis also acted as writers and producers for entertainments by Chapel performers.[12]

The Chapel enjoyed another advantage, a specific place in which to rehearse and perform—the chapel itself. Plans of Wressle (c.1600), the seat of the Percy earls of Northumberland, show how the chapel related spatially to the rest of the castle, and include dimensions for each room. Doorways provided convenient indoor access to the Nether Chapel and to the High Chapel from the Great Hall, the Lord's Bed Chamber, and the Dining Chamber. Such access certainly

---

[11] Hope, 300. The testament mentions mass books, processionals, graduals, twenty-one prick-song books, and eight antiphoners. Norfolk paid to have a prick-song book composed or copied, and for another 'messe of prykkd song and an anthume' (Collier, 314). Northumberland's many fine service books were confiscated by Wolsey on the Earl's death, and his heir had to go to great pains to retrieve them. *The Black Book* required that Chapel Gentlemen be 'sufficiaunt in organez playyng' (p. 135). Records for the purchase and repair of organs occur in many household accounts: see, e.g. Hope, 291; Collier, 170. Wickham (*EES 3*) stresses that plays requiring complex or sophisticated music were certainly composed with performance by choristers in mind (153–4).

[12] NHB 61, 92, 97, 199. The almoner appears in the list of Chapel personnel (see n. 7); Ian Lancashire, 'Orders' at 13 n.; Anglo, 37. Redford worked with Paul's Boys: Baugh, 359. For Heywood and Udall see Chambers MS 2, 203; Feuillerat, xiv; Ellis, 273; and Wallace. Hunnis was master of the Children of the Chapel Royal 1566–97: see Crow, v–vi, and Stopes.

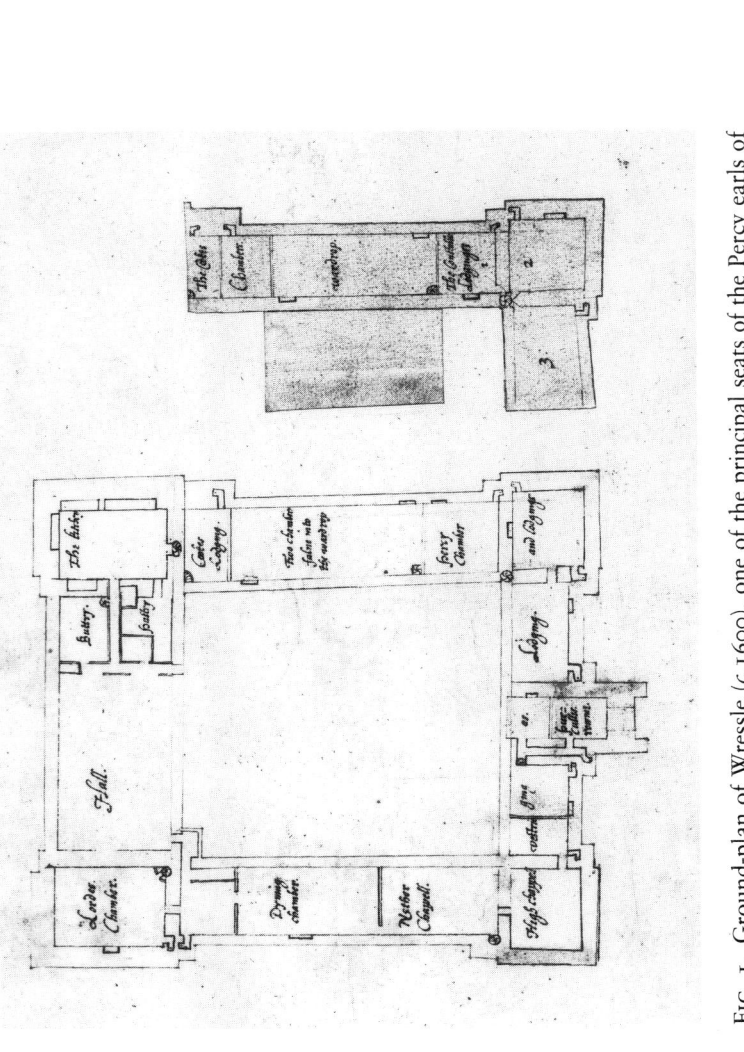

FIG. 1. Ground-plan of Wressle (c.1600), one of the principal seats of the Percy earls of Northumberland. The plan shows the playing spaces in the 'Lordes Chamber', the 'Dyning chamber', the 'Nether Chappell', and the 'High chappel' located conveniently adjacent to each other. From the West Sussex Record Office, Petworth Archives, 3538–47, reprinted by kind permission of Lord Egremont.

The Chapel

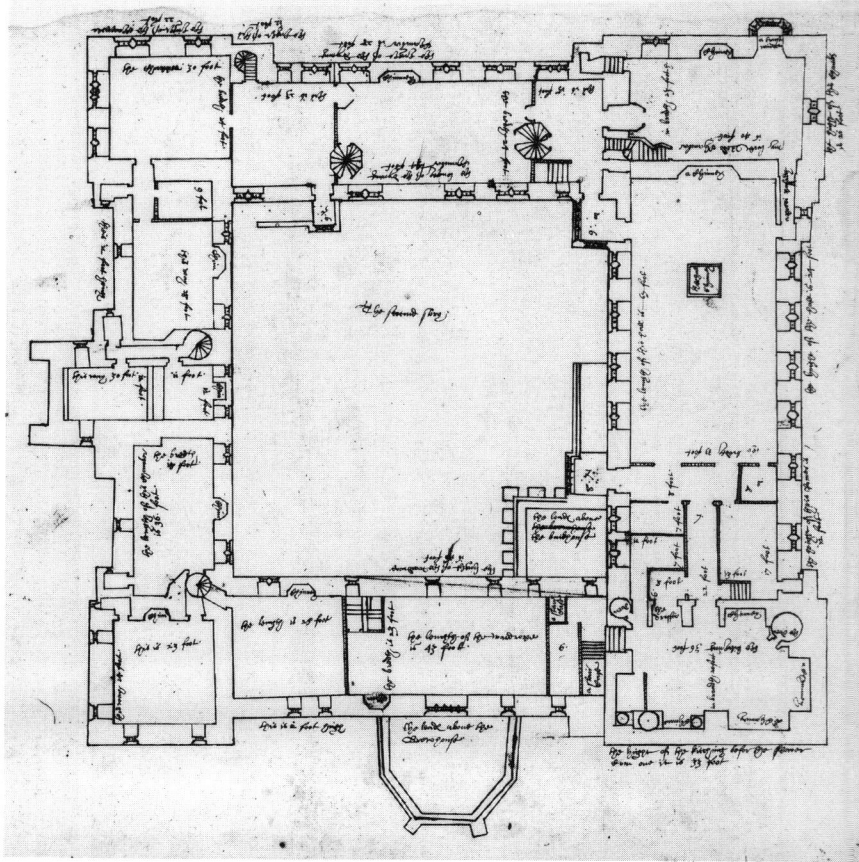

FIG. 2. The second storey of Wressle, showing the details and dimensions of the Chapel (upper left), the dining chamber (top centre), the lord's private chamber (upper right), and the great hall (right centre). Note the placement of stairways, galleries, and doorways that make the rooms adaptable playing spaces.

provided easy movement for the entire household to attend services, but, more important, it also allowed ceremonial processions through the house, and to and from the chapel. Furthermore, this spatial arrangement could permit the Chapel Children and Gentlemen to dress and arrange themselves in the chapel or vestry, then to move through the

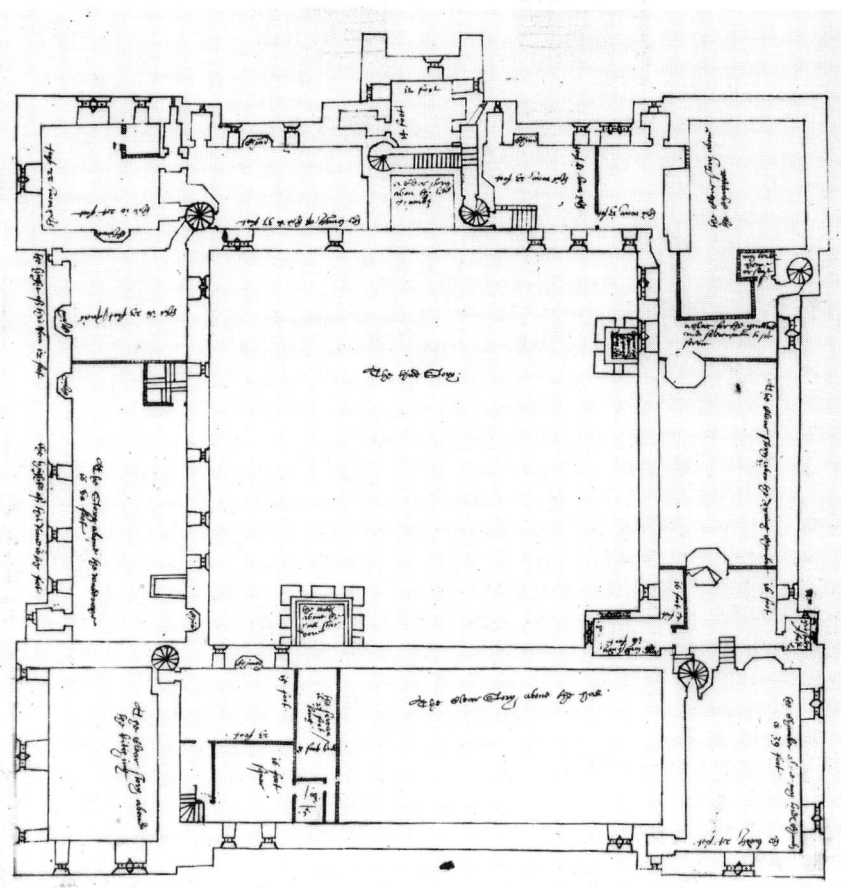

FIG. 3. The third storey of Wressle, further detailing dimensions and heights of chambers used for entertainments.

house to public performing spaces for concerts or disguisings. Just as the players would dress and enter from the kitchen, the Chapel could dress and enter from its own domain.

The largest room at Wressle was, of course, the Great Hall, which measured 63' x 33' x 24'; the hall was accessible from the Lord's private chamber both through a private passage and through a hall that connected with the Dining Chamber, allowing Percy to make a solo dramatic entrance into his hall if the occasion demanded. Percy's private room (40' × 23' × 21') and the Dining Chamber (44' × 24' × 28') were of comparable size, which suggests that the Lord's Bed Chamber was used not just for sleeping, but also for work and recreational space. Perhaps the Chapel sang privately here for the Earl.

Immediately beyond the Dining Chamber, the Chapel rooms were almost as large as the Great Hall itself, which attests to the chapel's importance as a gathering and performing place. A Nether Chapel, measuring 23' × 24' × 12', gave entrance to the High Chapel, which measured 30' × 24' × 22'. The ten-foot disparity in height between the Nether Chapel and the High Chapel contributed to the versatility of the performance space within the chapel. Above the Nether Chapel and overlooking the High Chapel, a rood loft provided space for the household to see services or for the Chapel singers to perform. Here, on Christmas morning, an angelic choir could sing the Gloria as the nativity play was enacted below. At the rear of this loft, a small balcony overlooked the adjoining Dining Chamber, allowing Percy's singers to entertain from above while his family and guests supped.

Adjacent to the loft, and accessible from the lower storey (the Nether Chapel) by a spiral stair, a small private balcony was set aside for 'my lordes pew of stat'; this arrangement allowed the Earl to make convenient and stately entrances to and exits from the services, and provided him with privacy, since it was probably hung with a travers. For theatrical purposes, this private balcony provided a high and prominent position from which God or angels could speak, and the travers could facilitate a discovery, a tableau, or a temporary exit, such as Jupiter makes in Heywood's *The Play of the Weather*, or the King in *Godly Queen Hester*.

All the features of the chapel rooms made them a remarkable theatre space. Working from the rood loft, the lord's balcony, and the High Chapel itself, Chapel personnel could create theatre-in-the-round, surrounding their audience with sight and sound. The Nether Chapel served as performance space, or as a tiring house, or as a gathering place for processional entries, while the nearby vestry provided additional dressing space, as well as a second entrance to the High Chapel.

Although not all noblemen were fortunate enough to retain a resident Chapel, most included space for worship within their manors. The arrangement of rooms at Wressle seems representative of other households, for gentry manors at Smithills Hall and Agecroft Hall in Lancashire, and at Woodlands Manor in Wiltshire show basically the same layout, albeit on a smaller scale. The Earl of Rutland's Haddon House, Derbyshire, is far larger than these manor houses, but the rooms are similarly aligned. The Haddon plan, however, shows no indoor access to the chapel, which would force the household to enter through the courtyard from the Great Hall. This plan, however, was drawn in 1782, so internal access may have been a feature of Haddon during the sixteenth century, before Protestantism discouraged clerical dramatic performances and isolated the chapel as a space dedicated solely to worship. The Haddon House Chapel, described by Edward King, was nevertheless a beautiful space:

Come we now to the Chapel, which is not less curious than the rest. Its entrance is from the first great court, under a low, sharp-pointed arch, looking more like the entrance of a cellar than that of a place of worship, and leading to a sort of anti-chapel, very low in height, and that has not a much better appearance. . . .

The chapel itself, has, at the entrance, two side isles, divided from the body by pillars and pointed arches, like a church: and in one of them are many long oaken benches, for the domesticks; the other side isle being taken up, with the pulpit, the desk, the ancient organ loft, and the stairs leading to them.

The organ is now removed; but the wainscotting of the loft, all edged with burnished gold, like that of the pulpit, the desk, and seats for the family, still remain.

These seats for the family, consisted of two large high pews, on each side of the body of the chapel, reaching from the middle nearly as far as the altar; and were large enough to hold many guests.

In the great windows, over the altar, and on each side, are some good remains of painted glass. . . .[13]

---

[13] King, 354–5. Emmison describes the chapel of Sir William Petre at Ingatestone Hall, Essex, on pp. 14–15. Although there is no evidence that Petre kept a full Chapel (he hired Paul's Boys), he maintained a chapel within his manor.

24 The Chapel

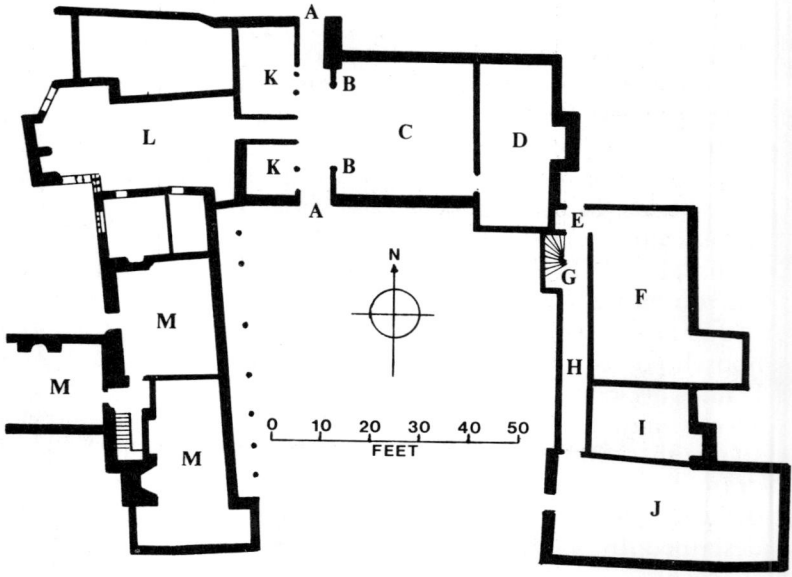

FIG. 4. Three sixteenth-century manor houses, drawn by Paul Miller after Avray H. Tipping, *English Homes*.

(*a*) (*above*) Smithills: The screens passage at A, the hall at C, and the withdrawing room at D are all fifteenth century, and echo the design of Wressle. The sixteenth-century east wing includes another withdrawing room at F, the vestry at I, and the chapel at J, all connected by a convenient stair and passage.

(*b*) (*opposite above*) Agecroft: The south wing still encompasses the chapel (E), vestry (I), and withdrawing room (H) pattern. Abutting this sequence of rooms is the hall (G) with the screen passage (F).

(*c*) (*opposite below*) Woodlands Manor: Shows a lobby and stair connecting the chapel (E) to the hall (C), clear indication that movement between these two locations was frequent and necessary. The customary and theatrically useful screen passage (B) separates the public spaces from the private chamber (H).

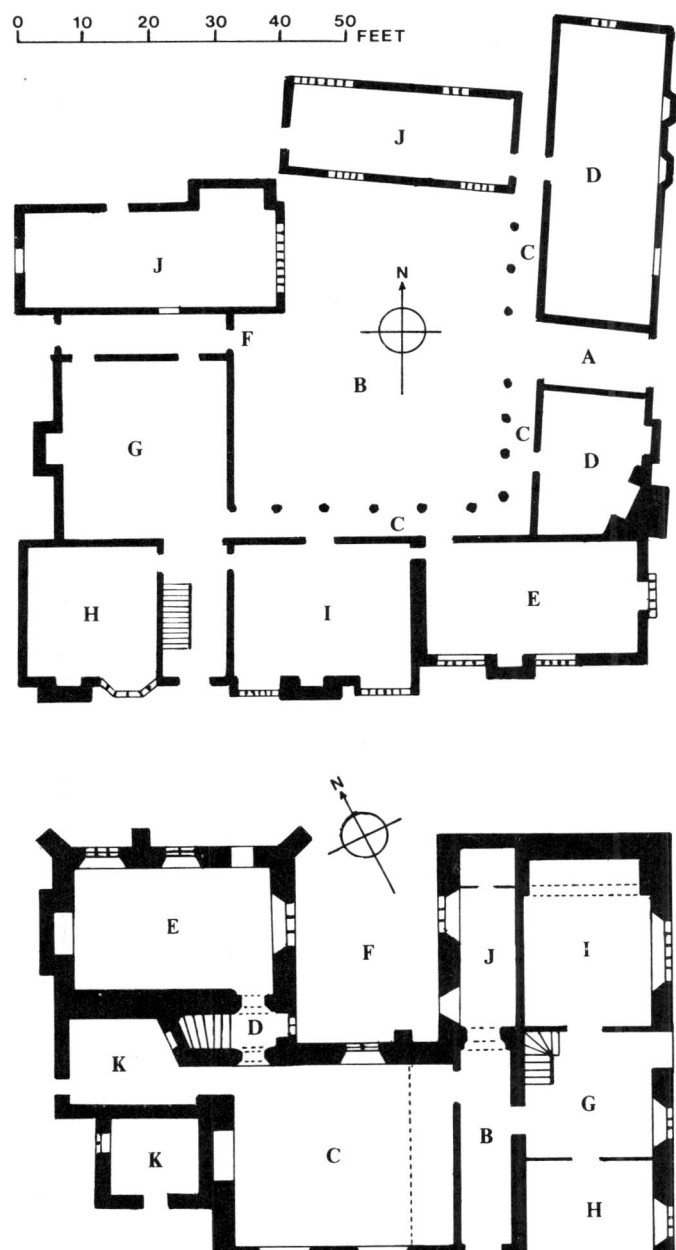

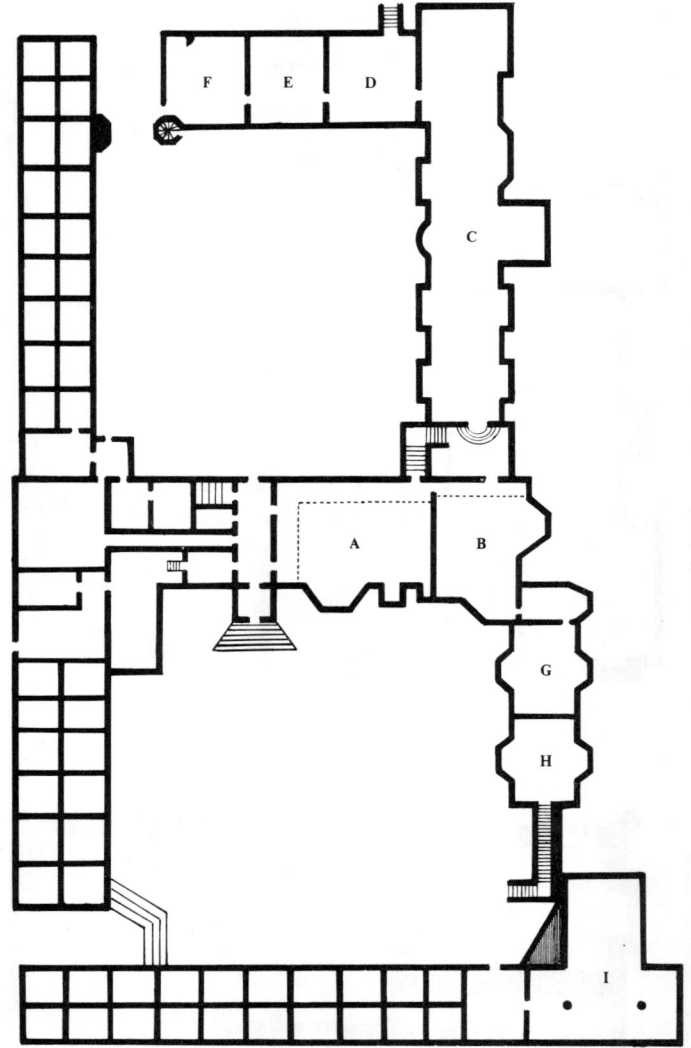

FIG. 5. Haddon House (*c*.1782), drawn by Paul Miller after Edward King, 'Sequel to the Observations on Ancient castles'. The Chapel (I) is quite a distant from the Great Hall (A) and Dining Chamber (B), allowing movement from one to the other through the private apartments (G, H) or the outside court, where stairs and the porch and screen passage (A) give entry. The great gallery (C), adjacent to the private rooms (D, E, F) might also be used as playing space. Dotted lines in the Great Hall indicate a gallery, useful for dramatic and musical entertainments, and the screens.

The Chapel 27

The chapels of the great households were visually glorious, richly furnished and provided with bejewelled and embroidered vestments, gilt statuary and vessels, beautiful arras, and expensive books.[14] Although the primary motive for such splendour was, of course, to glorify God and the household's patron, it could also be exploited for theatrical effect. The choir and lofts provided playing space, and the aisles an ease of movement and scope for ceremonial processions, just as cathedral aisles had for centuries. Here, the Chapel could stage religious plays; vestments became costumes, chapel structures became sets, and hangings became backdrops.

Such a performance was probably the motive for the expenditures of the first Duke of Norfolk just before Christmas in 1481, when the Duke spent £60 for six days' work on his chapel, carried out by three labourers, a plasterer, and a carpenter. At Christmas the next year, 'wyre' and 'hokes' were purchased for the chapel, along with 48 yards of linen and 6 yards of 'tewke', a canvas cloth. Three days later, payment was made for dyeing this cloth, and two days after, 42 additional yards of cloth were purchased and prepared. The Duke also paid for thread, cloth, 'shafftes', patins (wooden, thick-soled shoes), and points (laces for doublets and hose) for the Chapel Children. The cloth, hooks, and wires were used to decorate the chapel with hangings, perhaps for a discovery or setting. The workmen may have been repairing the chapel, but it is more likely that they were building a specific 'set'. The clothing purchased for the children was not specifically clerical; patins were worn outdoors to keep the wearer out of mud, or indoors to increase the height of the wearer, obviously an asset to staging, as the Greeks had found thousands of years before. Neither albs nor surplices are mentioned.[15] As is customary,

---

[14] Inventories of chapel furnishings indicate that the nobility spent vast sums on such matters: see Hope, 276, 278, 291, 329–31 for de Vere; F. D. Blackley and G. Hermansen, 121; McFarlane, 97, for a 1397 testament of Thomas of Woodstock and a 1415 testament of Henry Scrope of Masham. For Norfolk see Collier, 170, 380. Northumberland took care that his chapel linens were cleaned at the household's expense: NHB 192–3. Laundry expenses for no other group (not even the Earl's family) are listed among the accounts.

[15] Collier, 141, 325–6. It is possible that hooks and wires were used to move a star for a nativity play. Chambers notes that such was the custom for Epiphany plays (MS 2, 44). Percy's chapel was hung with arras for his daughter's wedding. The

the accounts include no explanation for these expenditures, yet the time of the year and the nature of the items purchased imply that the chapel and its personnel were being furnished for the Christmas season celebrations, which included dramatic as well as religious offerings.

PERFORMANCE: PLAYS, PAGEANTS, AND DISGUISINGS

At Northumberland's household, the Chapel was specifically directed to perform the 'Play of the Nativity uppon Cristynmes-Day in the morning', as well as the 'Play of Ressurection upon Estur-Day in the Mornynge', and the 'Play befor his Lordship uppon Shrofteusday at night yerely'. We should expect this sort of schedule, given the importance of the feasts, and indeed we find Chapels at Magdalen College celebrating Christmas and Easter with plays by 1481.[16] At Northumberland's, the Christmas and Easter plays were religious, perhaps even liturgical, and were performed in the chapel itself.

The Shrovetide play was different. Shrove Tuesday, unlike both Christmas and Easter, is not a religious feast but rather a secular festival, a final opportunity for the household to celebrate before the strict observance of Lent. Specifically ordered for the evening, its subject unspecified, the Chapel's Shrovetide play was likely to be a secular play, an interlude performed at or after a banquet that allowed the household to consume foods shortly to be forbidden and to enjoy amusements to be prohibited for the next forty days. Thus, Northumberland's Chapel was accustomed to performing in at least two distinct types of plays: the scriptural play and the interlude.

Texts for the scriptural plays performed within the great households either do not survive or have not yet been identified as such, so we must look to analogues from other sources. Household Chapels probably participated in the

accounts of Oxford, Norfolk, and Northumberland frequently record that noblemen supplied their Chapel Children with articles of clothing that were not specifically religious costuming.

[16] NHB 256–8; Wickham notes similar patterns of performance at Oxford and Cambridge: EES 3, 44.

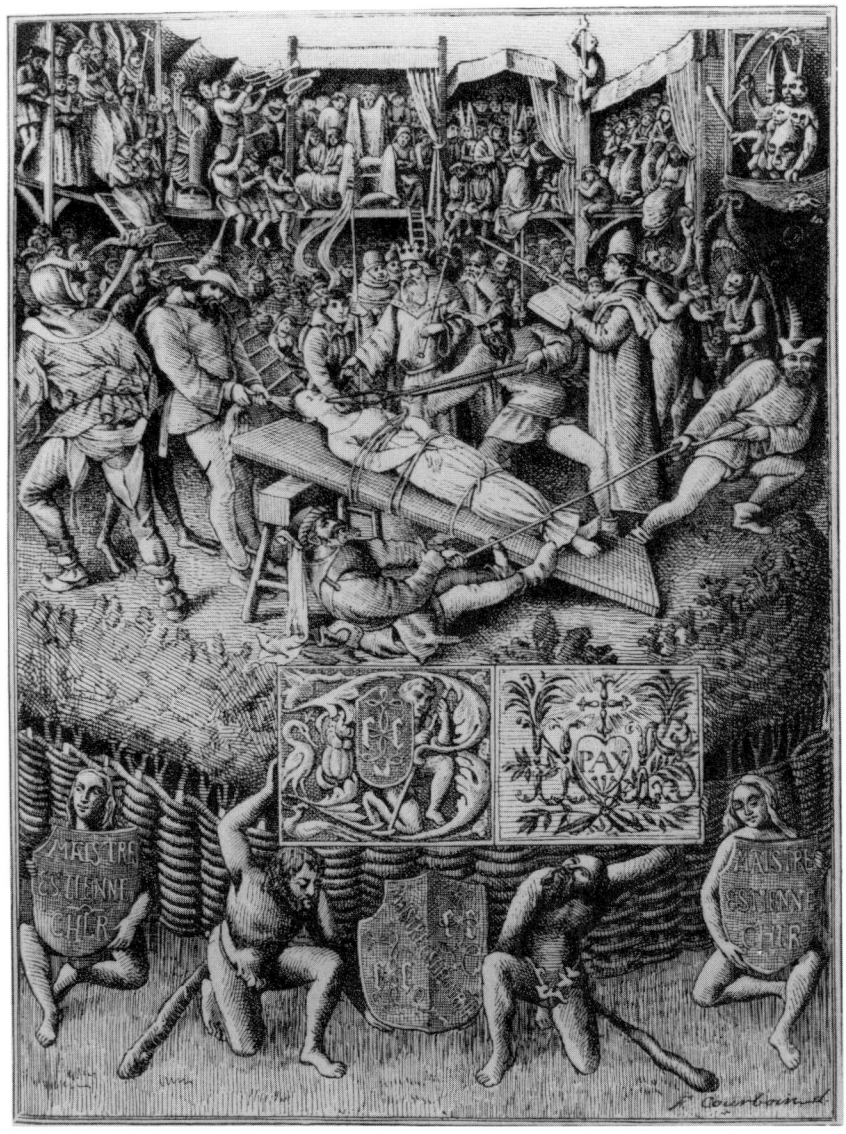

FIG. 6. Jean Fouquet's miniature 'The Martyrdom of St Apollonia', from Germain Bapst, 'Essai sur l'histoire du théâtre' (Paris, 1893). The collaborative efforts of a number of entertainers are preserved in this sketch of a miracle play in performance. At the upper level, an organ player is flanked by Chapel boys dressed as angels to his left and by trumpeters to his right.

Corpus Christi cycles, those enormous productions that utilized performers drawn from all stations of life. On the Continent, producers of mysteries and miracles had long made use of local organists and choristers; the Fouquet miniature of 'The Martyrdom of St Apollonia' accurately depicts the organist and the children who performed as angels on the upper left. JoAnna Dutka notes payments to the choirboys and men at Chester for singing, playing instruments, acting, and composing songs, and similar payments were noted down at Coventry.[17] Recent study has make it increasingly apparent that all production requirements for the cycle plays were sophisticated rather than simple, so, in the spirit of Tudor pragmatism, local churches and cathedrals were called upon to provide expert singers for elaborate musical effects.

Household Chapels may have assisted their parish brethren for the local Corpus Christi plays. William Peres, or Pyers, who was a member of Northumberland's Chapel, participated in the revision of the nearby Beverley plays; perhaps his Chapel colleagues performed in them. There is no record of payment to Northumberland choristers, but that does not preclude their participation, for the Chapel personnel were already salaried members of a household who would not require additional moneys, although they would certainly not have refused them. During the warm summer months the nobility were generally on progress, attending to the management of their other estates, so the number of the resident household would be significantly reduced, and the duties of the Chapel similarly lessened. Further, a nobleman would approve of his Chapel lending its talents to the civic productions, for the performance would reflect well upon him locally.

We should also expect great household Chapels to perform liturgical plays in Latin, such as the 'Quem quaeritis' performed at Easter. Church choristers had been performing these plays for centuries; since the great household Chapels

---

[17] Brown, 'Musicians in the Mysteries and Miracles', in Taylor and Nelson, *Medieval English Drama*, 88; see also Dutka, *Music in the English Mystery Plays*, 2; R. W. Ingram, 55–76; and Chambers, 2–9.

had duties and responsibilities identical to other churches, the Chapels may also have been performing such plays.

In addition to performing in plays, great household Chapels were expected to provide religious and secular concerts outside the chapel itself. At the Twelfth Night festival, described in the *Second Northumberland Household Book*, the 'hoole chappell' was directed to 'sing wassaill', a carol celebrating the service of the wassail drink at the evening banquet. Afterwards, the Chapel continued to sing 'such carrailles as they be perveid of'. When the Earl and his lady left the Great Hall for their private chambers at the end of the banquet, the Chapel, again singing, accompanied its patron. The Chapel of Henry VII was also expected to sing carols at Christmas. On All Souls' Day, Percy's Chapel performed the 'Responde callede Exaudivi at the Matynstyme for xij virgyns'. Again, the Chapel of Henry VII was also directed to perform on All Souls' Day. This practice dated back to the reign of Edward IV at least, for *The Black Book* stipulates that the All Souls' Day concert took place in the King's hall or chamber, not in the chapel itself; at this time the King made plans for his Christmas festivities, presumably in consultation with his Chapel.[18] Although other household accounts do not refer specifically to concerts such as these, frequent payments to the Chapel at Christmas, on New Year's Day, and at Easter indicate that during these holidays the Chapel was performing special entertainments for the household in addition to its customary religious duties.

The peculiar mixture of religious and secular art that the Chapel performed is perhaps symptomatic of its unique position within early Renaissance society. As religious ensembles functioning under the protection of secular patrons, the great household Chapels could afford, both financially and politically, to experiment with styles and themes that their unprotected brethren could not, as long as they

---

[18] Lancashire, 'Orders', 39–40, 43; Leland, iv. 235–7. BL Eg. MS 985, f. 29; NHB 342–3; Anglo, 'Court Festivals of Henry VII', 29–43. The Chapel Children consistently received twenty shillings on or around 1 November for singing the Audite, which Anglo suggests was a 'setting of the 48th Psalm for first Vespers All Souls'; *The Black Book*, 136.

subscribed to their patron's 'party line'. For centuries, the Church fathers had been equivocating about the spiritual merit of the theatre; some understood the educational and devotional value of religious drama, while many more railed against the theatre, forbidding their flocks to watch or perform in plays.[19] The Lollard 'treatise of miracles' playing' (c.1380–1410) fired a strong salvo against clerical participation in drama and, by 1511, John Colet, the Dean of St Paul's complained that priests were ignoring Church rules that forbade clerks to be 'Common players'.[20] Such ecclesiastical pressure was certainly instrumental in purging church performances of perceived blasphemies and in pressuring civic officials to restrain market-place performances, but harangues from the pulpit would have little effect on private performances, particularly when such churchmen as Morton and Wolsey were active patrons of theatre. Throughout this tumultuous period in the evolution of early English drama, clerks under noble patronage continued to perform, retreating from the public view of the cathedral to the private eye of the household. Closer attention to great household Chapels can provide theatre historians attempting to depict the evolution of drama from trope to tragedy with a neglected piece of the puzzle. Within great households, religious players continued to perform with relative impunity, marrying liturgical and secular effects to explore novel dramatic structures. This evolution is further reflected in the Chapel's participation in disguisings, a form which would never appear in the church, inn-yard, or city street. More than perhaps any other genre, the disguising encouraged Chapels to experiment with allegory.

Choristers had been performing in allegorical pageants almost as long as they had been performing tropes. Descriptions of civic pageantry for coronations, progresses, royal entries, and other public ceremonial occasions refer constantly to singing men and boys. In 1392, when the citizens of

[19] Lancashire, *A Guide to Dramatic Texts and Records of Britain: A Chronological Topography to 1558* has records of ecclesiastical censure from the 7th c. to the 16th c. Lancashire also comments upon the Church's attitude toward scriptural plays in his introduction, vii–x.
[20] 'Treatise of miracles' playing' in Hudson, 97–104; 'The Sermon on Doctor Colete, made to the Conuocation at Paulis', in Lupton, app. C, 295, 300–1.

London were reconciled with Richard II, the elaborate pageants celebrating the event included two angelic choirs 'with diuerse melodies and songen' and speeches addressed to the King and Queen in Latin. Both these qualities suggest the talents of the Chapel, religious contexts combined with secular effects. God and his angels sang at the door of St Paul's and at the Temple Bar; John the Baptist appeared in a pageant surrounded by a variety of trees and beasts. From the fourteenth century, local choristers had performed in such civic pageantry.

The 1415 pageant for Henry V's return from Agincourt,[21] attributed to John Lydgate, required two choirs of boy angels, one of patriarchs singing 'Cantate Domino canticum novum, Alleluia!', one of the twelve apostles, and one of twelve kings. As Withington notes,[22] the sacred music sung by these choirs was adapted from church ritual. Here we find the religious choristers involved in more spectacular pageantry than before, and offering their own allegory in the form of the twelve kings.

Lydgate's 1432 pageant series for the coronation of Henry VI employs many allegorical motifs found in the mummings he composed for the royal household. After passing a pageant whose chief character was a giant champion, the King was greeted by three empresses: Nature, Grace, and Fame. These were surrounded by fourteen angelic maidens dressed in white, who spoke and sang. The

---

[21] The title for the 1430 *Mumming at Hertford* states that it was commissioned by John Brys, Controller of the household. Texts for all the mummings may be found in *The Minor Poems of John Lydgate Part II*, ed. MacCracken. For the history of mumming and disguising see Welsford, particularly 30–41, in which she discusses the etymology of the word 'mumming' and attempts to distinguish it from the disguising. Wickham also discusses the development (*EES 1*, 195–8), as do many other scholars. The terms 'mumming', 'disguising', and 'mask' or 'masque' are often used indiscriminately both by 15th-c. and 16th-c. commentators and by contemporary scholars. For the purpose of this study, 'mumming' refers to a dumb-show or mime, 'disguising' to a dramatic performance that may incorporate elements of speech, music, dance, pageantry, and allegory. I have avoided using 'masque', to distinguish between early Tudor revels and the vastly different Jonsonian court entertainments. These distinctions are used for the sake of clarity, but should not imply that Tudor audiences perceived them. A glance at Edward Hall's chronicle shows that they saw no clear distinction even between a play and a disguising: e.g. Hall calls a political play that offended Wolsey a disguising (719).

[22] Withington, *English Pageantry*, i. 129–47.

description indicates that these maidens were actually choir boys, since they sang a 'roundelly in English with hevenly armonye' and they spoke 'lyke as clerkes write'.

The third pageant at Cornhill included Dame Sapience, the Seven Liberal Sciences, and Aristotle, who was 'most clerkly disputing'. Music's servant Boece and his 'scolers' performed 'with hevenly armonye' on organs, the instrument typically associated with the church. At St Paul's, the heavenly choir appeared and the King heard services, then proceeded to Westminster for the 'Te Deum'. Once again, the choristers were an integral part of the civic occasion, singing and playing instruments. Although Lydgate composed verse speeches for various characters, it is unclear whether these verses were actually spoken or displayed in writing accompanied by mimed action, as is found in his mummings, which I shall consider shortly.

The involvement of clergy and choristers in civic pageantry can be traced beyond the reign of James I. Just as the choirboys often served as the heavenly choir in the Corpus Christi plays, they provided the same services in the pageants. This was a practical arrangement, for a proper heavenly choir required extensive musical talent and training. It was clearly foolish to spend time rehearsing local children when church choristers could with little effort deliver a much more polished performance. In addition, production requirements for the civic pageantry were similar to those the Chapel was accustomed to fulfilling: the casts were large, mixed in age, and called for boys dressed as women; the entertainments required musical and rhetorical expertise; the occasions were specific and financially unprofitable; and the pageants themselves were elaborately appointed.

These values were also found in Lydgate's mummings, three of which were performed within the royal household, and represent the earliest extant texts of secular entertainments commissioned specifically as occasional pieces for a great household. All followed the same basic structure: a presenter read or spoke verses to explain the action which was mimed by the performers. This structure evolved into the disguising, popular at the great households of the Tudor era, in which, as we shall find, the Chapel plays a significant role.

The Chapel 35

Although no external evidence has thus far been discovered that Chapel members performed in disguisings before the reign of Henry VII, it is possible that they participated in the production of Lydgate's mummings at court. Both the Christmas *Mumming at Eltham* (c.1424) and the New Year's *Mumming at Hertford* (c.1427–30—also called a disguising)[23] required large casts of men and women. The *Mumming at Windsor* (c.1429) in particular seems to have required the participation of a Chapel.

Combining legend and religion to show how the fleurs-de-lis and ampulla became symbols of France, Lydgate's style in this composition is reminiscent of civic pageantry, and looks forward to the disguising. The plot of the mumming includes Clovis's conversion to Christianity by God through St Clotilda, the presentation by an angel to a hermit of a blue shield embossed with the gold fleurs-de-lis, and the baptism of Clovis by St Remigius, for which a heavenly dove delivered the golden ampulla. Lydgate compliments the ladies present by comparing them with St Clotilda, and pays tribute to Henry VI, who was of the line of St Louis, and therefore King of France. The themes expressed are courtly and specific to an occasion.

Lydgate himself probably spoke the verses, for in other mummings the headnote calls the presenter a herald or pursuivant, whereas here the headnote simply records 'made by Lidegate daun Iohn'.[24] He delivered fourteen stanzas and then informed the court that they would see the story enacted. The oration of this mumming (unlike Lydgate's others) preceded the performance because the action required the full attention of the audience for its complex visual, aural, and mechanical effects.

The characters include God (probably as the Trinity, for his threefold aspect is described at length), Clovis, St Clotilda, at least one angel, the hermit, and St Remigius. The action of the mumming is spectacular. The staging of Clovis's conversion was probably accompanied by a flash of light, as Saul's was in the Digby *Conversion of St. Paul*. The event

---

[23] See Firth for a discussion of the date of the *Mumming at Hertford* and political allegory. For the dates of the other mummings, see Pearsall.
[24] Lydgate, 691.

may well have been marked by an angelic chorus, for the oration was already done and the action would not have unfolded in silence. Had the dialogue and the music been performed simultaneously, the audience would have had to divide its attention between the two effects, resulting in a split focus that would have prevented full enjoyment of either effect. Trained Chapel singers would provide the angelic chorus.

Musical effects are again implied when the angel presents the hermit with the shield, and when the dove presents the ampulla. All these scenes require action which moves vertically; God, the angel, and the dove descend to men. God from 'þe heghe, hevenly consistorye . . . His eyeghe of mercy caste on Cloudovee' (8–12). The angel 'was frome heven sent' (31), and the dove 'brought adovne' (71) the ampulla. The last effect would be achieved by mechanical means with which we are familiar from the Noah and Pentecost plays of the Corpus Christi cycles.

This mumming demands sophisticated staging. First, a pageant device, which would allow height for the heavenly characters, a 'set' complete with a font for the baptism scene, and a place from which to operate the effects seem necessary to the staging. Barring that, the dais or gallery in the hall could be used, but heaven had to be differentiated spatially from earth by some means. Second, the costuming requirements are complex and extravagant. The angels and the Trinity-God require clothing according to their stations, which could have been easily adapted from ecclesiastical vestments as they were in the cycle plays. Clovis would have to be dressed in suitably royal garments to suggest his station and his spiritual significance as the first French king to be Christianized. The costumes of the hermit and the saints could have been less extravagant, but since the performance was a spiritual and political allegory performed for the royal court, even these costumes would have been lavishly iconographic rather than realistically simple. Third, special effects and properties included a flash of gunpowder, a highly decorated heavenly dove lowered by wires and bearing the golden ampulla, one of the central images in the mumming and surely one of the most elaborate. Last, the action implies the use of musical effects. In civic pageantry and the Corpus Christi plays, heaven was continually suggested by harmonic singing and the court would do the same. The oration, which preceded the action, introduced a silence to be filled with such harmony.

To a greater extent than the other two Lydgate mummings, this royal entertainment suggests a Chapel performance in the Great Hall. If we assume a choir of angels, the cast is large and requires trained voices. The mumming was an occasional piece, designed to be performed once only, with themes specific to Henry VI and his claim to the French throne; no other audience would be as affected as the royal household. The mumming depends upon sets, costumes, and props for its effect, suggesting close financial and artistic co-operation between the household and trained performers, a relationship common in great household Chapels.

Lydgate's mummings contain elements which reflect production values common to Chapel performers rather than to interluders or amateurs. As a member of the clergy himself, he was familiar with the performing techniques and capabilities of choristers, and this in turn affected his compositions. As the ancestor of the Tudor court disguisings, these mummings are significant, for if Chapels performed in these entertainments for Henry VI, we should expect to find Chapels performing disguisings for Henry VII and Henry VIII. Such is indeed the case.

Just as John Lydgate created disguisings for Henry VI, William Cornish, senior, and William Cornish, junior, designed disguisings for Henry VII. Descriptions and household accounts for some of these performances survive, clarifying the role of the Chapel in great household disguisings. Cornish senior, himself a member of the Chapel, figures significantly in these accounts, both as an actor and as an author, providing us for the first time with conclusive external evidence that Gentlemen and Children of the Chapel participated in secular entertainments.[25] For example, on Twelfth Night in 1494, *The Great Chronicle* records that the King entertained the mayor, the French ambassador, and the

---

[25] For an extended discussion of the relationship between Chapel players and the Renaissance drama see Wallace, *The Evolution of Drama up to Shakespeare*.

Spanish ambassador. Henry's players began performing a 'goodly Interlude', but they were interrupted by 'oon of the kyngys Chapell namyd Cornysh', who rode into the hall at Westminster dressed as St George, behind him a 'ffayer vyrgyn' leading a dragon that spewed fire. As Lydgate had done sixty-five years before, Cornish recited a 'spech made in balad Royall', then sang an anthem of St George 'whereunto the kyngys Chapell which stood ffast answerid Salvatorem Deprecare, ut Gubernet Angliam, And soo sang owth the hool antempn wyth lusty Corage, . . .'.[26] Again the Chapel was called on for vocal music. The virgin may have been a Chapel boy, but since she is required neither to speak nor sing, she may well have been a young lady. Cornish, a Gentleman of the Chapel, took the only speaking role. After this pageant, a series of complex dances was executed by 'xij lordes knights and Esquyers with xij ladies dysguysed'. In this three-part entertainment, the first two parts were performed by professional entertainers, the last by the lower echelon of aristocrats. The male disguisers, still in costume, returned to serve the banquet to the King and his guests, an interesting fact that establishes the social standing of the dancers as gentlemen ushers—noble servitors, not the noble guests who would appear during the reign of Henry VIII.[27]

The description of this entertainment shows that Chapel performers displayed certain characteristics not common to other professional entertainers. As in the Lydgate mummings, the staging was complex, the pageant device and costuming elaborate and expensive; the Chapel's artistic contribution was set within the framework of a larger entertainment, yet was still occasional and specific; and the vocal talents of the Chapel were exploited. Such a performance required the co-operation of the household administration to facilitate organization, to construct the requisite sets and costumes, to ensure thematic and stylistic harmony, and to pay the expenses.

Cornish also provided pageants for the 1501 marriage

[26] Thomas and Thornley, 251–2. For a different account of the same entertainment, see Kingsford, 200. Anglo examines this and other of Cornish's contributions to court revels in 'William Cornish in a Play, Pageants, Prison, and Politics', 347–60.
[27] Thomas and Thornley, 251–2.

celebrations of Prince Arthur and Princess Katherine. John Heron's accounts record four payments to Cornish:

Aug. 22–23	Item to William Cornyshe for disguysing	x^{li}
Sept. 8	Item for Cornyshe disguysing	x^{li}
Sept. 20	Item to Cornyshe for his pagent	x^{li}
Nov. 3	Item to Cornyshe for his iij pagenttes	xx^{li}

On 3 November, the Children of the Chapel were also rewarded, perhaps for some involvement with the revels, or for the annual All Souls' Day concert. The Chapel Children took part in two pageants: on 28 November they appeared dressed as mermaids, singing and drawing a pageant in the form of a tabernacle; on 19 November the Children entered singing in the towers of a pageant in the shape of a castle which bore eight disguised ladies. Afterwards, a ship pageant containing mariners entered, from which issued two ambassadors, Hope and Desire, who tried to persuade the ladies to welcome certain 'Knights of the Mount of Love'. The knights attacked the castle, won admittance, and danced with the ladies to complete the performance.[28]

Four types of entertainers were involved in staging this allegory: minstrels made music for the dance; Chapel Children sang; unidentified performers dressed as mariners and as ambassadors made 'spechis'; and knights and ladies mimed a battle and danced. The dancers, like their counterparts in Cornish's 1494 pageant, were ladies and gentlemen of the household. Accounts note that two shipmen's garments were given to two Gentlemen of the Chapel, so these performers were probably drawn from the Chapel rather than from King's interluders. If, as Sydney Anglo believes, Cornish was directly responsible for the composition of the disguising, his Chapel colleagues surely performed in it.[29] This pageant series, like that for Twelfth Night in 1494, requires that the Chapel and household co-operated and also confirms the suspicion that Chapel Gentlemen acted as well as sang.

In the 1511 'Golldyn Arber in the Archeyrd of Plesyer', three Chapel Gentlemen, Kyte, Cornish, and Crane, were

---

[28] Anglo, 'The Court Festivals', 37; *Spectacle*, 102–3.
[29] Stevens, 249; Anglo, *Spectacle*, 103.

FIG. 7. Ivory carving of 'The Siege of the Castle of Love', courtesy of the Victoria and Albert Museum. In a scene often enacted by court disguisings, armoured knights attack a castle defended by ladies throwing flowers, reminiscent of the defence of the Virtues in *The Castle of Perseverance*. Within the context of the scene, the trumpeters to the left and right appear to be martial or heraldic minstrels, but they may also suggest the minstrels who played thematic music for performances. The lions surrounding the carving call to mind the men disguised as beasts who often drew the pageant devices into the hall.

disguisers. The Christmas 1511 disguising of the 'Dangerous Fortress' featured the same three gentlemen as well as seven of their colleagues. Cornish, Crane, and Wentworth (another Chapel Gentleman) spoke during the Christmas 1515 disguising of the 'Pavillion in the Place Perilous'. In May 1515, six ladies' garments were provided for the Chapel Children to enact a May pageant, and at Christmas 1516, Cornish and the children performed *Troilus and Pandar* in Latin.[30] Chapel performers were clearly accustomed to delivering dialogue as well as song.

Henry VII frequently rewarded his Gentlemen of the Chapel for playing:

10 Jan. 1506	Item to the iiij pleyers of the Kinges Chapel	vj^{li} xiij^s iiij^d
1 Jan. 1507	Item to the iiij players of the Chapell that played affore the Kinges grace in rewarde	vj^{li} xiij^s iiij^d
7 Jan. 1508	Item to the v Gentlemen of the Kinges Chapell that played in the hall vpon xijth nyght afore the Kinges grace in rewarde	vj^{li} xiij^s iiij^d
25 Dec. 1508	Item to Master Kyte Cornysshe and other of the Chapell that played affore the King at Richemounte	vj^{li} xiij^s iiij^d
7 Jan. 1509	Item to diuerse of the Kinges Chapell that playde afore the King vpon xijth nyght	liij^s iiij^d [31]

These rewards were consistently higher than those the King gave to his four players, who usually received 20s. or 40s. It seems reasonable to assume that the King held the Chapel performers in higher regard than he did the players, or perhaps that Chapel productions were simply more spectacular.

Unfortunately, descriptions of these performances or specific accounts pertaining to them are lacking. All the payments occur during Christmas, which implies that Henry VII's household, like most educational, ecclesiastical, and noble households, was accustomed to watching a nativity play on Christmas morning. Two of the payments note that the Gentlemen played on Twelfth Night, presumably in the hall, since the household was assembled there. This entertainment was likely to be secular, occurring in the context of the banquet and festivities.

Although these are the only times the Chapel Gentlemen

---

[30] *L & P HVIII* ii/2, 1496, 1497, 1501, 1504, 1505.
[31] Anglo, 'The Court Festivals', 40, 41, 43, 44.

were referred to specifically as players, they received the same amount (£13. 6s. 8d.) consistently during the Christmas seasons of 1496–1500, 1502–3, and 1506–9. In 1501, the year of the royal marriage, the amount fell to £10. This curious fact would seem to indicate fewer responsibilities for the Chapel Gentlemen, but the importance of the occasion mitigates against decreased participation by the King's élite performers at this time. The Chapel Children may have been more active in the festivities, or perhaps the Gentlemen were paid for the occasion from other accounts. All payments to the Gentlemen occur on or about Twelfth Night, and are in addition to Chapel rewards for playing. In contrast, the Children of the Chapel were consistently rewarded with forty shillings on or about Christmas Day, sometimes for singing the Gloria (perhaps within a nativity play). In two years, 1496 and 1503, Cornish was rewarded at Christmas, as a performer or composer, for the season's revels. Like Edward IV and Percy, Henry VII heard a Chapel concert to celebrate All Souls' Day, for the Children were then frequently rewarded with twenty shillings, twice for singing the *Audite*. On 2 March 1498 the children were again rewarded, probably for an Easter performance; and on 13 March 1500 the Gentlemen were rewarded, presumably also for an Easter performance. The Gentlemen were also twice rewarded during the summer, 'to drinke with a buck'.[32]

These payments form an interesting pattern. Rarely was the Chapel as a whole rewarded; the Gentlemen and the Children often performed separately. The Children were responsible for performances on Christmas Day itself, possibly for a nativity play, and for the All Souls' Day concert. In addition they, rather than the Gentlemen, provided the vocal background music for the wedding pageants. The Gentlemen took part in the secular entertainments for Twelfth Night, and apparently on the occasion of a hunt during the summer. At Easter, both groups performed, but separately, and the nature of their individual performances remains unknown. If the Northumberland ordinances follow the example of the royal court, the Chapel would have performed a play about

[32] 'The Court Festivals', 27–44.

the resurrection in addition to Easter services. For the price of one Chapel, the household received two performing groups.

Henry VIII also saw pageants and plays that involved his Chapel Gentlemen and Children. By that time, the eminent nobility and the King himself often took part in the disguisings,[33] yet at times the identities of the disguisers were unspecified; in these cases, particularly when the performers spoke or sang, professionals, especially Chapel personnel, were participants. For example, in February 1510, the Gentlemen of the Chapel performed an interlude that was followed by a pageant and dance in which the King performed. In 1527/8, at the banquet house at Greenwich, the Chapel contributed to an elaborate entertainment: '. . . then entred eight of the kygnes Chappel with a song and brought with theim one richly appareled: and in likewise at the other side, entred eight other of the saied Chappel bringyng with them another persone, likewise appareled, these two persones plaied a dialog theffect whereof was whether riches were better then loue, . . .'. When the two, Riches and Love, could not agree, each called three knights, who staged a battle. The matter was eventually settled by 'an olde man with a siluer berd, and he concluded that loue & riches, both be necessarie for princes . . .'.[34] Again the Chapel performers were responsible for the musical and rhetorical elements of a pageant, while non-speaking roles could be taken by household members or aristocrats. The Chapel performance was immediately followed by noble maskers, including Princess Mary; the men, from a 'rich Mount' and the ladies, from a cave, met and danced, but they did not speak.

These are the only two occasions that Hall mentions the Chapel specifically as performers in secular revels. It is difficult to find a pattern in his references to the identities of

[33] In contrast to his son, Henry VII did not participate in court revels as a performer. Bacon tells us (albeit fifty years after Henry's death) that 'in triumphs of justs and tourneys and balls and masks (which they then called disguises) he was rather a princely and gentle spectator . . .'. Bacon, vi. 244. Many of Henry VII's nobles followed his royal example; when Henry VIII ascended the throne, however, this tradition changed quickly and dramatically. Hall frequently describes revels that starred the king and his coterie of young noblemen.
[34] Hall, 518, 723–4.

performers, for at times he is definite about the identity of noble disguisers, and particularly of the King, but when Hall fails to identify disguisers, we cannot always assume that they were professionals. Even when Hall stipulates that the King watched the performance, we cannot with any certainty state that courtiers were not involved and that the Chapel was.

Certain production values, however, indicate that professional entertainers, in particular Chapel performers, were often necessary. Whenever vocal music was called for, we should look for Chapel members. Whenever a participant was required to memorize and speak dialogue, we should look for an interluder or Chapel member. The nobility could be expected to don extravagant costumes, since they were eminently inclined to do so in everyday life; they could also be expected to execute the complex dances which were a sign of noble breeding. They could not, however, always be expected to spend their time rehearsing verses written by someone lower in the social hierarchy. Many of them lacked the talent, the time, and the inclination. Sir Thomas More was one of the few courtiers of the period who genuinely enjoyed oral interpretation, but his efforts were usually of his own composition. Noble poets like Surrey and Wyatt were probably similarly inclined, and, like Shakespeare, considered their privately circulated sonnets far more worthwhile than the expense of time and talent on dramatic doggerel.

When words were required to explain a performance in which noblemen took leading roles, either an expositor spoke or an explanation was displayed in writing. At the 1518/19 disguising to celebrate the betrothal of Princess Mary, 'a person called Reaport, appareled in Crymosyn satyn full of to*n*ges', entered 'sitting on a fle*n* horse wi*th* wynges & fete of gold called Pegasus. Thys person in Fre*n*che declared ye meaning of ye rocke & ye trees at ye Tournay.'[35] Report was a professional performer, probably the author of the mask, possibly Cornish junior. The allegory fits the Cornish style, and the entrance and performance of Report are similar to those of the St George that Cornish senior had acted in 1494. The second method of exposition, verses written on a placard

---

[35] Hall, 595.

attached to a pageant vehicle or presented to the king or queen, was extensively used, particularly at tournaments, which seldom involved the Chapel. Often, letters sewn on disguising apparel served the same function.[36] Hall never records that a nobleman took a spoken part in scripted dialogue for a court entertainment.

Such an elaborate disguising with dialogue occurred to honour Charles V on 15 June 1522. Again scripted by Cornish junior, the play involved three characters—Friendship, Prudence, and Might—who, with some assistance from two ironsmiths, attempted to tame a wild horse for its owner. After they had succeeded, men and women disguisers danced. As specific political allegory, designed to restate the alliance between Henry and the Emperor against the French, this was not a play that would prove profitable or mobile enough for a troupe of interluders. Since Cornish composed it, he must have used the Chapel Royal to enact it. As a complex, expensive, and occasional piece, this entertainment, like the Chapel performances under Henry VII discussed above, required the financial and artistic co-operation of the household for its organization and construction.

The household could justify paying expenses for an entertainment that it had commissioned. Various household members, from composers to carpenters, co-operated to stage a disguising, while the interluders operated more independently, on a much smaller scale, and on smaller budgets, although they could and did contribute plays to an evening's entertainment. Generally, however, the frequency of rewards to the Chapel and their participation in sophisticated revels

---

[36] This occurred at the 1515/16 Maying, when the King met two ladies in a chariot drawn by five horses, on which were seated five ladies. Each horse bore its name on its head, and each lady was labelled in the same way: 'humide . . . lady vert . . . lady vegetaue . . . lady pleasaunce . . . swete odour . . . lady May . . . with lady Flora . . .' (Hall, 582). On Candlemas Eve in 1519/20, a pageant device met the King and Queen as they returned from Evensong. A lady presented a bill in which four knights challenged all comers to a Shrovetide joust (Hall, 600–1). Shortly after Epiphany 1510/11, King Henry jousted for Queen Katherine at Westminster. On this occasion, the names of the four challengers, 'Cure loial', 'Bon voloire', 'Bon espoir', and 'Valiaunt desire', and the articles of the challenge were inscribed upon a tablet (Hall, 517). On 13 Feb. in the same year, Sir Charles Brandon entered the lists as a hermit, and presented a bill to the Queen, asking her permission to joust (Hall, 518).

indicate that the Chapel performers, unlike the players, were at the convenient and exclusive command of the patron of the household. As a result, the Chapel was able to and expected to perform entertainments that were more expensive, more visually and musically complex, and more specific to an occasion and a particular audience than were other performers.

In the noble households, the Chapel performed in similar fashion. Noblemen who did not retain a resident Chapel had to hire Chapel performers for specific occasions, a fact suggesting that these performances could not be staged by the more common household entertainers, such as minstrels or players. Manners, whose records do not include payment to his own Chapel, hired the choristers of Grantham to sing for his feast on St George's Day. In 1542, his own Gentlemen performed a New Year's Day mask, probably without complex vocal or rhetorical elements. Similarly, Edward Seymour, whose records also indicate no resident Chapel, hired Paul's Boys to perform on New Year's Day at Wulfhall, Wiltshire. Sir John Petre also imported Paul's Boys to Ingatestone, Essex, where they sang and performed in a wedding entertainment in 1559 and 1560.[37]

Noble households who did keep a resident Chapel could make far more effective use of its talents. When a patron imported entertainers, he had to make arrangements in advance, and to accept the entertainer's repertory, unless he went to the additional expense of commissioning an entertainment. Without such limitations, retained Chapels contributed more efficiently to entertainments of a large scope that utilized other household performers as well. Complex, multimedia entertainments with thematic and stylistic unity, similar to those found at the royal court, became possible. In contrast, aristocrats without resident Chapels would have to incorporate a prefabricated piece by an external troupe into the evening's entertainment, in which case aesthetic unity would be a happy coincidence, and efficient production a tribute to the quick adaptability of household officers and performers.

The Northumberland household revels are a good example

[37] HMC *4th Report*, 321, 323; Jackson, 174; Emmison, 76.

of this. While the scriptural plays and concerts of religious music were performed exclusively by the Chapel, on other occasions the Chapel combined its talents with many others to create the entertainment. During the Christmas season, Percy rewarded a youth as Abbot of Misrule, the Chapel provided a boy to play St Nicholas and other boys from Beverley or York acted the Boy Bishop. On Christmas Day and on Twelfth Night, the Chapel marched in procession with the rest of the household. At the Twelfth Night banquet, the Chapel sang secular carols, perhaps accompanied by the household minstrels, who were required to play during supper, the disguisings, and the henchmen's morris dance.[38] Chapel entertainers may have performed in the disguising itself, for the ordinance does not stipulate who was to perform.

The Howard dukes of Norfolk also watched this type of conglomerate entertainment. The resident Chapel performed and was rewarded on New Year's Day, visiting troupes of interluders performed, and disguisers danced. A 1482/3 list of disguising materials includes gold and silver paper and glue for property, set, or costume construction, as well as gunpowder and other chemicals for visual and aural effects.[39]

Oxford's Chapel appeared at the royal court of Henry VII in May 1506,[40] the only Chapel retained by a nobleman to do so. They may have performed for Rogationtide, Ascensiontide, or Whit Sunday, or perhaps this performance expressed traditional May-Day themes in secular songs or was a disguising like the May pageant, discussed above, that Henry VIII's Chapel Children performed. On 1 January 1491, Oxford rewarded his Chapel and minstrels twenty shillings each. This notation is immediately followed by a bill for disguising materials and a pageant,[41] once again suggesting that the Chapel had some involvement with the disguising. The eighteenth Earl's absorption with Lyly, Blackfriars, and children's companies certainly indicates a long-standing family interest in choristers and their dramatic activities.

[38] NHB 254, 256, 257; Lancashire, 'Orders', 14–15.
[39] Collier, 144–5, 336, 339, 340.
[40] Anglo, 'The Court Festivals', 41.
[41] Collier, 517.

The disguising was one of the most popular of great household entertainments. The Howards, de Veres, and Percys produced disguisings, as did Henry VII and Henry VIII, while the Seymours, Petres, and Manners imported them. As early as 1443/4, Humphrey Stafford paid for one at his seat at Writtle, and in 1452/3, Queen Margaret of Anjou paid for a Christmas disguising. Even the turmoil of the War of the Roses did not prevent the Pastons from watching disguisings.[42] Such performances included acting (either in mime or dialogue), singing, music, dancing, and often a pageant device complexly staged, with a unified artistic intent, by a variety of performers.

The accounts of Henry VII and Henry VIII indicate that the Chapel contributed to these performances as writers, composers, and performers. In contrast, the king's players are rarely mentioned in connection with the disguising. Further, the household absorbed the cost of staging a disguising, often allowing the performers to keep their costumes, financial assistance that interluders did not receive. Since the household expected a sophisticated level of performance from the Chapel and was prepared to pay for it, the patron, in effect, became the producer; and consequently the household administration completely controlled the form and content of the disguising, providing a strong bond between Chapel artists and their patron, a bond that the interluders did not enjoy to such a great extent.

There are several types of performance we can be sure did not involve the great household Chapels. Normally, they did not perform at other households, so they could not establish the artistic links between aristocratic households that patronized players could. Since a noble household could not afford, economically or politically, to stage tournaments, its Chapel did not undertake the allegorical pageants that so often accompanied them. There is no indication that aristocratic households ever staged public entries, those elaborate pageant series that welcomed important visitors to cities and towns during the early Tudor period.

---

[42] Turnbull, 23; Myers, 'The Household of Queen Margaret', 88; Gairdner, *The Paston Letters*, 314.

PLAY TEXTS

Many extant play texts show no evidence of Chapel involvement. Plays such as *Hick Scorner* and *Mundus et Infans* employ small casts of male actors, require no complex music, and are general enough in theme and simple enough in staging requirements to provide profitable touring scripts. These scripts were designed for players.

However, other play texts do show the influence of the Chapel. The nativity plays of the Corpus Christi cycles were probably similar to those staged within the great households. Motter notes that as early as 1378, the students or choristers at St Paul's were accustomed to producing a religious play at Christmas, and speculates that these plays were also modelled on the civic cycle plays, a likely theory since recent scholarship shows increasing evidence that local clerics and schoolmasters were the authors of the miracle plays.[43]

The shepherd plays, in particular, employ production techniques that the Chapel had mastered. The Wakefield Master's *Secunda Pastorum* in the Towneley Cycle requires a cast of seven (including two women and one boy) and a heavenly choir. These parts can easily be filled by the guild in a civic performance but, within a household, the cast is too large for an interlude troupe. The play is too specific in plot and theme to be a viable touring piece. As a nativity play, it could be performed at Corpus Christi within the context of the 'creation-to-doomsday' temporal structure, or on Christmas morning itself, a day on which household Chapels were directed to perform precisely such a play.

The musical requirements of the *Secunda Pastorum* are quite sophisticated, and have elicited frequent comment from scholars.[44] Choristers could produce the complex harmony required for a heavenly chorus. More significantly, harmony and disharmony contribute to the thematic structure of *Secunda Pastorum*, where spiritual quality is reflected in musical expertise. Mak's dissonant singing betrays his evil nature and offends the shepherds' ears, while the shepherds,

---
[43] Motter, 128.
[44] Carpenter, 'Music in the *Secunda Pastorum*', 696–700.

in turn, sing with less expertise than the angels. Thus, music contributes metonymically to the aesthetics of the dramatic structure. This fact and the musical terminology employed in the play[45] provide ironic statement if the play is performed by a Chapel. At the same time as the performers are paying tribute to the birth of Christ, they are playing tribute to their own talents.

Besides referring to musical terminology, which was of particular interest to a Chapel, the *Secunda Pastorum* alludes to specific Chapel functions. The second shepherd says 'as euer rede I pystyll' (100);[46] reading the epistle was the responsibility of the 'Pistler', not a layman and certainly not a peasant-shepherd. Mak misquotes from the Compline service (266). The play contains further liturgical references, missing from other shepherd plays, to lauds (180), to the mass for the dead (252), to the Paternoster (104), and to the Creed (350).

Such liturgical allusions should not be completely unexpected in biblical plays that celebrate the feast of Corpus Christi, yet there are further references within the *Secunda Pastorum* that make the play a specifically seasonal piece. The angel-choristers sing the Gloria, with which they were familiar from singing Christmas services. The third shepherd, a boy, calls upon St Nicholas (118), who was often played by one of the Chapel Children at household Christmas festivities.[47] Furthermore, the *Secunda Pastorum* is full of comments about winter weather; each of the three shepherds complains of the cold, frost, and wind (ll. 57–8, 61–2, 128, 748), and the first observes 'thyse nyghtys ar long!' (182). The York Chaundelers' pageant neglects to mention the

---

[45] Robert Withington, 'Thre Brefes to a Long', 115–16.
[46] Line references are drawn from Cawley.
[47] At Northumberland's household, the Chapel sang the Gloria during the procession to the chapel on Christmas morning. (Lancashire, 'Orders', 14). In Henry VIII's royal household, similar payments were recorded. *L & P HVIII* ii/2, 1444–1518 *passim*. See NHB 256 for a reward given to one of the Children of the Chapel, probably for playing St Nicholas; if a boy playing St Nicholas visited from outside the household the Chapel child's reward for playing the role was halved. Henry VIII rewarded a 'St. Nicholas Bishop', whose identity was unspecified; the term suggests a child played St Nicholas and the Boy Bishop (*L & P HVIII* ii/2, 1469, 1480). BL Add. MS 59900, f. 54 (1544–5 accounts of Henry VIII) records rewards to the Chapel Children on St Nicholas's Day 'as hath byne accustomed'; see also Chambers, *MS 1*, 363, 369.

temperature, as does the Wakefield *Prima Pastorum*, and Chester's references are brief and unspecific.

References to winter weather would hardly be highlighted at the outdoor summer Corpus Christi performances, but they would be appropriate to indoor winter performance at Christmas. Set requirements for the *Secunda Pastorum* suggest either simultaneous stationary performance or indoor performance. The play requires a minimum of five loci: a general space, perhaps a field; Mak's house; the 'crokyd thorne' setting; a raised space for the angelic choir, and the stable. Four of these do not require elaborate sets, but Mak's house is equipped with seats of some sort, perhaps a fireplace (for he offers to build a fire [495]), a bed for Gyll, and a cradle. Lines in the play repeatedly call attention to a door (305, 362, 404, 478), which actually forms the focus of comic business, as Gyll hesitates to draw the latch when her husband has ordered her to 'open the hek' (305–6), and rushes to 'spar the gaytt-doore' (327) against the angry shepherds. These set devices are not easily mobile, and mime seems out of the question.

References to the Christmas season, to Chapel functions, and to extensive sets do not indicate outdoor processional performance at Corpus Christi. Rather, these references, as well as the dramatic structure of the *Secunda Pastorum*, suggest staging by parish choristers or a great household entertainment by a Chapel, a religious body functioning within a secular context. The *Secunda Pastorum* is a religious play that embraces the secular elements of Mak, his sheep trick, magic, and humour; pointed topical criticism of unruly retainers and the perils of marriage command 88 of its 753 lines (11.7 per cent of the entire play), while only 115 lines actually concern the angels' tidings, the shepherds' travels, and the adoration of the Christ child. The remainder of the play enacts the pseudo-nativity of Mak's sheep/son, and reflects the upside-down order of the Christmas Feast of Fools. A. C. Cawley has noted that the Wakefield Master was not a cloistered monk, but rather a cleric with a wide experience of secular life,[48] a description that applies perfectly to the Gentlemen of the great household Chapels.

[48] Cawley, xxx–xxxi.

It is certainly curious that the Wakefield plays include two complete scripts of drastically different shepherd plays, while no other cycle series duplicates a particular play. It is also curious that the *Secunda Pastorum* seems so seasonally specific, and that it required trained choristers to produce its musical effects. The Earl of Northumberland's Chapel was directed to provide just such a play on Christmas morning at his seat at Wressle, about 30 miles from Wakefield, and midway between that city and Beverley. The Earl's chaplain, William Peres, contributed his talents to the Beverley plays; perhaps one of the Percy Chapel Gentlemen travelled west and assisted at Wakefield. Since five plays in the Wakefield cycle (the Towneley plays) are in parts identical to York's, it appears that a great deal of sharing was going on. The *Secunda Pastorum*, the type of religious play a great household Chapel would be expected to perform, may have been shared between Wakefield and a local household.

Another text that utilizes Chapel performance techniques is *Wisdom Who is Christ*, composed between 1460 and 1474. Scholars have disagreed widely in their attempts to isolate the auspices of the play. Smart favoured a monastic household; Chambers believes schoolboys performed it; Malloy suggests students at the Inns of Court; Wickham proposes a sophisticated collegiate staging; Eccles concludes that the play had civic auspices; and Gatch attributes the play to the Bishop of Ely's household in Holborn. Bevington believes that the play is a developmental step toward reducing the cast size to that of an interlude troupe, and agrees with Smart, suggesting St Edmundsbury Abbey as the place of composition.[49] Yet a priory, with many performers at its disposal, would not attempt to double parts to produce a manageable touring script.

An analysis of *Wisdom*'s staging requirements can to some degree resolve these disagreements. The play needs actors who speak dialogue, seven mute boys, dancers, and at least three minstrels.[50] With doubling, the thirty-eight characters may be played by six speakers and seven children, which is,

---

[49] Eccles, xxxv; Bevington, *From 'Mankind' to Marlowe*, 50; Wickham, *EES 3*, 152, 289 n. 45.
[50] All references to the play are drawn from Eccles.

as I have already shown, the average number of performers in great household Chapels. The boys may have doubled as the dancers, but the minstrels are crucial to the performance. All these performers could be found within a household that retained minstrels and a Chapel.

The play requires 'trumpes', a 'bagpype', and a 'hornepype'; as the chapter following demonstrates, noble households almost always employed trumpeters for heraldic purposes, and often retained bagpipers as waits, and pipers as minstrels. It also requires liturgical singing in Latin. Mind, Will, and Understanding identify themselves as treble, mean, and tenor (617–20), and sing 'Quid retribuam Domino pro omnibus que retribuit mihi? Calicem salutaris accipiam et nomen Domini inuocabo', a trope which the Chapel sang. Five virgins (who could be Chapel Children) sing 'Nigra sum sed formosa, filia Jerusalem' from the Song of Songs. Soul sings 'wyth drawte notys as yt ys songyn in þe passyon wyke', a song from Lamentations for Holy Thursday.[51] Other songs of this nature are scattered throughout the script.

Many other characteristics of the text suggest that it was staged by a resident group of trained and subsidized individuals. For example, the processions and dances in *Wisdom* necessitate either extensive rehearsal time or a group experienced in such performances. The thirty-eight characters needed many costumes; even with doubling and minor additions to costumes to suggest new characters, their number precluded comfortable touring. Banns or pleas for donations, each a feature of non-private auspices, are conspicuously absent.

The script of *Wisdom* reflects the aesthetics of household performances in several ways. The multimedia effect employs drama, music, and dance, just as performance at court did. The play, like great house revels, is unsuited to public commercial auspices. It requires the co-operation of different types of entertainers—singers, dancers, minstrels, and players—who could not support themselves without patronage. The theme, a psychomachia in miniature, is expressed in terms that would appeal to a sophisticated audience. The

---

[51] Eccles, 119, 146, 149, 205 n., 215 n.; Wickham, *EES 3*, 152.

style of *Wisdom*, unlike that of *Secunda Pastorum*, is generally sober and didactic, bursting only occasionally into exuberance with the dances. Internal evidence suggests private auspices, and the variety of performers necessary indicates performance in a conservative noble or ecclesiastical great household.

The anonymous *Mankind* shows similar evidence of Chapel involvement, but is far more high-spirited.[52] Mercy appears as a 'semely father' (209), and Mischief addresses New Guise, Nowadays, and Nought as 'fayer babys' (427), a joke that is appropriate if the tricksters were Chapel Children. Latin is used extensively in the script, by Mercy and Mankind for religious effect (228, 292, 321, for example), and by the vice figures for comic effect (e.g. 57–60, 124–34, 324–6, 475, 687–93, 779–81). References to learning the 'neke-verse' (520) and to hearing evensong (551) have specific meaning for clerical performers.

Complex staging requirements make *Mankind* a difficult, but not impossible, play for a small independent troupe to manage. Minstrels are required to play dances (72), and the vices sing, albeit bawdy songs rather than the complex liturgical singing generally associated with choristers. Although at first glance the set requirements seem simple, the property list is extensive, including a substantial gallows (805) and a large number of stolen church goods. The gallows set piece and purloined plate would be easily supplied by a household.

The structure, theme, and mood of *Mankind* suit the aesthetics of performance within a noble household, perhaps as Wickham believes, at Christmas (for a Christmas song is parodied), when Percy's Chapel and the Chapel Royal were known to have staged plays. Several features of *Mankind*, however, do not suit Chapel performance. First, the doubling of Mercy and Titivillus would be unnecessary. Second, the irreverence of the vices and the lewdness of the music are inappropriate to Chapel style which, while it could be boisterous, was usually not bawdy. Third, the plea for donations (460) indicates a touring script. Production requirements and form suggest household Chapel auspices, and we

[52] References to *Mankind* are also drawn from Eccles.

could excuse aberrant qualities on the rather weak logic that the twelve days of Christmas tended to be saturnalian anyway. Yet the fact remains that the content and style of the play strongly suggest travelling interluders. Perhaps *Mankind* was originally a household play, produced by patronized interluders to satirize their privileged competitors with linguistic jibes and simplified yet sarcastic music and dance. Alternately, perhaps the text of *Mankind* that survives was adapted and developed from a less *risqué* Chapel play by interluders in need of a script.

Godly Queen Hester, which Bevington accepts as a Chapel play,[53] also utilizes production techniques common to Chapel performances. The play needs a large cast, for Aman enters with many men, the Pursuivant enters with many maidens, and a banquet is prepared on-stage. More significantly, Hester says:

> Call in the chapel to the intent they may
> Sing some holy himpne to speed us this day   (p. 277).

At this point, the Chapel did just that. The costumes of sixteen speaking characters and the supernumeraries, and the staging requirements, preclude touring.

The dialogue (composed of intellectual *débat* and oration, both courtly and educational forms), the theme, and the style of the play indicate an élite audience. As in Lydgate's mummings and Tudor disguisings, biblical allegory is carefully manipulated to protect author, producer, and performers while still making a political point: although the King is directly responsible for the persecution of the Jews in the biblical source, in *Godly Queen Hester* the King is clearly innocent, which indicates that the playwright was editing history to prevent royal censure or displeasure, and to thrust the blame for the political scheming solely upon the ignoble counsellor. Cast size, the number of costumes, the complexity of the staging, the necessity for a number of female roles, the actual summoning of a Chapel, and the sophistication of the music imply Chapel auspices. Bevington suggests that the

[53] Bevington, *From 'Mankind' to Marlowe*, 30; References to *Godly Queen Hester* are drawn from Farmer, 245–87.

chapel structure itself was the place of performance, since a travers or enclosed pew, to which the King retreats for most of the play (a wonderful visual image of the ruler's indifference or naïvety), was often available there. Yet a travers could be easily constructed for the hall, which frequently included a convenient minstrels' gallery (as did Percy's manor at Wressle), and the service of the banquet would be more easily accomplished there.[54]

Henry Medwall's plays, *Fulgens and Lucrece* and *Nature*, written for the household of Archbishop Morton, also create problems for a troupe of players, but may be easily staged by a combination of household entertainers. The two-part structure of the plays makes it clear that they were designed for performance in the Great Hall during a banquet; *Fulgens* was probably composed for a specific occasion, perhaps the visit of the Spanish and Flemish ambassadors to Lambeth at Christmas.[55] Both plays require complex staging and costuming, which would make touring difficult. *Fulgens* calls for a dance of mummers (II. 389) and at least one and probably more musicians (II. 386). *Nature* begins with a ceremonial procession, and requires costumes for twenty-two characters. Some of these, particularly those worn by the virtues, could have been adapted from ecclesiastical vestments which the household possessed.

The composition of the casts for both plays also indicates Chapel involvement. Bevington, following Brandl, tentatively suggests that *Fulgens* was staged by a professional troupe, with the assistance of two boys. Nelson is hesitant about assigning the plays to professional actors, suggesting rather that roles in both *Fulgens* and *Nature* were filled by household performers, including children from Morton's

---

[54] Based on this reference in particular, Bevington suggests that *Godly Queen Hester* was actually produced in the chapel. Yet the simple presence of a travers does not support the assumption. Henry VIII watched Anne Boleyn's coronation banquet from one (Hall, 304–5), so they were used in the great hall. Further, in *The Play of the Weather* the character Jupiter also enters a travers, yet Bevington suggests this was a set structure in the great hall (*From 'Mankind' to Marlowe*, 40). Serving a banquet, as is called for in *Godly Queen Hester*, within the chapel would have presented staging problems easily avoided if the great hall were used.

[55] Medwall, 2–3. References to the plays are drawn from this edition. Moeslein provides the most recent biography that helps to establish the details of Medwall's career under Morton's patronage.

Chapel, a conclusion with which Moeslein concurs. Performance of *Nature* at Eton or King's College, Cambridge, which Medwall attended from 1475 to 1483, is possible but unlikely, since most recent editors date the play between 1495 and 1500.[56] Nelson and Moeslein's solution to the casting difficulties is much more practical than Bevington and Brandl's postulation of a large troupe of actors with two child apprentices, and it reflects the co-operative effort of various household professional entertainers that we have observed elsewhere.

Rastell's *Four Elements* sharpens the issue of itinerant interluders versus conglomerate groups. The shorter version, in which Rastell tells us 'ye may leve out muche of the sad mater' of the full version, allows for unaccompanied song and simple dancing, thus providing an easily mobile script for five players. In contrast, the full version, designed for household performance, incorporates a disguising, which required dancers, minstrels, and additional costuming.[57] Rastell perceived the differences between the offerings of a troupe of actors and the offerings of household entertainers acting in consort, and tailored his play to accommodate both sorts of performance.

With the works of Heywood, Udall, and Redford, we find the beginnings of a divergent courtly tradition: plays employing casts composed exclusively of child choristers. This technique is hardly surprising, since all three were schoolmasters accustomed to producing school plays. Another explanation for this development may be found in the change in the nature of household revels under Henry VIII. As the nobility increasingly took central roles in the disguisings, culminating in the exclusively noble cast of the Jonsonian masque, the Chapel performers found themselves gradually excluded. Consequently, these performers sought other vehicles for their talents. Choristers espoused the tradition of Paul's Boys, who had been performing and touring independently and successfully. This division gradually evolved into

[56] Bevington, *From 'Mankind' to Marlowe*, 44; Medwall, 5, 19; Moeslein, 5–10; Brooke, 73.

[57] References to *The Interlude of the Four Elements* are drawn from Axton's edition; see also Wickham, *EES 3*, 113, 153, for a discussion of the musical requirements of *Four Elements*.

the active competition between professional boys' companies and adult troupes against which Hamlet so eloquently speaks.

But this tradition belongs to the professional theatres, not the great household auspices, and as such is outside the scope of this study. Although external boys' companies performed at court under Edward VI and Queen Mary,[58] resident Chapels continued to participate co-operatively in great household revels.

This chapter has examined the qualities which made the Chapel a unique performing body, and the dramatic activities in which it participated. Extant primary sources testify that the participation of the Chapel in great household revels was frequent and complex, and indicate that there is still extensive work to be done in order to re-evaluate the Chapel as a household performing group. Lost sources present a particular difficulty here. The disguisings, which were frequently staged at many households, were too ephemeral to be scripted and too ambiguously described even when they are documented. Texts of scriptural plays presented within great households seem to have disappeared, one hopes only temporarily. Chapel involvement in selected extant interludes is summarized in Table 1.

Based on the ideas presented in this chapter and an analysis of the texts, the chart assesses Chapel involvement in the interludes by isolating performing techniques that the Chapel was documented to have contributed to other great household entertainments.

Throughout this chapter I have delineated the six characteristics of the Chapel that determined its performing techniques. First, the size of the Chapel made possible entertainments that required a large cast. Doubling was unnecessary, for the Chapel could assemble a multitude 'on stage', something no other troupe of professional entertainers could achieve. Second, since the Chapel was composed of both men and boys, parts for women and children could be easily filled. Third, the Chapel were salaried entertainers and, as such, were not dependent upon touring to support

---

[58] For a convenient list and details of the records of such performances, see Feuillerat, xii–xv.

TABLE 1. *Chapels and Interludes*

Date[a]	Title	Cast Requirements[b]	Doubling[c]	Occasional[d]	Elaborate Set/Costumes/Properties[e]	Music & Dance[f]	Chapel Involvement[g]
1460–3	Wisdom Who is Christ	38+; 12w, 7b	?	No	C, S, P	Yes	Yes
1465–70	Mankind	7+	1	Xmas?	P	Yes	?
1495	Everyman	16	Yes	No	No	No	No (Foreign)
	Nature	22; 2w, 1b	Yes	?	C	Yes	Yes?
1497	Fulgens and Lucrece	7+; 2w	?1	Yes	C disg.	Yes	Yes?
1508	Mundus et Infans	2	Yes	Yes	No	No	No
1513–14	Youth	6; 2w	Yes	Yes	No	Yes	Yes
1514	Hick Scorner	6	Yes	Yes	No	Yes	No
1518	Four Elements (short version)	8+	No	No	C disg.	Yes	?
	Pardoner and the Friar	7	Yes	No	No	No	No
1519	Four PP	4	No	No	No	Yes	No
1520	Johan Johan	3; 1w	No	No	No	No	No
1520–2	Magnificence	14	Yes	Yes	C, P	Yes	No
1527	Gentleness and Nobility	4	No	No	No	No	No
	Calisto and Melibea	6; 2w	Yes	No	No	Yes	No
	Godly Queen Hester	16+; 1+w	No	Yes	S, C, P	Yes	Yes

TABLE 1 (*cont.*)

Date[a]	Title	Cast Requirements[b]	Doubling[c]	Occasional[d]	Elaborate Set/Costumes/ Properties[e]	Music & Dance[f]	Chapel Involvement[g]
1530–3	Weather	10; 2w, 1b	No	No	No	No	?
1533	Love	4; 1w	No	No	P	No	No
1537	Thersites	5; 1w, 1b	No	Xmas?	S, P	No	? School, Interluders
1538	Three Laws	14	Yes	No	No	Yes	No
	God's Promises	9	Yes	No	No	Yes	No
	John the Baptist	8+	Yes	No	No	Yes	No
	Temptation of Our Lord	5	Yes	No	No	Yes	No
	King Johan	14; 1w	Yes	?	C	Yes	No
1539	Wit & Science	21; 5w, 2+b	?8	Yes	C, P, S?	Yes	Yes
1547	Impatient Poverty	8; 1w	Yes	?Xmas	No	Yes	?
1552	Roister Doister	15+; 4w	No	?	C, S, P	Yes	Yes ?School
1553	Gammer Gurton's Needle	10; 4w, 1b	No	No	S	Yes	?School
	Respublica	12+; 6w	No	Yes	C	Yes	Yes
1555	Jacob & Esau	11; 3w, 1b	No	No	C, S	Yes	Yes
	Wealth & Health	7	?1	No	No	No	No
1555	Jack Juggler	5; 2w, 1b	No	Xmas	S	No	?School

[a] The dates of the plays are drawn from the most recent editions, and from *The Revels History of Drama in English*, vol. ii; these generally agree with T. W. Craik's in *The Tudor Interlude*. Most are uncertain: Bevington's *From 'Mankind' to Marlowe* and recent editions of individual texts should be consulted for more specific discussions of dating.

[b] The rubric '+' indicates that supernumeraries are required to fill non-speaking and/or musical roles. Particular casting requirements within the full cast number are indicated by a number followed by a 'w' (woman) or 'b' (boy).

[c] I have indicated 'yes' when doubling is *specifically* mentioned in the text or when the structure of the play indicates overwhelmingly that the author intended doubling to be employed. Occasionally I have noted cases when a limited number of characters may have been doubled.

[d] A positive response in this category means that either the text or external evidence indicates that the play was composed and performed for one specific occasion. A negative response, however, should not rule out the possibility; it simply indicates that the text has yet to be linked to a particular occasion or location. Many of these plays could have originally been occasional pieces that were adapted for touring or were composed with future touring in mind.

[e] The particular element or elements that were elaborate are indicated by 'S' for set, 'P' for properties, and 'C' for costumes. Again, the assessment is based on an analysis of the texts; those that require large numbers of costumes and properties or complex sets are noted.

[f] These are noted when the text or rubrics actually mention them within the context of the play. Many of the plays that do not specify music (which have been labelled 'no') would probably have included musical elements anyway.

[g] I have indicated those plays in which the talents of the Chapel could have been put to use. The conclusion is based upon the characteristics weighed in the chart, as well as references within the texts and external accounts. The chart demonstrates that, although Chapel performers were not involved in the production of all extant interludes, they did participate in some. More important, the aesthetics of Chapel performances, once noble households had explored and embraced them, affected the structure and style of much Renaissance drama. Further study of the disguisings and scriptural plays, which will be possible once more primary source materials are discovered and catalogued, should yield further evidence of this.

themselves. Patronage allowed them more freedom than the interluders in choosing material or undertaking entertainments at the specific request of the household, and their position in the household allowed the Chapel members to work with quite separate kinds of entertainers, such as minstrels, interluders, noble dancers, or even bearwards. Chapel entertainments did not have to be commercial properties, and so could afford to refer specifically to an occasion and could expect financial support and co-operation from the household for that occasion. Fourth, the Chapel had access to elaborate costumes, sets, and properties drawn from its own and the household's resources. The nobility spent vast amounts on valuable chapel furnishings, which could be put to use in entertainments. Fifth, the Chapel had continuous access to a definite playing and rehearsal space—the chapel rooms of the household. In addition, it had the use of other spaces with which it was familiar: the great hall and private chambers of their patron. Unlike touring troupes of interluders, the Chapel could perform entertainments designed for a particular location. Sixth, the training and social status of the Chapel enabled it to perform more sophisticated works, designed for a courtly audience, than the common players could; the Chapel's facility for music, rhetoric, and Latin prompted it to undertake entertainments that exploited these talents, and consequently reinforced its claim to a social standing superior to other household entertainers.

These qualities, combined with the fact that the Chapel was the only troupe of professional entertainers that operated strictly within the physical confines of great households, contributed significantly to the style, structure, and aesthetics of performance within the great households.

2
The Minstrels

> 'Do come,' he seyde, 'my mynstrales,
> And geestours for to tellen tales,
>   Anon in myn armynge
> Of romances that been roiales,
> Of popes and of cardinales
>   And eek of love-likynge.'
> *The Canterbury Tales* VII. 845–50;
> B^2 2035–40

Chaucer's description of Sir Tophas, surrounded by a variety of minstrels commanding a vast repertoire of songs and stories, is a satiric, yet accurate, representation of the medieval and Renaissance patrons who recognized the value of minstrels as versatile professional entertainers. Some were retained minstrels, residents in the household, while others were itinerants who ranged in class from professional musicians with noble patrons to vagrants who could carry a tune on a pipe. The frequency and variety of minstrel performances at the great households could easily give modern readers the impression that these entertainments were chaotic in planning and aesthetically eclectic, but contemporary accounts show that minstrels, like anyone associated with noble households, had legislated privileges and duties, were subject to the organizational procedures of the household administration, and made specific contributions to the production values of multimedia theatrical performances.

As most researchers have found, any investigation of the role of minstrels in medieval and Renaissance society is fraught with problems, due to the tremendous quantity and varying quality of manuscript references to these performers. The most frustrating problem is, unfortunately, also the most fundamental: the confusion in terminology. Entertainers such as jesters, jugglers, acrobats, and poets were called 'minstrales', 'histriones', and 'ludentes'.[1] In order to reconstruct great household minstrel performances and to assess the effect of their artistic values on the style of household revels, it is necessary to sift through these slippery terms to discover what types of musicians the nobility retained, and what they expected these resident musicians to do.

Depending upon their artistic function within the household, which was often determined by the types of instruments they played, retained minstrels served two functions: they provided heraldic and recreational music. Heraldic minstrels played loud instruments, chiefly wind instruments and drums, to attract and focus attention for ceremonial purposes. Recreational minstrels could be soloists, usually playing strings or keyboards, who provided music that was itself the focal point, and that could be enjoyed on more private occasions. Consorts or broken consorts, however, were the most generally useful entertainers, mixing string and wind instruments to provide occasional music and dance music for feasts and entertainments at the great households. The particular functions of each of these two groups demonstrate that the households had specific artistic and social demands which their minstrels were expected to fulfil.[2]

HERALDIC MINSTRELS

Heraldic minstrels included trumpeters (and sometimes sackbuts), drummers, and waits, whose primary function was, put simply, to make loud, impressive sound, designed to command quiet and to accentuate the arrival of an influential

---

[1] Chambers has discussed the various entertainers within the minstrel class in *The Mediaeval Stage*, i. 48, 59, 66, and ii. 230–303. Wickham also treats the problem in *Early English Stages 1300–1660*, 1, 181–2, 264–5; see also Woodfill, 57–8. The evolution of the minstrel class into more specific troupes is also discussed in *MS 1* 63–9, and *MS 2*, 185–7, and in *EES 1*, 268–9. Whether this trend is indicative of specialization within the minstrel class or is a result of more detailed record-keeping within household and civic accounts is, as yet, undetermined.

[2] These divisions should in no way be considered pigeon-holes; they simply facilitate an investigation of an extremely complex group. There were certainly overlappings within the groups, and period accounts often do not distinguish among them, just as they make no distinction between play and disguising.

personage or the presentation of a significant event, analogous to the entering player's cry of 'room' in the interludes. For presentational purposes heraldic minstrels used auditory spectacles to impress audiences with the social superiority of nobles and noble actions. Noblemen recognized the subliminal value of the artistic impression, and consequently virtually all, from knights to kings, retained heraldic minstrels.

The list of minstrels rewarded at Edward I's massive Whitsun feast in 1306, preserved in BL Add. MS 24459 and edited by Constance Bullock-Davies, confirms this idea. Of the 119 minstrels listed, 29 were heraldic minstrels accompanying their patrons. Most aristocrats travelled with a pair of trumpets, and the King retained a pair who were to attend him at all times.[3] The King's four watchmen, or waits, were also present, 'blowing or piping' for the audience, in addition to performing their customary duties such as sounding the hours at night and rousing the household in emergencies.[4] Seven drummers, called taborets and nakerers, completed the list of heraldic minstrels.

During the late fifteenth and early sixteenth centuries, the number of heraldic minstrels retained by the nobility increased dramatically. Edward IV's regulations, based on precedents set by previous monarchs, stipulate that the King retain two trumpeters, the same number attached to a noble patron during the reign of Edward I; but by the accession of Henry VII the number of trumpeters attending a noble patron

---

[3] Bullock-Davies, *Menestrellorum Multitudo: Minstrels at a Royal Feast*, 10–12, 19, hereafter referred to as *MM*. Edward rewarded two trumpeters of the Prince of Wales, Prince Thomas, the Earl of Lancaster, the Earl of Hereford, Sir John de Segrave, Sir Robert de Monhaut, Sir Henry de Beaumont, and Sir Robert fitz Payn.

[4] *MM* 51. Although the particular instruments that waits played are rarely specified in household or civic accounts, they are almost always referred to as 'blowing' upon instruments. Basing his conclusion on a 1330 wax seal, Rastall postulates that household waits usually played shawms. From July to Oct. 1511 Henry VIII retained a 'backpipe wayte', which indicates that waits could play other wind instruments as well (*L & P HVIII* ii/2, 1453). Carole Janssen (59) implies that the Norwich waits played viols and recorders although she cites no evidence for her assumption. By 1568, the waits of London played coronets and viols. Thomas Morley's *First Book of Consort Lessons*, dedicated to London's waits, mentions them playing lute, bandora, cittern, and viol: Lasocki, 23–8. From a general reading of Tudor musical history and accounts, it seem that civic waits did, of necessity, evolve from watchmen to more generally useful musical consorts. Since households retained a number and variety of professional musicians, household waits tended to retain their functions as watchmen.

tended to be six or more. Whereas the fourth Earl of Northumberland retained two trumpeters, his son employed six.[5] By 1481, Howard records show that the Duke of Norfolk retained five trumpeters.[6] At the royal court, where a trumpeter's services were more frequently in demand, the number was far higher. Henry VII retained twelve trumpeters and rewarded many others.[7] Henry VIII paid wages to a varying number of trumpeters at various times, but the total never drops below that of his father.[8]

It is interesting to speculate about this general increase in the number and use of heraldic minstrels from the fifteenth to the sixteenth century, as the Tudors consolidated their power, and the values of the aristocracy changed from feudal to Renaissance ones. One of the reasons for this increase was certainly the parallel increase in ceremonial activities that prolonged peace and relative prosperity not only allowed but almost required. Rather than continually demonstrating their prowess on the battlefield or their authority on the estate, the aristocracy were cultivating the talents of the businessman, the diplomat, and the courtier, roles that demanded an understanding of and ability to manipulate signs and symbols. Tudor noblemen were becoming increasingly aware of how an extravagent artistic performance contributed to their own prestige.[9] For centuries the popular imagination

[5] A. R. Myers, *The Household Book of Edward IV: The Black Book and the Ordinances of 1478* (Manchester: Manchester University Press, 1959), 132; NHB 254; Lancashire, 'Orders', 12.

[6] Collier, 53. One of the five was paid separately and received a smaller amount. He may have been an apprentice, a non-resident, or a part-time employee. This would decrease the number of Norfolk's resident trumpeters to four, an even number more consistent with the numbers recorded in other accounts.

[7] Price, 10; Woodfill, 296; Lafontaine, 1–3. Henry VII rewarded trumpeters retained by Prince Arthur, Princess Katherine, 'therle' of Spain, Irish trumpeters, Spanish trumpeters, and 'straunge' trumpeters: Anglo, 'Court Festivals', 29–33.

[8] Price, 12; Woodfill, 296–8; Lafontaine, 2–5. Wages to trumpeters are noted in *L & P HVIII* ii/2, 1458; BL Add. MS 7100, ff. 2, 33; BL Add. MS 59900, f. 44ᵛ; BL Arundel MS 97, f. 3.

[9] McFarlane and Stone provide a historical analysis that is crucial to a thorough understanding of the social and political history of the period, and to a conception of the way that history affected the nature of the noble classes. Both explore how the economic and philosophical shift from feudalism to bastard feudalism necessitated attitudinal shifts on the part of the Tudor aristocracy. Retainers had to be courted and impressed into remaining loyal. Consequently, ostentation, generosity, and artistic spectacle became valuable tools for ensuring a stable and reliable household structure.

had recognized that heraldic music signalled an important social event. The aristocracy, realizing that they could use this recognition to impress the populace ideologically with the concept of nobility, exploited the presentational nature of heraldic effects in art as well as in life.

Edward IV's regulations dictated that his heraldic minstrels provide '. . . blowinges and pipinges, to suche offices as must be warned to prepare for the king and his houshold at metes and soupers, to be the more redy in all seruyces, and all thies sitting in the hall togyder, whereof sume vse trumpettes, sume shalmuse and small pipes.'[10] Hall's chronicle is filled with references to the performances of heraldic minstrels at ceremonial occasions, at military encounters, and during civic pageantry, when trumpets, drums, sackbuts, shawms, pipes, and even cannons were called upon to produce an impressive sound.[11]

It is frequently difficult to characterize the musical style of this 'sound' since period accounts lack detailed descriptions, and manuscript texts for heraldic music from the fifteenth century seem not to have survived. Many scholars have concluded from this that most of these musicians did not, or could not, read music, that their performances were formulaic, traditional, and perhaps occasionally improvisational, and that their craft was learned by rote through apprenticeship. This conclusion is clearly in error. As early as 1306, one of Prince Edward's choristers was sent to Shrewsbury Abbey to learn 'the minstrelsy of the Crwth'; the Prince also requested that Sir John de London lend the clerk who had trained the Prince's boys to sing to his sister, the Countess of Hereford, so that her singers could learn the style. In 1358/9, Queen

---

[10] *The Black Book*, 131.

[11] Further examples of the varied use of heraldic minstrels abound, e.g. in the spring of 1481 Norfolk's trumpets and drums accompanied him to Scotland aboard the *Mary Howard* (Collier, 6, 53); When Princess Margaret travelled to Scotland for her wedding in 1503, she was accompanied by 'trompetts in disployed Banneres, in all the Departyngs of the Townes, and in the Intryng of that sam, playing on their instruments to the Tym that she was past owt' (Leland, iv. 267). Henry VII rewarded trumpeters in Jan. 1500 that 'blew when the King came over the water' (Anglo, 'Court Festivals', 35), His son frequently paid trumpeters for accompanying a nobleman overseas (*L & P HVIII* ii/2, 1451, 1455, 1456, 1461; 3.2; 1533ff.). Many household accounts record rewards to trumpeters retained by other noblemen, who may have been visiting (Collier, 116, 447; NHB 254). For references to heraldic minstrels in civic pageantry, see Withington, *English Pageantry*.

Isabella rewarded one Walter Hert, recently returned 'de scola Menestralcie' in London.[12]

The social and martial importance of heraldic music in particular implies sophisticated technique and superior performances. Elaborate and dramatic fanfare for plays, disguisings, and tournaments, and crucial signals for battles would not be entrusted to amateurish or poorly trained tooters.

Peter Downey's discovery of a mid-sixteenth-century correspondence concerning such heraldic musicians shows beyond doubt that trumpeters were musically literate and gifted artists in great demand by the courts of Denmark and Saxony. On 3 February 1557, King Christian III wrote to Elector Augustus of Saxony:

> We hope that YH [Your Highness] will have paternal and R [Royal] concern that some of our best trumpeters, who could play on all sorts of instruments, have left our service. Therefore, although we still have a few (who are good trumpeters and instrumentalists), we nevertheless require some good replacements as we wish them to practice the Italian style. Knowing that YH's trumpeters play the Italian style better than others, we would really and truly like to have some of these, as many as you can spare.
>
> Furthermore, we hope that YH would paternally and R like to help us by permitting us, through your trumpeters, to obtain the Italian blowing-at-table and cavalry signals, just as YH's trumpeters play them, written down in musical notation and with a descriptive commentary, so that ours may be able to establish the same style properly.
>
> We also need a timpanist: could YH, through your trumpeters, send us an apprenticed youth who can play timpani, and, moreover, a trumpeter, who is also an apprenticed youth, and who can play the Italian style and also cornetts, schwerpfeiffs and other instruments at court? We would also like YH to inform us of the fees and maintenance for good employ, for we are also troubled with these trifling things. All of these things, as stated above, will be used at court so that YH will not complain that we have presumed to trouble YH so much.[13]

---

[12] Stevens, 63, 312–13; Bullock-Davies, *Register*, 155–6.

[13] Downey, 325–9. The letter is preserved in the Royal Archive, Copenhagen 'Auslendises registrant de annis 1556–57', 220–4.

This letter proves many theories about the particular qualities of court trumpeters that have thus far been merely conjectural. It demonstrates that good heraldic minstrels were valuable to the court for both domestic and martial duties. King Christian required not only that his trumpeters be talented, but also that they master a particular style, indicating that many different trumpet styles existed (perhaps named for their geographic origin), and that some styles, like styles in costume and art, were considered chic or superior. Most important, we learn that court trumpeters were definitely musically literate, that they were indeed capable of learning written scores and communicating these in writing to other households.

Apprenticeship was still, however, the chief method of training new trumpeters to play and read the elaborate music they would perform; apprentices undoubtedly came cheaper than fully trained experienced trumpeters. Although King Christian calls his final request for advice on proper payment of trumpeters 'trifling things', his concern shows that good heraldic minstrels were difficult to find and to retain. Musicians of this calibre could easily find employment elsewhere if they felt underrated or underpaid.

Augustus's reply to King Christian is equally enlightening.

... in all friendliness we must inform YRH that recently all of our Italian trumpeters (and also the other Italian instrumentalists, apart from two who are not trumpeters) have returned to Italy, apparently because they did not get enough money for their monthly wage, despite the fact that we gave them, in addition to board and clothing, two hundred gulden per year service payment. Thus, we have no Italian trumpeters at present, only Germans who have learnt the Italian style. But as none of these is an instrumentalist, in order to maintain our instrumental music, we have written to Italy for others so that we may once more provide for the same; YRH may rest assured that we will be most diligent not to forget him.

Similarly, our timpanist died only half a year ago and we have had to use the [apprentice] he had trained. However, we are most willing to send YRH a boy who had been learning from him for some time, as soon as he has mastered [the art of] the [drum-]beating.

Furthermore, we are sending YRH the Italian signals for 'Boots and Saddles', 'Mount Up' and 'To the Standard', as well as a few signals, such as 'Retire' and 'The Watch'; moreover, a sonata which our trumpeters use for blowing-at-table, which is set in music and is played in six parts, according to the Italian trumpeters' method, which the trumpeters will easily understand. And as the sonatas for blowing-at-table are many and are often changed, we have sent YRH the most common and most used example...[14].

The mere existence of such a detailed correspondence, the fact that sovereigns would take the time to negotiate such cultural exchanges, shows the importance of qualified heraldic minstrels to the royal courts of Europe. Augustus's trumpeters knew their value, and did not hestitate to leave his court for greener pastures, which indicates that they considered themselves valuable professionals in great demand, not mere servitors desperate for a job. When his timpanist departed for celestial pastures, Augustus was clearly dissatisfied with being forced to 'use' the apprentice, even though the beleaguered youth, not fully trained himself, was knowledgeable enough to pass on, at least in oral form, the basics of his art.

The last, and most interesting paragraph of the letter shows that heraldic music was diverse and complex. Clearly, military signals must be specific and properly executed in order to preserve the State, but need they be fashionable in style? The fact that they were argues that, even on the field of battle, patrons were concerned with dramatic effect. The six-part sonata that marked the entrance of the patron to supper was a sophisticated composition, yet Augustus assumes that retained trumpeters 'will easily understand', and that they will be capable of learning 'the most common and most used example' and of improvising upon it to provide variety at public occasions. These relatively brief letters surely demolish any misconception that heraldic music served merely as traffic signals, short simple measures blown by lower-class musical illiterates.

Although this correspondence originates in northern Europe and dates from the mid-sixteenth century, its implications may be applied to England and to previous years. Downey

[14] Downey, 325–9.

maintains that the Italian style of trumpeting began its influence at the end of the fifteenth century and travelled northward.[15] As Sydney Anglo has pointed out, Henry VII was certainly aware of and influenced by the Burgundian court entertainment styles. His son was also sensitive to new artistic fashion from the Continent, for in 1538 he was raiding the Doge of Venice's court to recover the Bassano brothers, Italian recorder players who had been resident in England 1531–6.[16] The English court was not a cultural backwater and would have retained musically literate, talented, and expensive trumpeters like those of King Christian and Elector Augustus to provide the dramatic effects court life demanded.

For example, trumpet fanfare could create a mood. One of the duties of household trumpeters was to play at the doors of their patrons on New Year's morning, a service for which special rewards were recorded in accounts of royal households, Northumberland's household, and Rutland's household during the sixteenth century.[17] Rather than indicating the movements of a nobleman or drawing attention to a visual event, these performances set a celebratory tone for the New Year's Day festivities, heralding the arrival of the idea of seasonal rebirth and producing an exuberant mood within the household members. Whereas the trumpeters usually performed in reaction to aristocratic movements, on New Year's morning the aristocrats reacted to the musicians.

Dramatic performances made similar use of heraldic instruments. JoAnna Dutka's detailed study *Music in the English Mystery Plays* reveals that wind instruments were used in the Corpus Christi plays more frequently than any other instruments, probably because the potentially boisterous and chaotic nature of the huge audiences, whether indoors or not, necessitated the use of loud instruments for control and attention. Yet civic pageantry, which was also staged in the midst of public tumult, often employed the quieter music of

---

[15] Downey, 328.
[16] Anglo, *Spectacle*, 98–9; Lasocki, 23.
[17] *L & P HVIII* ii/2, 1444; BL Add. MS 7100, f. 14 (Henry VIII); Anglo, 'Court Festivals', 43–4. (Henry VII also rewarded the Queen's minstrels for playing on New Year's morning.) NHB 257 (Northumberland also rewarded the minstrels on New Year's Day). HMC 4: 359, 371.

strings, voices, and keyboards.[18] A second reason for the preponderance of wind instruments in Corpus Christi plays was that the minstrels who played them were accessible; it was easier to find and hire a piper with his own instrument than, for example, a virginals player. In the case of Corpus Christi plays that were staged processionally, the use of wind instruments solved a logistical problem, being mobile. Just as we do not include cellos in marching bands, the producers of processional plays were practical enough to note that the use of certain instruments, particularly the larger strings and keyboards, would present production difficulties.

Although the guilds used heraldic music for practical purposes, they were not ignorant of its artistic potential. Because of the traditional connections with consequential personages and momentous events, heraldic instruments could underscore the special significance of a character or a dramatic moment; thus the idea of King Herod's pretentious nobility was accentuated because he was attended by trumpets. Similarly, horn players costumed as angels emphasized the gravity and exultation of the Last Judgement at Chester, York, and Towneley.[19] The flourishes and fanfare symbolized the significance of the doctrinal moment by exploiting the social and ceremonial connotations for theatrical effect.

At the royal court of Henry VII, heraldic instruments were used frequently and in great numbers to fulfil their primary political function and to contribute to the artistic effects of household revels such as the tournament and the disguising. Richard Gibson's revels accounts reveal that the trumpeters who played at tournaments were costumed at the household's expense, so that their physical appearances complemented the composite aesthetic effect. If the household were interested in sound effects solely for the purpose of commanding attention, there would have been no need for the costumes, since livery would have been sufficient and far less costly.

At the February 1515 tournament at Greenwich, the trumpeters and 'drombyllslads', or drummers, like the noble

---

[18] Dutka, *Music*, 83–7; Withington, *English Pageantry*, i. 132–97.
[19] Dutka, *Music*, 82–7.

jousters, their horses, and other retainers, were costumed in blue and white. In May of the following year, when the king produced a two-day tournament at Greenwich, his attendants and fourteen trumpeters were provided with blue costumes for the first day and yellow for the second, again echoing the colour schemes of the tournament.[20] Although the practical function of the drummers and trumpeters, which was to provide 'great triumphe' as the company 'entered the felde wyth trompettes, dromslades and other minstrelsey'[21] did not necessitate that they be thematically associated with the principal actors, nevertheless the minstrels were not separated, visually or spatially, from the events to which they were drawing attention. They were costumed to be within the context of the theatrical event, to contribute to the illusion, while at the same time providing aural focus for it.

In disguisings, trumpeters served the same dual function. On the evening of 13 February 1511, when Henry held an elaborate joust and revels at Westminster to celebrate the birth of his short-lived first son, the household was treated to an interlude and concert by the Gentlemen of the Chapel, a knighting ceremony, and a period of dancing. Then 'the trompettes at thende of the Hall began to blow' heralding the approach of an elaborate pageant device, focusing audience attention and, as Stevens notes, covering the undesirable noise emitted by a heavy wheeled vehicle drawn by straining men. Here the trumpets were used for practical purposes. The same morning, however, six trumpeters had entered the field dressed as foresters in green velvet, standing on a pageant device 'like a forest with rockes, hilles and dales, with diuers sundrie trees . . .'. The pageant was drawn before the queen, at which point the 'forsters blew their hornes', the pageant opened and four knights emerged.[22] In this case, as with the other tournaments, the trumpeters were an integral part of the illusion, costumed actors playing roles compatible with the allegory represented by the pageant device, while at the same time highlighting the principal dramatic moment, the opening of the pageant.

[20] *L & P HVIII* ii/2, 1507, 1509–10.
[21] Hall, 584–5.
[22] Hall, 517–18; Stevens, 250.

74 The Minstrels

Heraldic instruments such as trumpets, drums, and fifes could, on occasion, provide dance music for a disguising, as they did at Wolsey's household, when trumpets accompanied a dance of old men and nymphs. In France, a banquet in honour of the English ambassadors included trumpets and fifes playing for dances. Henry VIII also used a drum and fife, again appropriately costumed, for a Shrove Sunday disguising in 1510.[23] Thus, the minstrels added a third function to their others; besides focusing attention on the dancers and creating an appropriate mood for the entertainment, the music became itself an integral part of the performance. When they heralded the movements of a noble patron, they acted independently, but when they participated in revels they were integrated within a larger group, co-operating with other household entertainers, and responsible for blending themselves and their art with a larger artistic concern, under the direction of the designer of the entertainment.

Although heraldic musicians were involved in some capacity in most of the extravagant ceremonial and theatrical performances at the great households, they were rarely the centre of interest. In contrast, recreational musicians, and especially those retained as soloists, were, and they bore little resemblance to heraldic musicians, for they played different types of instruments and different types of music. In addition, their duties and privileges placed them in a different relationship to the household and its patron.

SOLOISTS

The soloists retained as household musicians sang or played stringed or keyboard instruments, the most popular being the harp (sometimes called the cithara), psaltery, lute, organ (or regals), and virginals.[24] Quieter in tone and volume than heraldic instruments, solo instruments were often used as accompaniment for voice, obliging the audience to attend to the performers themselves and preventing solo musicians

---

[23] *Venice*, 4 (4 Jan. 1527); *L & P HVIII* ii/2, 1432; Hall, 513. Stevens believes that pipe and tabor frequently provided dance music at noble households (247, 256, 301). Other musicians who provided dance music will be discussed shortly.

[24] See Appendix B for a survey of solo instruments.

from functioning as effective heralds. Consequently, soloists are rarely mentioned in connection with large household revels such as disguisings, tournaments, or public ceremonial occasions. They played for select groups, often within the private chambers of their patrons rather than in the great hall. Instead of drawing attention dramatically to moments or movements as their heraldic brethren did, soloists diverted their audiences while quietly attesting to the civilized good taste of their patrons.

Edward I's string minstrels, harpers, luters, or viol-players entertained the King in his chambers when he was ill, when he was bored, or when he felt sleepless. The King's drummer, Martinet, twice acted more as a playmate than as a musician when he played for the princes in the royal nursery. Henry VIII retained 'Benet de Opiciis, player at organs, ... to wait on the King in his chamber'. Another organist, Dionisus Memo, performed a four-hour concert in Queen Katherine's chamber before the King and Queen, their attendants, and the ambassadors of Venice and the Empire.[25]

Whereas heraldic minstrels were generally responsible to the household administration, soloists were more directly in the control of the patron himself. Consequently, soloists could have enjoyed, to the limited degree allowed by the boundaries of the social hierarchy, a more personal relationship with the nobles they served. These minstrels could become personal favourites of a patron, reaping the financial rewards of such a position while balancing precariously on whims that dictated rising and falling fortunes. Zuan Piero, an Italian luter, lost the King's favour to 'a lad who played upon the lute' only to regain it with the help of Memo, the King's favorite organist. Anne Boleyn's favourite luter, Mark Smeton, lost far more than favour by cultivating the wrong patron.[26] Friendly relationships between patron and soloist

---

[25] MM 19, 136; L & P HVIII ii/2, 1472; Giustinian, ii. 97.

[26] Giustinian, ii. 75. Marqués de Molins reported to Spain that Mark Smeton played to the Queen while she was in bed, that she ordered her ladies to dance, and that she danced with him herself. Since the Spanish sentiment toward Anne Boleyn was less than warm (*The Calendar of State Papers Relating to Spain* refers to her constantly as 'the concubine'), the report is suspicious. But the fact that it was communicated indicates that such an occurrence was at least possible, if not probable. Stevens, 245. Molins, 55.

must have been forged, for the public accepted the possibility that their Queen enjoyed a sexual relationship with her lute-player.

Like heraldic minstrels, soloists reaffirmed the idea of nobility. Consequently, minor aristocrats who lacked the resources to retain trumpeters, drummers, and groups of minstrels managed to afford one musician. Such a patron was Wood, Treasurer of Norfolk's household in 1480, who kept one musician in his pay and livery.[27] Noblemen who could afford several musicians still enjoyed solo private performances, perhaps because the luxury of being able to command music at any time or any place reinforced their personal sense of wealth and power. In addition, retention of a virtuoso performer allowed a nobleman to display the excellence of his personal taste and, by extension, the artistic sophistication of his court. When Henry VIII ordered Memo to play for the ambassadors and required his court to attend to the young luter who had become a personal favourite, he expected to receive as much adulation as the performer did.

It is difficult to determine the form and content of these solo concerts. Although music for soloists represents a large percentage of extant musical manuscripts, many of these are from late in Henry VIII's reign, many are for keyboard, lute, or voice, and many appear to be for the use of noble amateurs rather than professional musicians. For example, no manuscript sources for harp music have, as yet, come to light, which makes performances difficult to characterize, and forces music and theatre historians to rely on speculation and analysis of traditions. Constance Bullock-Davies suggests that harpers composed and sang elegies and victory songs, since they often accompanied their patrons to battle.[28] Chambers and Stevens believe that harpers recited poetry, accompanying themselves with varying skill on their instruments.[29]

[27] Collier, xxi.
[28] *MM* 20–1. Her assumption is supported by Norfolk's accounts, which indicate that the Duke took Thomas, his harper, and his heraldic musicians on the voyage of the *Mary Howard* to Scotland in 1480 (Collier, 6).
[29] *MM* 27; Stevens, 281, 284; Chambers, *MS* 1, 73. Bullock-Davies, Chambers, and Stevens note that the early Renaissance harper was probably a descendant of the medieval troubador or scôp. Much of the evidence for this idea is limited to folklore and oral tradition, since accurate descriptions and manuscript music are

An item in Norfolk's accounts gives further evidence about the music of harpers: 'Item, the same day, my Lord made comenaunte with Willm Wastell, of London, harper, that he shall have the sone of John Colet, of Colchester, harper, for a yere, to teche hym to harpe and to synge . . .'.[30] This notice is unique in household accounts, and suggests certain qualities that differentiated harpers from other soloists and from heraldic musicians. As with many other minstrels, musical talent and training tended to be in the family, much like any other business; John Colet's son probably learned the fundamentals of harping from his father, was sent to London to polish and update his skill, then returned to Norfolk's household. Unlike Augustus's trumpeters or Henry VIII's organists, the boy was taught to play the harp and sing, but not to compose or read music, implying that what he learned he learned by rote. One reason that harp music does not survive is perhaps that most harpers were musically illiterate, improvising or singing lyrics to a general storehouse of memorized music.[31]

If harpers performed in the manner outlined above, several conclusions about the nature of their performances present themselves. Since the song was a prominent part of the performance, audiences had to listen for they could not fully appreciate the harp if they considered it background music and continued to converse or watch other performers. If harpers composed elegies and victory songs, their lyrics were lacking. Stevens quotes Puttenham's *The Arte of English Poesie* in support, to show that in the Elizabethan period, harpers still recited: 'we ourselves . . . have written for pleasure a little brief *Romance* or historicall ditty in the English tong of the Isle of great *Britaine* in short and long meetres, and by breaches or divisions to be more commodiously song to the harpe in places of assembly, where the company shall be desirous to heare of old adventures and valiaunces of noble knights in times past . . .' (Stevens, 281). The tone of this excerpt, and the words 'old adventures' and 'times past' indicates that by Elizabeth's time, this type of harp concert was more a nostalgic curiosity than a contemporary and fashionable kind of entertainment.

[30] Collier, 300.
[31] The idea that many musicians could not read music is supported by Stevens, 284, and by Price, 1–3. References from popular literature and private accounts indicate that training in harp playing was considered part of a nobleman's education, yet training in musical literacy is never mentioned: see Morris, i. 244; *The Black Book*, 45. Stevens, 284, comments that household accounts rarely note payments for songbooks or copyists, further supporting the idea that many musicians, amateur and professional, could not read a score.

specific to a household; although the music could be drawn from general traditions, the lyrics commented upon people and places known to the audience. Within the household, this music preserved personal and family accomplishments, and when performed outside the household, it reinforced the prestige of the family. In addition, since the harpers commanded a large repertoire of popular songs, the members of the household could request that favourite selections be played in impromptu fashion. The performances of harpers would then require less planning and simpler structure than other performances. In addition, these suppositions preserve the role of the family harper as bard in the Celtic and Anglo-Saxon tradition, as preserver of history, much as the African griot preserves tribal and clan accomplishments to this day.

Luters, the Renaissance heirs to medieval harpers, seem to have lost the bardic identity while inheriting some of the qualities of their musical ancestors. Since song was often part of the performance, the audience again had to listen. Accounts also indicate that solo lute performances were often unplanned and informal, and that they did not require complex organization on the part of the household administration. Therefore, the methodology and artistic effect of a solo lute performance would resemble those of the harp performance. Although lute-song music survives, indicating that some luters could read music, little of it can be dated before 1540. Both Stevens and Price believe that the survival of manuscript lute music is due more to the increased interest in music-making among the noblemen themselves rather than to a significant increase in musical literacy among professional musicians.[32]

Musical literacy was certainly one of the talents of solo organists and singers, many of whom were drawn from the ranks of Chapel performers, whose training included reading music. This skill affected the types of performances a nobleman could expect from singers and keyboard artists.

[32] For a discussion of lute-song books see Stevens, 7, 109, 130, 278–9. Stevens also discusses the compositions for lute by Henry VIII (111–12). He considers Wyatt as a composer of lute-song, but concludes that Wyatt's poetry was not composed specifically as music (133–8); see also pp. 274–83 for an examination of amateur lute-playing by noblemen. Price also considers this phenomenon at length as does Page.

Memo may well have been following a score for his four-hour concert in the Queen's chamber, but even if he were not, his repertoire would reflect a knowledge of sophisticated musical styles from the Continent. The complexity and length of these performances, combined with the respected social position of the clerical organists, would prevent organ concerts from being impromptu and informal, as the offerings of luters and harpers could be. Organ concerts required planning to make the instrument itself, unless it were a portative, available at the time and place where the concert was to be given. These factors indicate that the organ solo, sophisticated in style, in content, and in execution, was a more structured performance than a harp or lute solo.

Extant music for organ is, of course, mostly religious, yet secular music for keyboards does survive, so organists were not limited to liturgical concerts. Memo himself was a composer and wrote 'a very fine vocal quartet' for Henry VIII which expressed his loyalty to his earthly king, not to his heavenly one.[33] It is a mistake to assume that de Opiciis and Memo, Henry VIII's principal solo organ players, were incapable of providing music that reflected social as well as religious values.

Secular songs also form a large percentage of extant manuscript music, indicating that this was a particularly popular form of entertainment, but it is difficult to discover exactly who was singing these songs. Henry VIII supposedly composed songs, further evidence that interest among Tudor nobles in vocal music was intense.[34] The inclusion of songs in extant interludes, which I will examine in detail later, confirms that singing was a fundamental part of the Renaissance notion of entertainment. Yet, curiously, rewards to solo singers in the household accounts occur only rarely. One such seems exorbitant: in 1313/14 the singer William de Milly, resident in court for only thirty-seven days of the year,

---

[33] Stevens surveys extant music from the early Tudor period, 3–7; Giustinian, ii/75.

[34] According to Stevens and Price, singing was considered an important facet of noble life; young noblemen were taught to sing, and their parents entertained each other with singing in private. Some of the extant music is complex, though, indicating that it was written for professionally trained singers such as the Chapel Gentlemen and Children: Stevens, 1–23, 111–12, 130–1.

was receiving wages at two shillings a day, equivalent to the wages of a knight. Perhaps secular song was usually provided at a cheaper rate by the musically literate Chapel singers, explaining some of the unspecified rewards to Chapel Children and Gentlemen.[35] Solo singing probably took place in private or on less formal occasions, since descriptions of court entertainments rarely refer to solo singing as part of the larger household revels.

Since the chronicles usually report public events and household accounts record moneys expended through regular administrative channels, information about private solo performances is rarely preserved. The extant references, however, do give some idea of the social and economic rewards that such performers could expect. Dionisus Memo was a respected virtuoso performer who so pleased the king that:

> said Majesty has included him among his instrumental musicians, nay, has appointed him their chief, and says he will write to Rome to have him unfrocked out of his monastic weeds, so that he may merely retain holy orders, and that he will make him his chaplain. In this case a piece of fine fortune will have befallen him, for to be a royal chaplain is an honourable appointment and very profitable; . . .[36]

Memo's social and economic privileges were due in part to his status as a priest, yet his virtuosity on the organ attracted Henry's initial attention and prompted him to retain Memo as a solo performer. He surely had no dearth of chaplains but had to offer Memo a desirable position to prevent him from seeking more lucrative and prestigious employment elsewhere.

---

[35] Perhaps Norfolk's singer 'litle Richard' was at one time a Chapel chorister. Accounts that record expenses for his clothing also detail expenses for Chapel Children, yet he was treated separately. Apparently he was not resident within the household, for 'Willm Davyes, prest of Neylong' was paid for boarding him. In addition, Richard was frequently employed as a messenger for the Duke, riding great distances, which implies that he was a young man rather than a child. Perhaps he began service in the Duke's Chapel and was retained as a soloist and personal servant when his voice changed. Norfolk also employed two adult singers, Nicholas Stapleton and William Lynsey; whether or not they were Chapel Gentlemen is impossible to determine solely from the available records (Collier, 124, 163, 389; expenses for Richard's various errands are recorded on 114, 126, 128, 151, 208, 211, 216, 220).

[36] Giustinian, i. 296–7; ii. 97. By the following year, Memo had indeed become the King's chaplain.

As chief of the instrumental musicians and a royal chaplain as well, Memo garnered double privileges, double salary, and increased control over the household music.

Other soloists also reaped benefits from their unique positions in the households. One of Edward I's harpers was a King of Heralds, a position at the top of the hierarchy of household musicians. In the fourteenth century, William Le Sautreour grew rich as the psaltery player for three queens, often travelling with his patroness; John de Brabant, a visiting vielle player from the court of Hugh le Despenser was rewarded with forty shillings from royal household accounts, eight months' wages for a royal harper.[37] Norfolk's harper and singer served as personal messengers. Wages and rewards delivered to solo musicians through John Heron, Henry VII's Treasurer of the Chamber, were consistently higher than those paid to other retained musicians, further indications that the position of a household soloist was socially and financially more comfortable than that of the other musicians.[38]

Although these soloists contributed significantly to the leisure entertainment of noble patrons, they were not as frequently or as generally useful as other household minstrels, nor were they as influential in the development of dramatic structure and style. Consorts, and particularly mixed consorts of string and wind instruments, were retained by most noble households, and were expected to provide music for many different types of occasions. Consort participation in court ceremonials, disguisings, and plays contributed more directly to the theatrical aesthetics and public relations of household revels than did the concerts of soloists or the playing of heraldic musicians, and their touring activities enabled them to communicate these effects to other households, to cities, and to ecclesiastical and educational institutions all over England.

CONSORTS: RESIDENT AND TRAVELLING

Hundreds of pages of household and civic accounts have recorded the journeys of the itinerant troupes. Financial

---

[37] MM 77–9, 91–2, 98–104.   [38] See Appendix B.

FIG. 8. BL MS Harleian 1527 f. 36ᵛ, from a French *Bible Moralisée* (c.1250–75), shows four minstrels during a meal playing fiddle, symphony, harp, and psaltery.

accounts, however, merely establish the quantity of minstrel troupes and the frequency with which they travelled, rarely preserving even the most rudimentary description which could provide modern observers with insight into the performance style. Information from ordinances and descriptions of royal court activities help determine what instrumentalists comprised a typical household troupe, and how these troupes contributed to the cumulative artistic effects of the entertainments.

From the mid-fifteenth century and through the early Tudor period the number of minstrels in troupes retained by noble patrons remained consistent at three or four. Shrewsbury accounts for 1457 mention payments to four minstrels under the patronage of each of the Dukes of Buckingham, York, and Exeter; in contrast, Durham Priory accounts from the mid-fourteenth century, when they record numbers at all, usually mention two, and use the term 'histriones' which could possibly indicate performers other than minstrels. Edward IV kept four minstrels and a wait resident within his household; two were heraldic minstrels, and the other two were string-players who were resident only if and when the King wished. In the early sixteenth century, the Earls of Northumberland and Oxford retained three household minstrels each, as did Queen Elizabeth of York, Queen Katherine of Aragon, and Queen Katherine Parr. Even Cardinal Wolsey, perhaps one of the most flamboyant patrons of the period, employed only four in his resident minstrel troupe. The lists of household minstrels retained by Henry VII and Henry VIII include greater numbers of resident minstrels, but this phenomenon is not indicative of the practices of most great households; the frequency and complexity of theatrical and ceremonial activity at the royal court required greater manpower than did the smaller courts.[39]

Just as the numbers remain consistent, so does the

---

[39] Chambers, MS 2, 241–2, 250; *The Black Book*, 131–2. Non-resident but liveried minstrels raised the total of Edward IV's minstrels to thirteen. NHB 201; Hope, 319; Nicholas, 100; BL Add. MS 59900, f. 68^v; Cavendish, 20. It is difficult to list the number of household minstrels retained by Henry VII and Henry VIII, since the numbers changed from year to year, and the accounts are sometimes fragmentary, sometimes misleading. Woodfill lists Henry VII's musicians in 1509: 4 sackbuts and shawms of the privy chamber; 8 still shawms; 3 minstrels; 4 minstrels of the chamber (including 2 luters); 3 taborets; and 15 or 16 trumpeters. At the time of his death, Henry VIII retained: 8 viols; 6 sackbuts; 6 flutes; 2 luters; 13 singers; 1 virginalist; 3 harpers; 1 bagpiper; 1 Welsh minstrel; 8 musicians; 8 minstrels; and 1 rebec player (Woodfill, 296–7). Henry VIII's accounts for 1544–5 in BL Add. MS 59900 list monthly wages for: 17 trumpeters (f. 44); 2 lutes; 2 rebecs; 1 harper; 1 wait (perhaps the bagpiper?); 1 viol; 4 sackbuts; 1 taboret; 2 minstrels; 2 drumslades (ff. 44–5^v); 2 virginals players, Heywood and Burton (f. 59^{r-v}); 6 Italian viols; 3 minstrels (f. 69); and 1 Welsh minstrel (f. 149^v).

composition of the minstrel troupes. Northumberland retained a taboret, a luter, and a rebec player. Similarly, Oxford retained a taboret, a luter, and a fiddle player. Katherine of Aragon's minstrels included a taboret, piper, and rebec player. Although Northumberland and Oxford seem to lack wind minstrels within their troupes, their taborets were probably capable of playing pipe and tabor. Northumberland's waits, who visited the royal court in August 1499,[40] could also have combined with his minstrel troupe since, given their northern homeland, they were probably bagpipers. Queen Katherine's troupe lacks a luter, but she may have employed one as a soloist, or have commandeered one of her husband's when the need arose.

Retained minstrels could expect to receive livery, room, board, and wages for the days when they were actually resident at court; in addition, the household would on occasion underwrite expenses for such supplies as horses, weapons, or war gear if the minstrels were on their master's business. Some minstrels, like Richard Pilke and his wife Elena, were paid as waferers as well as minstrels, and travelled with the king's household in 1311/12.[41] Payments for instruments and repairs to instruments also appear occasionally in household accounts, and rewards from patrons or visiting dignitaries and grants of land provided perquisites for certain talented or highly valued minstrels.

In return, the patrons expected their minstrels to be available to play at any time. Trumpeters were indispensable since they signalled the meals, movements, entrances, and exits of the nobility. Other minstrels were required to perform at major holidays such as Christmas, Easter, and Shrovetide, as well as at important family occasions such as weddings, christenings, funerals, and visits from important guests. All the minstrels were expected, like any retained employee, to take their orders from the household administration and to obey household regulations that prevented them from overstepping the boundaries dictated by their

---

[40] NHB 201; Hope, 319; Anglo, 'Court Festivals', 35. Northumberland's taboret and Oxford's luter received higher wages, perhaps for acting as troupe marshall or leader. It is also possible that they received higher wages for extended duties or for special talents. [41] Register, 51.

social positions. Edward IV's regulations are quite specific on this matter, and indicate that the minstrels in particular had to be warned to behave themselves: 'The king woll not, for his worshipp, that his minstrelles be too presumptuouse nor to familier to aske any rewardes of the lordes of his lond; . . .'.[42] The regulations prevented the minstrels from abusing their privileged status as 'The King's Minstrels' to pressure the nobility into paying them, but did not actually require them to refuse an offer. Most household account books show that, despite the ordinance, the nobility offered rewards, and the minstrels no doubt accepted them. Since *The Black Book* cites the practices of Henry II as precedent for these traditions, the retention of household minstrels, as well as the history of their abuses, reached back to the twelfth century, at least in the minds of the compilers of the household book.

In addition to playing music, household minstrels were expected to teach music to aristocrats and to repair the instruments they owned. Minstrels were responsible for teaching Lady Frances Manners the guitar and probably the lute, for a lute and a set of song books were purchased. Her husband apparently played the viol. A nephew of Lord Willoughby was taught to sing and play the virginals. By the sixteenth century, teaching music had become one of the regular duties of household musicians, for Braithwait comments that they were expected 'to teach the Earle's children to singe and play upon the Base Violl, the Virginalls, Lute, Bandora, or Citerne'.[43] Although there is no indication that the household minstrels were able to construct instruments (these were usually purchased from artisans external to the households), they could and did string, tune, and make minor repairs.

In order to play frequently, to teach, and to take care of family instruments, the minstrels would have to be resident within the household on a regular basis. Indeed, in 1318, Edward II required that four household minstrels be available all the time: 'Item ij trompers soient, et ij autres ministralx soient, al fois pluis, al foitz meins, qi ferrount lour minstraucie

---

[42] *The Black Book*, 132.
[43] HMC 4: 4, 381, 412–14, 432, 532; Jones, 232; see also Rastall, 16.

devaunt le roi a toutz lez foitz qi luy plerra. Et mangerount en chambre ou en la sale solonqu qils serrount comaundez. . . .'[44] Similarly, over a century later Edward IV required continuous service from his two trumpeters and two other minstrels.[45] The frequency of theatrical activity and ceremonial events at the courts of Henry VII and Henry VIII demanded that household minstrels be in continuous residence with the king. The nobility also required frequent service from their minstrels, and not all occasions could be planned far enough in advance to allow all the minstrels to leave their patron; all great households required that some minstrels be available at all times.

This raises the most troublesome conundrum inherent in any investigation of Tudor minstrelsy. Household, civic, ecclesiastical, and college accounts record that hundreds of minstrel troupes in the livery and under the patronage of a nobleman were travelling all over England every year. If the households required such frequent service from their minstrels, how could they be permitted to travel so far and so often? If household minstrels received food, clothing, shelter, and wages from their patrons, why would they have to travel at all? Any rewards they received would have to be spent to purchase the necessities that the household supplied if they remained at home. Yet these troupes did travel while maintaining some sort of relationship with the household.

Bullock-Davies's investigation of the household minstrels of Edward I indicates that many of these men were not the poor vagrants scraping for a living that they have been imagined to be. Rather they were middle-class family men, who owned homes in London and property elsewhere, and received land grants from the King. Living on their savings, they retired to their homes or to a comfortable life at one of the monasteries under the King's patronage. Hugh de Naunton, one of the King's harpers, came and went from his London home to court frequently, but with no regular pattern. Exchequer accounts carefully recorded his movements and paid him wages only when he was actually present in the household, a system of accounting followed for all

[44] Rastall, 8.
[45] *The Black Book*, 131.

royally retained minstrels.[46] Many royal musicians earned their fortunes through investment and business, not by splitting twenty-shilling rewards with other musicians while visiting at noble households.

Henry VIII went to some trouble to acquire and retain a talented consort of recorder-players, the Bassano brothers of Venice. Resident in the English court from 1531 to 1536, the family returned to the Continent to take service with the Doge of Venice, the precise reason for their departure from England remaining unspoken. Perhaps, like Augustus's trumpeters, they felt undervalued or underpaid. What is certain is that Henry felt their lack, for from 1536 to 1540 he was busily negotiating for their return. One brother, Anthony (a maker of instruments as well as a player), had returned to England in 1538, perhaps to whet Henry's appetite, perhaps to negotiate for his family. Henry needed little encouragement, for he agreed with Edmond Harvel, his Venetian agent, that it would be 'no small honour to His Majesty to have music comparable with any other prince or perchance better and more variable'.[47] By 6 April 1540, 'Aluixus, John, Anthony, Jasper, and Baptista de Bassani, brothers in the science or art of music', were back on Henry VIII's payroll, holders of trade monopolies in Gascon wine and living rent-free with their families at the dissolved Charterhouse monastery. From then firmly established at the English court, three generations of Bassani served the Tudor monarchs.

The Bassano brothers, like Memo and the Italian trumpeters of the Denmark–Saxony correspondence, were 'hot properties'. Royal patrons were obviously aware of fashionable trends in music, could spot talented players, were not above raiding other courts to entice unique musicians away, and were prepared to be generous in order to keep them

---

[46] PRO E 101.371.8; MM 21–2, 64–5. William de Roos, the King's viol player, had the modern equivalent of £900 stolen, not an amount we would expect a poor travelling player to possess (MM 91–2). William Le Sautreour, the Queen's psaltery-player was rich enough to own property and to loan money (perhaps an early usurer?); his home was robbed of goods to the value of £20,000 in modern currency (MM 98–101). Stevens mentions several minstrels who practised other non-musical trades, such as dealing in counterpanes, beer, wool, and wine (Stevens, 315–16).

[47] Lasocki, 23–8; see also L & P HVIII xiii, 537; xiv/1, 163; PRO SP, 1/153 f. 215; PRO C 66/690 m. 38. For more information about the Bassano brothers, see Selfridge-Field.

satisfied. It is difficult to imagine musicians such as these enduring the rigours of the road to entertain provincial crowds for small rewards.

Not all retained minstrels were this fortunate, of course, but some were able to support themselves quite comfortably on their earnings. Clearly, household administration was prepared to accommodate various wage and time structures for different types of minstrels. Some, particularly the heraldic musicians, were resident on a regular basis and were generously recompensed for their services. Others, resident only during particular and limited times and paid on a daily basis, would be free to tour or to attend to their own businesses, as their financial conditions allowed.

Edward IV's *Black Book* further supports this idea. Of the Kings thirteen minstrels, some '. . . are strengmen, coming to this courte at v festes of the yere, and than to make theyre wages of houshold after iiij^d ob. a day if they be present in court; and than they to auoyde the next day after the festes be don.'[48] These 'strengmen', or players of stringed instruments, did not simply 'drop in' to the royal household. Rather, their visits were planned and regular, and the duration of their stay was legislated. They arrived at times when the demands of the revels required that the number of available minstrels be augmented, and left when their services were no longer needed, when they could place an unnecessary burden upon household expenses. In return for their services, these musicians could call themselves 'The King's Minstrels', and enjoy the welcomes and financial rewards that such a title encouraged. A 1520 charter for the royal minstrels mentions names that never appear in the King's accounts as household minstrels, further indicating that some royal minstrels were actually resident while others simply acquired the name and livery in return for limited service.[49]

The organization of Edward IV's minstrels provides a clue to the nature of the travelling patronized troupes. Perhaps noble households retained three or four minstrels as resident entertainers, and allowed others to use the nobleman's name in return for planned but infrequent visits. Thus, patronized

---

[48] *The Black Book*, 131–2.
[49] Stevens, 300.

troupes could appear at far-flung locations while the patron could still depend upon the services of some of his musicians. It is also possible that minstrels travelled with their patrons, and that rewards given by other households and by cities indicate the presence of troupe and patron. A third possibility is that some minstrels would be given leave to travel while their lord progressed to his various estates, visited noble kinsmen and allies, or 'broke up' his household, keeping only a few dozen retainers about him. At such times the patron would still require the services of his heraldic trumpeters, but would have found other minstrels expendable.

Unfortunately, scholarly investigations of the movement patterns of minstrels are still in an embryonic state which prevents solid conclusions. Once primary materials are collected and examined, touring patterns for minstrel troupes may become clearer and may be matched to the movements of patrons to determine whether these minstrels actually travelled independently of their patrons, what times of year they tended to tour, what locations they frequented, and what motives existed for the tours.

During Christmas 1507, for example, the Duke of Buckingham's household was entertained by forty-one minstrels, far more than he could possibly have retained on a regular basis. His household accounts record that he fed 459; since his own household in 1511 numbered 225, the others must have been guests.[50] Household minstrels would be unlikely to abandon their patrons during Christmas, when their services were crucial to the celebrations and rewards liable to be generous, unless the patron was not planning to remain at home. Just as Edward I's guests brought their own musicians to his 1306 Whitsun feast, Buckingham's noble guests probably brought their household minstrels along to Thornbury, Buckingham's ducal seat.

---

[50] Rawcliffe, 88, 94. The players of the Duke's brother-in-law, the Earl of Northumberland, also entertained during this Christmas season. Since the Earl's Twelfth Night order specifies that he was to be entertained with a play in his own household, the presence of his interluders at Thornbury suggests that perhaps the Earl was also there (Lancashire, 'Orders', 12). Similarly, Northumberland's players entertained at Henry VII's Twelfth Night in 1493, suggesting that Northumberland spent that Christmas at court, where he had been raised as a ward of the King's mother (Anglo, 'Court Festivals', 28).

FIG. 9. BL Royal MS 14 E IV f. 244ᵛ, a fifteenth-century miniature from a Flemish manuscript shows John of Gaunt at table with the King of Portugal. To the right, shawms play from a balcony while gentlemen ushers serve the royalty and clergy. To the right an older retainer, perhaps the Chamberlain, looks with disapproval on a courtier arranging the tip of his fashionable shoe.

The Minstrels 91

Visiting minstrels frequently entertained at noble and royal households. Rewards in these accounts were basically of two types: payments to minstrels from other households and cities; and payments to unidentified entertainers. Notices of rewards of the first type do not yield much information, since they usually record only the name of the patron, indicating that the household administration felt that the identity of the nobleman was more important than who his minstrels were or what they performed. Payments of the second type are more enlightening, and often more entertaining to the researcher, for they record details of unique performances.

Edward I was entertained by '... John de Coton, a Lombard, making his minstrelsy with snakes', and by '... Bernard, the Fool, and 54 of his companions coming naked before the King, with dancing revelry'. Royal accounts of 1331 record a land grant to one 'Roland le Fartere' for 'making a leap, a whistle and a fart'. Matilda Makejoy, one of the very few female minstrels on record, entertained with dances and acrobatics in 1297, 1306, and 1311. Henry VII rewarded minstrels 'that played in the Swan', one of his ships, and seamen who 'rowed vpe and down syngying' at Greenwich. His son was particularly generous to 'Two women out of Flanders that did pipe, dance and play' before the King, rewarding them an exorbitant £8. 6s. 8d.[51] These 'novelty' performers posed no great threat to resident minstrels, for their acts were self-contained, their appeal limited, and their appearances infrequent (often they performed once only), effectively preventing them from competing with retained minstrels or contributing in any significant manner to the theatrical styles of a household.

The logistical and organizational relationship between the visiting minstrels and the household administration remains a mystery; minstrels could not simply knock on the gate and ask to see the lord. While household regulations never mention what procedures were to be followed for the presentation of itinerant musicians, the Earl of Northumberland's regulations do record an elaborate system of payments to visiting minstrels under the patronage of a nobleman;

---

[51] MM 66–7; PRO E 101.375.8, ff. 14^v, 32^r; *Register,* 108–9, 174; Anglo, 'Court Festivals', 27, 43; *L & P HVIII* ii/2, 1450.

amounts of rewards depended upon the rank of the patron, whether he was a 'speciall Lorde Frende or Kynsman' to the Earl, and how frequently the troupe visited the Earl's household.[52] Northumberland, like Edward IV, expected certain minstrels to visit him on special occasions, so his household planned the visits and allocated specific payments. There is no similar system of payments for civic or unpatronized minstrels who visited Northumberland's household, which suggests either that their visits were unexpected and unplanned or that Northumberland found no need for a specific reward system that carefully reflected the social hierarchy and political alliances.

When a troupe of musicians arrived and the household could not or would not hear them, they might still be paid. Such an event occurred on 8 January 1542 at the Earl of Rutland's household when three minstrels from Nottingham and six players from Derbyshire were rewarded 'because they played not'. The Earl was in residence, for a juggler who 'shoyd hes connyng in mackyng off a lyght for the banckyt' was rewarded.[53] Perhaps Rutland's household administration had already designed an entertainment for his banquet and visiting entertainers, especially those without a patron's name or even a powerful city's patronage to recommend them, could not be accommodated within its structure. This idea is further supported by Northumberland's Twelfth Night ordinance. Although his accounts and regulations demonstrate that he listened to visiting troupes from various noblemen, his ordinance does not indicate that these visitors participated in the evening's revels. Rather, the Twelfth Night festivities seem designed to utilize household minstrels who rehearsed with other entertainers and who were familiar with the structure and order of the revels.

Noble households had to design, construct, and plan polished and artistically sophisticated entertainments, particularly for important occasions. Neither the arrival nor the repertoire of visiting minstrels was under the control of the household administration, and entertainments offered by masterless itinerant minstrels undoubtedly varied considerably

[52] NHB 253.
[53] HMC 4: 322; Woodfill, 268.

in quality, frequency, and style. Patronized troupes may have offered music that was more consistent in style and quality, since no nobleman would have been willing to risk his reputation by dressing substandard minstrels in his livery, but their arrival and particular talents were still bound to be somewhat unpredictable. Consequently, the household depended chiefly upon its resident minstrels to execute disguisings and the elaborate multidimensional revels that often accompanied ceremonial banquets. Visiting troupes could, perhaps, entertain upon these occasions, but their performances probably took place before or after the planned entertainment. Not once do Hall's descriptions of Henry VIII's revels ever mention that a visiting troupe performed within the context of his court revels, although the accounts show that Henry did frequently reward such troupes. Clearly, noble patrons were never foolish enough to depend upon external performers to execute the centre-piece entertainment at important secular festivals or religious feasts.

Resident mixed consorts provided incidental, dance, and ceremonial music. Just as Northumberland rewarded his trumpeters for a heraldic fanfare on New Year's morning, he also rewarded

... his Tabret Lute ande Rebek upon New-Yeares-Day in the mornynge when they doo play at my Lordis Chambre doure for his Lordschipe and my Lady xx^s ... And for playinge at my Lordis sone and heir Chaumbre doure the Lord Percy ij^s. And for playinge at the Chaumbre dowres of my Lords Yonger Sonnes my Yonge Maisters after viij^d. The pece for every of them. ...

John Heron recorded payments by the King to the Queen's minstrels on New Year's morning, probably for a similar service.[54] Like household trumpeters, minstrel consorts set a festive mood for the holiday.

Northumberland's minstrels also played a concert during his Twelfth Night festival, but this music was not the focal point of the entertainment as it had been on New Year's morning;[55] instead, it provided aural background which would not detract from the service and enjoyment of the

---

[54] NHB 343–4; Anglo, 'Court Festivals', 31, 32, 34, 38, 40, 41, 43, 44.
[55] Lancashire, 'Orders', 40, 42.

banquet. With great regularity, Hall records such performances at the royal court, where banquets were frequent occurrences and the music of consorts or mixed consorts was indispensable. Although detailed descriptions of such occasions at the noble courts are lacking, the practices of the royal court provide a model which smaller courts could imitate to the best of their financial and artistic abilities.

MINSTRELS IN PERFORMANCE

Thus far I have been discussing various types and degrees of the minstrel class primarily as makers of music, but many minstrels, particularly resident consorts, played a vital role in the theatrical life of the household, chiefly by assisting in the design, composition, and performance of the disguising. On these occasions, the minstrels often became an integral part of the visual representation while providing the music for professional performers and aristocratic dancers.

On Twelfth Night at Northumberland's household, the minstrels' role in the disguising and morris was both presentational and functional. Although the household book records wages to a troupe of three minstrels, the ordinance mentions 'iiij Minstrallis suche as the lord haith at that tyme . . .'. Since the order never mentions the inclusion of visiting performers, and its syntax continually implies that the order is intended specifically for household personnel, perhaps one of Northumberland's resident trumpeters or waits joined his minstrel consort for the occasion. The four were directed to stand on the side of the hall and to play as the disguisers entered, made their obeisance to the Earl, and danced. When the disguising required both female and male dancers, the minstrels split into two groups, one accompanying the men, the other the women. After the initial dances, the disguising was interrupted by the arrival of a pageant device, out of which poured the henchmen, who, again accompanied by the minstrels, executed the morris dance, then departed with the pageant. The disguising resumed, the minstrels playing basse and round dances as the men and women danced together.[56]

[56] Lancashire, 'Orders', 35–6.

Northumberland's Twelfth Night ordinance is prescriptive rather than descriptive, so it raises as many questions as it answers. It preserves a pattern for disguisings in general, indicating specific forms to be followed by performers but omitting the content; yet several conclusions may be drawn from observing this form. The minstrels were responsible for four types of music: presentational or heraldic, thematic, morris dance, and basse and round dance. First, they served as heraldic minstrels, playing to announce the arrival of the disguisers as they took their assigned positions in the hall. Second, they provided unspecified 'mood' music for the initial part of the disguising. Since the disguising was a costumed allegory, requiring that the performers impersonate unusual people or imitate animals, the music for these dances must have been specific to the teme or plot of the entertainment. For example, music to accompany a disguising based on classical motifs, such as we find in Lydgate's mummings, would differ from music designed to accompany a performance by wildmen, such as we find at the royal court.[57]

As the pageant device bearing the morris dancers entered, the music shifted again in tone and style. Within the structure of the revels, the morris functioned in the same manner as the anti-masque did in a later time: it interrupted the style and presentation of the disguising to introduce new and different themes and plots. Although very little is known about the Tudor morris dance, it seems that this performance was a noble imitation of a traditional folk form, a boisterous fool's wooing danced by performers wearing bells and often miming sword-play with wooden staves.[58] Perhaps the pipe and tabor players provided this dance music, as they did at folk festivals. The energetic nature of the dance and the competing noise of bells ringing and sticks banging would require a change in style and volume in the music provided by the minstrels.

The fourth movement of the disguising, the basse and round dances, required another shift in musical style. The basse dance, formal and stately, provided a dramatic contrast

---

[57] Hall, 580–1.
[58] Chambers, *MS 1*, 195–7; Lancashire, 'Orders', 30–1.

to the departing morris. Stevens explains that music for this dance was usually provided by sackbut and shawms, reinforcing the notion that Northumberland's waits and trumpeters formed part of the consort for the evening, since there is no extant evidence that he retained a sackbut. The round, a less formal dance executed in a circular pattern, was often accompanied by rebec, lute, and pipe and tabor, a consort which precisely mirrors Northumberland's retained troupe.

The dramatic structure of this disguising pattern was complex, the dramatic mood established by the visual portion of the disguising continually announced and underscored by the music. In addition, artists would never simply recycle old scenes and effects for such an important religious and secular household festival, but would design fresh and fashionable entertainments if they hoped to please their patron. This artistic complexity indicates extensive co-operative effort among the individuals who designed, rehearsed, and executed the disguising; in order to devote the time required for this co-operative effort, the musicians involved would have to be resident rather than visiting.

The staging details, such as moments of entrance and exit, the physical positions of the performers, and the placement of the disguising within the context of the evening's entertainment, were dictated by the ordinance. The content, however, would vary from year to year. Since the minstrels played such an important role in the execution of the disguising, it is possible that they played an equally important role in its design, particularly at the noble households that did not have as many versatile and brilliant designers to draw upon as the royal courts.

Northumberland's ordinance does mention a 'maister of the disguisings' specifically in reference to the pageant device. This unidentified official was probably responsible, as was Richard Gibson at Henry VIII's court, for the financial aspects of the entertainments and for supervising the construction of costumes and sets. Depending upon his artistic qualifications, he may also have contributed to the visual and thematic design. Regardless of what man or group actually designed the disguisings (they cannot be said to have been actually scripted), the minstrels would have to have been consulted about the musical aspect of the revels, particularly if thematic music were required.

There are indications that minstrels were more directly responsible for dramatic entertainments particularly during the medieval period. Edward I's court minstrels produced and presented spectacles during the central courses of banquets, for example at the Whitsun feast, when minstrels entered carrying a gilded swan pageant device, ornamented and draped with precious cloth. Apparently they invited the new knights 'to vow some deed of arms before the device'. The idea that minstrels organized and staged such performances is further supported by a payment preserved in PRO E 101.370.16 for 29 May 1307: 'Regi Capiny Joha*nn*i de Cressy et aliis menestrall*is* ludent*ibus* miracula et fac*ientibus* menestralc*ias* suas coram Regi*n*a de dono Regis per m*anus* Guilloti de Psalt*er*io xl.^s' The man referred to as 'Regi Capiny' was James de Cowper, a harper and King of Heralds within the royal household, and John de Cressy was a minstrel-taboret.[59] Of course, isolated payments of this kind cannot form a solid basis for the conclusion that minstrels customarily composed and executed plays, but the reference does indicate that some relationship existed between the minstrels and dramatic entertainment.

This relationship may be explored on the firmer ground provided by Hall's descriptions and the supplemental information preserved in household accounts during the reigns of Henry VII and Henry VIII. For example, John Heywood was retained primarily as the King's virginals player, but he also wrote plays. Although other minstrels in the King's household cannot be positively identified as playwrights, minstrels did participate as musicians, dancers, and actors within the household revels.

Gordon Kipling argues convincingly that disguisings at the court of Henry VII were designed and executed exclusively by professional entertainers, not by disguised aristocrats.[60] Until Henry VIII revolutionized the style of court revels, courtiers remained spectators; the line between the illusion, represented

---

[59] *MM* xxx–xxxv, 77–9; *Register*, 34; Rastall, 7.
[60] Kipling, 3–8.

by professional and entertainers, and reality, represented by noble patrons, remained firm. Consequently, entertainers were drawn from the ranks of household retainers.

As the previous chapter has demonstrated, Chapel performers definitely participated in the disguisings as singers, actors, and possibly as dancers. Kipling implies that wardrobe officers may have performed the dances, but he does not offer any ideas about the identities of female disguisers. Some, but not all, of the royal household musicians would be required to play music; others may have performed as dancers. After playing music for the same dances for years, minstrels would have had to have been singularly obtuse not to know the steps; in addition, on at least one occasion, and probably on many more, a minstrel taught a young nobleman the art of dancing.[61] It is possible, therefore, that some of the disguised dancers in Henry VII's revels were household musicians. Even after noble dancers invaded the disguisings during Henry VIII's reign, minstrels still performed as dancers, for at the February 1511 disguising called 'The Golden Arbor in the Orchard of Pleasure', which celebrated the birth of Henry's son, 'the mynstrels, which were disguised also dau*n*ced',[62] and the event is not remarked upon as particularly unusual.

Hall's descriptions of the royal court disguisings indicate that minstrels were often considered an integral part of the visual as well as the aural representation. On 14 November 1510, for example, a disguising for the ambassadors from Spain and the Empire took place in the Queen's chamber. First, the King and fifteen others 'came in with a mommery' and 'played with the Quene and the straungers', then departed. 'Then sodenly entred vi. mynstrels, richely appareled, plaiyng on their instruments', followed by fourteen torchbearers, who ushered in two groups of six disguisers each, one group of men dressed in green and white decorated with gold and silver, and one of women dressed in crimson satin decorated with pomegranates and gold, 'strynged after the facion of Spaygne'.[63] Richard Gibson's revels accounts confirm that the minstrels were visually integrated, for the

---

[61] One of the king's minstrels was paid to teach Lord Roos to dance shortly before his marriage to Anne Neville (HMC 4: 281; Woodfill, 266).
[62] Hall, 519.
[63] Hall, 516.

expenditures include the minstrels among those to be costumed at the household's expense. Gibson's accounts also add details that Hall neglects to mention, and present a slightly different picture of the disguising. According to Gibson, the Revels Office constructed costumes for six minstrels, three of blue sarcenet, and three of crimson. In addition, he records that three 'brought in the mummers' and three 'brought in the ladies', the same staging directions used in Northumberland's Twelfth Night disguisings. The musicians who accompanied the ladies were probably those in crimson 'dresses',[64] their colours complementing those of the female disguisers.

Minstrels were visually inseparable from the staged illusion in many other court disguisings as well. At the 1511 pageant of 'Dangerous Fortress' the minstrels rode in on the pageant device, danced, and kept their costumes, 'old garments' drawn from the wardrobe's stock.[65] For 'The Rich Mount' Twelfth Night disguising of 1513, six minstrels dressed in blue and yellow rode in playing music on the device. Four others, tamburine and rebec players dressed in 'garments spangled with copper from the King's old store', played for the dance. All the minstrels were permitted to keep their costumes.[66] In this disguising, one group of minstrels provided the presentational and thematic music, while another provided dance music. The two groups were distinguished both by spatial placement and by costumes that differed in colour and style.

For the 1515 Twelfth Night disguising 'The Pavillion in the Place Perilous', six minerals costumed in blue and white entered on the pageant, playing sackbuts, shawms, and viols. A mock battle ensued, accompanied by four drumslades dressed in violet and yellow. Another minstrel, dressed in yellow, also performed, but his particular function went unrecorded. Again, the minstrels were costumed and placed according to their dramatic function. Those who provided thematic music were placed on the set, costumed to complement the overall effect of the illusion. Those who provided

---

[64] *L & P HVIII* ii/2, 1492–3.
[65] Hall, 518–19; *L & P HVIII* ii/2, 1497–8.
[66] Hall, 535; *L & P HVIII* ii/2, 1499–1500.

music to accompany the dramatic action of the battle took their place elsewhere and, although still in costume, were differentiated by their colours. Like the disguisers, the minstrels were playing roles within the context of a dramatic structure.

Although minstrels were involved in some capacity in most theatrical events at the royal court, no evidence has yet been found to indicate that they produced their own independent dramatic performances. Based on the fourteenth-century references and on the dramatic values inherent in minstrel performance, I suggest that they did.

Carole Janssen has discovered that minstrels under civic patronage did produce their own dramatic performance in 1556, when the waits of Norwich staged a pageant entitled 'Veritas Filia Temporis', an allegory that utilized sophisticated production values of set, speech, and music. Although the play was actually written by the local schoolmaster, John Buck, the musicians apparently took full financial and artistic responsibility for the staging. Janssen postulates that Robert Suckling, the eldest of Norwich's five waits, assumed the role of Father Time, delivering numerous verses to explain the elaborate pageant device and drawing comparisons between Norwich and Rome in compliment to Catholic Queen Mary, whose motto was 'Veritas filia Temporis'.[67]

The elaborateness of the pageant, a round pavilion 'Richelie adorned full of targettes with a morien on the toppe staunding naked with a targett and a great Darte in his haunde', and the ability of a musician to deliver rhetorical explanation testify that the waits possessed the artistic expertise and experience to stage a play. Their long association with civic pageantry gave them the opportunity to observe theatrical techniques in the dramatic performances of other groups and the ability to put these qualities to polished use in performances of their own. The complexity of this pageant indicates that civic waits were accustomed to acting and playing music for such performances, and that earlier texts or references to minstrel plays may yet be identified.

Extant interludes, although not directly attributable to minstrel composition or production, indicate that minstrels

[67] Janssen, 57–64.

and minstrelsy had made a significant impact upon the Renaissance idea of dramatic entertainment, particularly since the liturgical drama was practically opera, its dependence upon the subtleties of music was so thorough. A cursory glance at the surviving plays shows that an overwhelming majority include some type of music. The conclusion generally drawn is that song and instrumental music were simply inserted to provide respite from rhetorical elements or to provide an additional element of entertainment without a particular relationship to the text. Upon closer examination, however, the relationship of musical performance to dramatic text is far more complex.

In the interludes, music functions just as it did in the household revels, for both presentational and thematic effect. Some plays also require that minstrels play while characters dance, just as minstrels played for professional and noble disguisers. Further, many interludes required minstrels as part of the performing group, which means that players had to be minstrels, had to travel with minstrels, or had to stage their plays at locations where they could depend upon access to a resident troupe.

Most music in the extant interludes is vocal rather than instrumental, and was probably performed by players who could sing with varying degrees of skill. Often the songs were unspecified, leaving the actors to choose popular ballads, part-songs they had rehearsed, or simple descant. When lyrics for song were included in the text, they were often sung to the tune of popular melodies.[68] Instrumental music is rarely described or specified, leaving the minstrels to select a rehearsed piece from their own repertoires—a practical solution to the problems of interluders who had to depend upon musicians external to their own troupes.

Examples of presentational music are found in the crying of banns for Corpus Christi plays and moralities such as *The Castle of Perseverance*. Here instruments, probably trumpets and shawms that civic waits could have played, were used to attract public attention and to direct it to the verses spoken by the vexillators. Characters like King Herod were also

---

[68] Bevington gives examples of this from *Horestes* and *The Marriage of Wit and Widom*. See also *EES 3*, 288 n. 39.

attended by players of heraldic music to reaffirm the social superiority of the character. Just as drummers played to accompany the mock battle in Henry VIII's 1515 'Pavillion in the Place Perilous' disguisings, drummers were also used in the plays to set the tone for battle. In *Rafe Roister Doister*, probably a school play, Rafe and his retainers attack the home of Christian Custance to the accompaniment of drums (IV. vii). Similarly, in *Horestes*, trumpets and drums punctuate the battle scenes. Vocal music could also be used for heraldic effect; such songs are frequently used in the plays to mark the entrances and exits of characters, to signal act or scene divisions in plays composed according to classical models, and often to signify the end of the play.[69] 'Intrat cantantes', 'cantent et exeant', and 'omnes cantent' are the most common stage directions found in the interludes.

In addition to providing focus, music was used to accompany dancers. *Fulgens and Lucrece* and the full version of *Four Elements*, plays designed to be performed in households that retained minstrels, require—without specifically describing—disguisings and dances that interrupt the action. Similarly, as I have discussed in chapter one, *Wisdom Who Is Christ*, which may be a household play, includes three disguisings, albeit on a much smaller scale, and specifies the three types of minstrels who play the dances. In *Mankind*, in its surviving form probably not a household play, New Guise calls 'ande now, minstrellys, pley the comyn trace!' (72) so that the vices may dance; the minstrels here were probably cast members and the 'comyn trace' a well-known tune. In other plays where single characters or small groups of characters danced, they probably did so to the accompaniment of a single instrument that could be played by an interluder, or to the *a cappella* accompaniment of their own voices.

Dance music and heraldic music certainly contributed to the theatricality of the plays I have mentioned above, but did not actually form part of the dramatic structure. In some plays, however, music was used in a far more complex

---

[69] A few of the numerous examples of this use of music include: *King Johan* (639, 763, 1338); *Rafe Roister Doister* (I. i; I. iv); *Weather* (end); *Wit and Science* (225, 988, end); *Respublica* (I. ii, beginning; II. iii, end; end of play); *Mankind* (161).

fashion, to reinforce themes, to forward plot, to establish and develop character. In these plays, as in household revels, the music is inseparable from the dramatic structure; sound is used as sub-text, to complement, comment upon, and develop the visual and rhetorical aspects of the plays. Obviously, such plays have need of well-trained singers and minstrels, and were written by men who had particular knowledge of and interest in the subtle uses of music, mostly schoolmasters, parish priests, and patronized clerics.

In religious drama, the harmonies of heaven and the cacophonies of hell had long ago become conventional signifiers for good and evil, chaos and order, triumph and defeat, and other similar oppositions, so music could be used in the interludes to indicate the moral and social status of a character. By the mid-fifteenth century, English drama is already beginning to show signs of the reformers' censorship, for often secular singing and dancing, two of the most natural, most popular, and most easily accomplished of human pleasures, indicate an evil nature. Thus, the vices in *Mankind* demonstrate their degeneracy and corrupt the audience by leading them in a lewd song (235–43). In *Youth* Pride and Riot include Youth in their song (472–5). Sensual Appetite in *Four Elements* enters with a frisky song (416–20), and Folly in *Magnificence* lures his victims to the stews by singing a song 'in their ear' (1225–7).

John Bale was particularly adept at exploiting music as an index of moral stature. Each act of *God's Promises* ends with the singing of an antiphon accompanied by organ to communicate a positive religious mood. In marked contrast, he used music in *King Johan* to stress the hypocritical nature of the vices. The perfectly innocent lyrics of Psalm 137 are insidious when placed in the mouths of Usurped Power and Private Wealth (759–60). Sedition also often acts as choir master (824, 1055, 2409), but none of the positive characters ever sings. Here Bale manipulates music in a subtle fashion to make the audience aware of the dangers of blindly (or deafly) accepting conventional signification, and, by extension, of unquestioningly following traditional political or theological dogma.

Music was also used simply to provide diversion, and

beguile the time. In these cases, the characters who sing are not particularly good or bad, but they are usually simple, and the implication is that music a fairly harmless waste of time. In *Fulgens and Lucrece*, A, B, and Jone sing to amuse themselves (1125), as do Mage Mumble-Crust, Tibet Talkapace, and Annot Alyface in the boys' play *Rafe Roister Doister* (I. iii. 16; 50–60; II. iii. 56–88). Instrumental music is also used in *Rafe Roister Doister* to pass time and to develop Rafe's character as a noble patron and courtly lover (I. iv. 1; III. iii. 150; V. vi. 45). Similarly, one of the symptoms of Callisto's lovesickness in *Callisto and Melebea* is his preoccupation with music (Farmer, 52–3).

Wit and Science, probably a play for the choirboys of St Paul's, of whom Redford was master, makes extensive and subtle use of musical effects and therefore merits more detailed discussion. This play specifically requires that a consort of viols perform both as minstrels and as characters within the play. Other characters, both good and evil, use music to develop theme, plot, and character. Without the use of music as dramatic shorthand and the availability of performers who could both act and play, Redford's dramatic structure would have been quite different.

Music makes its first appearance at line 224, after Tediousness has slain the protagonist, when Honest Recreation, Comfort, Quickness, and Strength surround Wit and sing a seven-verse song that brings him back to life. Here music is used as a charm to effect a resurrection, as the medical charms of the doctor vitalize the hero in the St George plays of the folk tradition. Such a magical transformation was far more efficiently and effectively expressed through music, which was, in certain forms, considered spiritual and mystical, than through speech.

Later in the play, music is combined with dance to act metaphorically, as well as to further plot and character. Wit calls for a basse dance, to which Honest Recreation replies

> Nay, sir; as for bassys,
> From hence none passys
> But as in gage
> Of marriage   (289–92).

This reference depends upon audience recognition of a specific cultural code, unfortunately lost to most twentieth-century viewers and readers. In the social and moral hierarchy of dance, the basse, executed slowly and formally by couples, suggests courtliness and conventional morality. Honest Recreation refuses to dance the basse, encourages Wit to throw off the gown given to him by Lady Science, calls 'Go to, my men, play!' to her minstrels, and dances the more lively galliard. Again, the dance functions metonymically, for at the end of it Wit falls into the lap of Idleness, the initial step on his road to degeneracy.

A consort of four viols is required to sing and play their instruments (620–72) to entertain Lady Science and her mother Experience, just as minstrels provided solace for their patrons by playing in the private chambers. This consort does not, however, simply enter, play, and exit. The minstrels, assigned the roles of Fame, Favour, Riches, and Worship, deliver lines that are crucial to the revelation of Lady Science's character, since she establishes her modesty and spiritual purity by refusing their services. The minstrels' lines cannot be omitted, so the play must have been staged under the auspices of an institution or household that retained viols; otherwise these minstrels would have to have been hired and rehearsed. The lines are limited in number (Fame, Favour, and Riches have six lines each; Worship has eight) and could be quickly learnt, but the very presence of scripted dialogue for the minstrels as well as their appearance at various points in the play where they sing and play specific music, argue that Redford had a resident troupe in mind, and indicate the minstrels could and did perform as actors.

Music is also used to effect the reconciliation between the protagonist, Wit, and his intended bride, Science. Wit and his company sing a verse of 'Wellcum my nowne', and are answered by Science and her company singing the second verse. Alternating in this fashion, they approach each other and meet in the centre of the playing space. Here, the content of the song communicates mood, emotion, and plot, while the form of alternation provides aural reinforcement for the visual movement.

At the end of the play, the four viols enter once more to

play and sing 'Remembreance', the music and lyrics for which have not been discovered. Afterward, the entire company makes its obeisance, then exits singing an unspecified song. In this instance, the concert and song were used to signal that the play was at an end and to echo its joyful denouement.

If Redford's play was indeed intended for boys—as its academic theme surely suggests[70]—the presence of these minstrels raises many questions about the play's production methods. Complex vocal music would be no problem for choirboys or their master, but did schools, like households, retain the consort of viols and broken consort required for the dances? Boys in choir schools were often trained to play keyboards for religious services, but were they also trained to play more 'courtly' instruments to prepare them for later employment in great households? Or did schools indeed retain professional minstrels to teach and perform within their walls? A third possibility is that most choirboy scripts were intended for eventual touring, not to public spaces in towns and cities, but to the private and lucrative auspices of the great households of the nobility and the clergy, who could be depended upon to provide resident minstrels. The centuries-long record of Paul's Boys hiring themselves out for all occasions certainly indicates that the playwrights who composed entertainments for these trained young actors would be aware of the need for touring scripts, the availability of sophisticated support staff at the upper-class locations the boys frequented (choirboys were not to be found performing at taverns, fairs, or guild-halls), and the expectations of these élite audiences for complex musical structures and effects.

Wit and Science is unusual in its use of many kinds of music for many different dramatic purposes, but it is not unique. The presence of music, and particularly song, in the majority of miracle, mystery, and morality plays indicates that the Renaissance audiences not only accepted, but actually expected, music to be a versatile component in dramatic technique. Like Tudor dramatists, the designers of entertainments originating within the great households or

---

[70] *EES* 3, 76; Motter, 131.

intended for eventual production there recognized the value of music and those who provided it, and consequently incorporated both into the aesthetic fabric of great household performances. Ceremonial and recreational minstrels added another artistic dimension to the visual and rhetorical elements of the entertainments, piling on new effects to provide melody, harmony, and counterpoint in both a literal and a thematic sense. Through co-operative efforts with other professional entertainers, minstrels helped to weave together the various theatrical values that culminated in artistically sophisticated, multimedia performances. To the aristocratic patron, these performances were socially and politically advantageous, for the more complexly layered, varied, and expensive the entertainments, the more they enhanced his reputation for intellect, wealth, largess, and taste, all of which translated ultimately into power.

3
Playwrights and Players

> A.   I trowe your owyn selfe be oon
>   Of them that shall play.
> B.   Nay, I am none.
>   I trowe thou spekyst in derision
>   To lyke me therto.
> A.   Nay, I mok not, wot ye well,
>   For I thought verely by your apparell
>   That ye had bene a player.
> B.   Nay, never a dell.
> A.   Than I cry you mercy:
>   I was to blame. Lo, therfor, I say
>   Ther is so myche nyce aray
>   Amonges these galandis now aday
>   That a man shall not lightly
>   Know a player from a nother man.
>   *Fulgens and Lucrece*, 43–56

At a banquet before a noble audience at Cardinal Morton's household, the characters A and B indulge in a comic exchange that examines two of the more enigmatic qualities of household players: their social status and their ambiguous identities. B is clearly insulted to be considered a player because players' reputations were unsavoury—an idea so frequently set forth that it has become inexorably linked in the popular imagination with the life-styles of early and even modern actors. Interestingly, the second characteristic, the ambiguous identity of the players, implies cause for their questionable position within the hierarchy.

No one knows who is a player and who is not. On the literal level, the close proximity of audience and actor, as well as the lack of distinction in costuming, produces confusion. A's comment on the similarity between the garish dress of the actors and the extravagant dress of the audience was intended to be humorous, yet jests are founded on facts, and a glance at any Tudor chronicle or wardrobe account will convince the reader that the aristocratic taste in clothing was far from sombre. The king, the clergy, and even the playwrights were for once in agreement when they attacked, through proclamations, sermons, and satires, the vanity of fashion.

On a more subtle level, this confusion of identity is symptomatic of the situation in which early Tudor players found themselves, for their function within the household was often occasional, and their relationship to the household hierarchy was unlegislated. As previous chapters have demonstrated, social standing within the household was closely connected to legislated responsibilities and privileges, but none of the early household books record detailed prescriptions for the selection, use, maintenance, or *raison d'être* of the players. Consequently, because their position in the 'great chain' of the households was questionable, so was their reputation.

This confusion of identity permeates to a still deeper, more symbolic level, for noble audiences, and in particular patrons, were keenly aware that they were playing on a larger stage. As both producer and chief spectator of the drama, the patron of a great household was as much the focus of attention as his players. The court observes Claudius and Gertrude during *The Murder of Gonzago*; all attend to Theseus and Hippolyta during *Pyramus and Thisby*. In both cases, royal reaction to content and style is as important, if not more important, than the play itself.

In order to understand the function of the drama within the great households, it is crucial to examine the relationships forged among patrons, players, playwrights, and audiences. These relationships are, like the drama itself, complex and multidimensional, for they carry economic, social, political, and artistic implications.

The loosening of this Gordian knot must begin with three fundamental considerations. First, what plays did household troupes enact and who was responsible for the creation of their scripts? Second, what procedures dictated the interaction among players, patrons, and audiences both inside and outside the household? Answering this question entails not only an awareness of practical staging requirements and the logistics of performance, but also a consideration of the organization and function of player troupes. Third, and perhaps most important, what motivated players to seek patrons and patrons to retain players?

Attempting to characterize the repertoire of the early Tudor players instantly produces another nest of snaky questions. How many plays did a typical troupe prepare for production at one time? What factors influenced the preservation or disappearance of these texts? None of these questions can be answered conclusively at this time, but by examining records and internal evidence from dramatic texts, I hope to shed a flickering light on the mystery.

Civic, monastic, school, and household accounts from the early Tudor era demonstrate that hundreds of players under the patronage of the nobility were touring the country. Rarely do these pre-Elizabethan accounts preserve any information about the plays these troupes enacted, preferring instead to record the identity of the troupe's patron. The earliest extant reference is to *The Play of Saint Catherine* by the choir boys at Dunstable about 1110. We know that Lady Honor Lisle purchased a text of an interlude called *Rex Diabole* for her household in 1538.[1] We know that the Queen's players acted 'the market of mischief' at Norwich in 1546,[2] and that 'Bale and his fellows', probably under Cromwell's patronage, were enacting Bale's virulent scripts in 1538 and 1539.[3] David Galloway has unearthed in Norwich civic records a reference to a play 'at the gyldhall of zacheus', probably by the Marquis of Dorset's players about 1551–2.[4] In 1542, 'the Suffolke men' performed 'their play of the battle betwixt the Spirit, the Soul and the flesh . . .'.[5] We know that the King's players performed the 'play of Self-Love' at Sir Thomas Chaloner's household on Shrove Monday sometime between 1551 and 1556.[6] Printers'

[1] *L & P HVIII, Addenda*, ii, vol. i, pt. 2, no. 1362.
[2] Murry, ii. 362.
[3] *L & P HVIII* xiv/2, no. 782, p. 339; and Fairfield.
[4] Galloway, 31.   [5] *L & P HVIII, Addenda*, i/2, no. 1547.
[6] Chambers, *MS* 2, 201. BL Lansdowne MS 824 (The Accounts of Sir Thomas Chaloner), f. 17. F. 13ᵛ is dated 5 Edward VI, 2 Jan. (1552), which makes it likely

inventories yield titles and texts of additional interludes, but do not connect these works with specific auspices or troupes. Thus, beyond these seven references, we have virtually no external evidence of what plays a particular troupe enacted. To complicate matters, of these only Bale's plays are extant, a fact which prevents extensive textual investigation.

Yet even the fragmentary evidence these references provide, the titles of the lost plays, is still helpful to theatre historians. With the exception of the Norwich play and, as we should expect, the *St Catherine* of the Dunstable choirboys play, all appear to be moral interludes rather than saints' lives or biblical plays. Evidence for civic patronage of the cycles and parish patronage for many saints' plays is conclusive: the production requirements of such plays placed them far beyond the financial and physical resources of a small troupe of players. The early moral interludes, however, were within the itinerant troupes' scope, and Richard Southern and David Bevington have assumed that these comprised the itinerant troupe's repertoire in their discussions of playing requirements.

The number of surviving texts reflects only a small fraction of the plays that must have been available to players. Hundreds of troupes toured England in the early Tudor period, and each probably had more than one play ready for performance during a given tour. For example, the Earl of Oxford's players appeared at Henry VII's court twice in the space of two years, from 1496 to 1498:[7] it is highly unlikely that they performed the same play for both occasions, so they must have had a repertoire of at least two plays. Since they also toured, they might have needed several scripts. The anonymous *The Book of Sir Thomas More* (c.1590) refers to a troupe called 'My Lord Cardinalls players' (which Chambers erroneously describes as the King's players)[8] that

that the reference to the play on f. 17 is within one or two years of 1552. Another reference on f. 17 mentions that ten shillings was 'payd among the maskers at dyn', perhaps for the same occasion. This reinforces the idea that masks and disguisings were not generally performed by players, but by the Chapel or by other performers; see also Motter, 1, 10.

[7] Anglo, 'Court Festivals', 30–4. For information on touring, see the Malone Society Collections vol. 2, pt. 3 and vol. 7; Murray, *EDC*.
[8] Chambers, *The Elizabethan Stage*, ii. 81, henceforth *ES*.

claimed a repertoire of seven plays, again all moralities or interludes, including '. . . the Cradle of Securite, hit nayle o' the head, impacient povertie, the play of foure Pees, diues and Lazarus, Lustie Iuuentus, and the mariage of witt and wisedome'.[9] Except for 'hit nayle o' the head' these plays are actually extant. From these references to Oxford's players and the fictional players attached to Wolsey, it appears that a troupe needed from three to seven scripts memorized and prepared in order to function efficiently and profitably.

If each of the scores of patronized troupes had a repertoire of three or four plays, certainly a conservative estimate, there must have been hundreds of plays available to them even considering that one popular script may have been shared by a number of troupes. If the Earl of Northumberland rewarded twenty troupes at Christmas 1511–12, each must have intended to present a different script.[10] The number of extant interludes is only the proverbial tip of the iceberg compared with the vast numbers of scripts that have been lost to us.

Many of those lost plays may never have existed in written form. As Shakespeare much later notes, players were adept at, sometimes overly fond of, improvisation. Hamlet's advice to the players cautions them: 'let those that play your clowns speak no more than is set down for them'; the rustics' rehearsal of *Pyramus and Thisby* is another case of player improvisation at work. By the mid-sixteenth century, the *commedia dell'arte*, which raised improvisation to an art, was flourishing on the Continent and undoubtedly influencing theatre in England. The famous apocryphal anecdote of Sir Thomas More as a young henchman in Cardinal Morton's court, stepping into the interlude and making 'the lookers on more sporte then all the plaiers beside',[11] indicates that the players, although they may not have appreciated the external interference, were accustomed to its style.

In order to stretch their repertoire, the players could rely

---

[9] *The Book of Sir Thomas More*, 918–22.
[10] NHB 45. The total outlay was 33s. 4d., with 20d. being the typical reward for each play.
[11] Roper, 5. Wickham agrees with these methods of script production among the players, *EES 3*, 125.

upon their own minds and talents to compose plays that probably varied considerably in quality. In addition, they could 'borrow' lines and plots from other sources; the texts of fellow players, contemporary ballads, gossip, current events, folktales, folk plays, and popular literature could be pillaged to provide outlines for dramatic performances suitable for touring. Renaissance players were surrounded with material for plays—Greek and Latin dialogues and tales remembered from school days; biblical parables preached from the pulpit; histories portrayed in civic pageantry and remembered by elders—not to mention the rich visual suggestions presented by carvings, stained glass, tapestries, and paintings. Although their creative resources were rich, the players were not, a fact which would preclude their purchasing or commissioning texts, at least during the early Tudor period. At that time, sophisticated works of literary merit could have come only from some sort of sponsorship, be it educational, ecclesiastical, or aristocratic.

A curious anonymous letter found among Sir Thomas More's correspondence indicates that the texts of these early interludes were valuable and well-guarded commodities:

> As to what you furthermore write to me, that I should find or acquire for you interludes or comedies in English or in the vulgar tongue, I have finally acquired them by the greatest exertion of effort. For up to now, they are rare and the owners of them are so inconstant that to exert or to strive with respect to such may justly be denominated or called almost a vain effort. For which reason, in order that I might satisfy your wishes, I have with assiduous exertion of effort and with flattering words finally softened the soul of an owner. I have acquired it on condition that as soon as you transcribe the original you will then return it to me so that I may restore it to the owner.[12]

If scripts were so difficult to acquire, it is highly unlikely that itinerant players would own them or carry them about on their travels. New texts probably remained in manuscript and in the possession of their commissioners, who allowed their players to memorize them for performance. Play texts seem to have been printed only when patrons recognized a specific

---
[12] Nelson, xxix.

advantage in doing so, perhaps after a text was too well known to be valuable as a touring vehicle, or when a piece of propaganda merited wider circulation, or when an inherited manuscript might bring in a bit of cash.

PLAYWRIGHTS

In today's world of copyright protection and freelance playwriting, it is easy to underestimate the importance of patronage during the early Tudor period. Even in the eighteenth century, patronage had degenerated to such a degree as to prompt Samuel Johnson to ask in his famous letter to Lord Chesterfield: 'Is not a patron, my Lord, one who looks with unconcern on a man struggling for life in the water, and when he has reached ground, encumbers him with help?'[13] During the early Renaissance, however, literary patronage provided the lifeline. As Samuel Moore noted: 'The fundamental difference between mediaeval and modern conditions is in the fact that the mediaeval writer directed his work, not to the world in general, or the "public," but to a very definite and restricted circle. He addressed himself to his patron and his patron's family, friends, and neighbors.'[14] Tudor patrons possessed the financial and material resources to commission or encourage the composition of dramatic texts. They had the means to assure the theatrical production of such texts, and they retained players to communicate the material to other households and in other cities. Were noble households, like schools and the Inns of Court, the sources for many of the extant early Tudor interludes in English?

Ian Lancashire has argued that, due to financial hardship, civic and parish patronage decreased during the late Tudor era, and that noble patronage increased to the point where most known playwrights of most interludes had their plays enacted at royal or noble courts.[15] Recent scholarship has seriously considered the problem of attributing anonymous extant moral interludes from the early Tudor era to definite auspices, and in most cases the auspices are noble or ecclesiastical households. T. W. Craik suggests that the

[13] Johnson, 152. [14] Moore, 369–92.
[15] Lancashire, 'Patrons and the English Moral Play'.

political interlude *Wealth and Health* was written for Queen Mary's interluders at the start of her reign. Ian Lancashire has conducted extensive research in this area, attributing *The World and the Child* to the household of the Earl of Kent about 1508, *The Interlude of Youth* to the fifth Earl of Northumberland's court about 1513, and *Hick Scorner* to the Duke of Suffolk's court about 1514. Gatch suggests that *Wisdom* belongs to the household of the Bishop of Ely at London.[16] Further research may yet reveal connections between other contemporary anonymous interludes and household patrons.

The pervasiveness of noble patronage for dramatic composition becomes even clearer upon consideration of the fact that almost all known dramatists were either in the service of a noble household, or were closely connected with a noble patron. Many found patronage at the royal court, but many also formed attachments with other Tudor noblemen and with prelates; almost all were clerically trained, and most served as schoolmasters or choirmasters at the nation's leading educational institutions.

Observation of civic pageantry and folk forms of theatre endowed the playwrights with a rich storehouse of mythological and historical allusions, and at the same time supplied native English structures to hang them on. Centuries of mystery and miracle plays provided the thoroughly English biblical background and the unique sense of the synchronic flow of time and the indeterminacy of space. In schools where they taught, these men participated in stagings of classical plays in Latin and Greek, which provided them with classical models of structure and theme, in scholarly disputations that influenced the *débat* structure of interludes, and in musical performances that taught the value of multimedia representations. But perhaps the most distinguishing characteristic

---

[16] Craik, 'The Political Interpretation of Two Tudor Interludes: *Temperance and Humility* and *Wealth and Health*', *RES*, NS 4 (1953), 98–108; Lancashire, 'The Auspices of *The World and the Child*', offers the Earl of Kent as sponsor for the play. Lancashire's *Two Tudor Interludes* suggests that *The Interlude of Youth* was composed for the fifth Earl of Northumberland, and that *Hick Scorner* was composed for Charles Brandon, Duke of Suffolk. Nelson connects *Fulgens and Lucrece* and *Nature* with Cardinal Morton's household in *The Plays of Henry Medwall*. Gatch suggests the Bishop of Ely's London palace as auspices for *Wisdom*.

of these dramatists was their participation in court circles, their intimacy with those in power. At royal and noble courts, such playwrights were not only able to watch the latest styles in entertainment, they were also able to keep abreast of the latest political manœuvres, social gossip, and prevailing trends in policy. With no need to save pennies through doubling or scrimping on sets and costumes, no need to court popular appeal to make a profit, and protected and encouraged by patrons to promote certain philosophies, the early Tudor dramatists enjoyed a relatively free rein for the era, so long as they remained within the pale of their patrons. The fact that Tudor monarchs found it necessary to exert control and even ban certain types of plays indicates that playwrights were taking full advantage of their freedom. These factors create a socio-political profile that distinguishes early Tudor dramatists from their less worldly predecessors and their entrepreneurial descendants.

For far too long early Tudor dramatists, and the plays they composed, have been considered second-rate, simply filling theatrical space and time until the 'real' artists come along. Even Glynne Wickham, one of the premier defenders and admirers of early drama, seems to fall into the trap of apologizing for these men, stating that 'a dawning consciousness of dramatic genre', among other influences, 'served also to translate the medieval and Tudor play-maker, or maker of interludes, into a man of letters, and thus into the modern playwright or dramatist who hopes to earn his living from writing'.[17]

This comment, and particularly the use of the term 'play-maker' clearly implies a hierarchy of dramatic quality that I believe is more a product of historicity, of our own imposition of modern tastes and horizons of expectation, than of objective judgement on the basis of early Tudor aesthetics. In addition, modern audiences are frequently unable to comprehend the cultural codes, iconography, and allusions that would have been familiar to early Tudor audiences; consequently, we tend to blame the messenger for our own inabilities, dismissing the drama we cannot decode.

[17] *EES 3*, xxi.

If Wickham means merely to return to contemporary terminology by echoing the 'maker of interludes' that we find in sixteenth-century documents, I have no objection, but the remainder of his comment implies that, on the contrary, he is disregarding the meaning of the word 'wright', which has, since the seventh century, referred to a craftsman or artisan. Early Tudor dramatists were certainly 'men of letters', often men charged with teaching those letters to the next generation. While men such as Bale, Skelton, and Heywood may not have picked up the receipts at the gate or owned a percentage of the action, they certainly did hope to earn their livings, and comfortable ones at that, from the continuing patronage of those who commissioned or produced their scripts.

Royal patronage was, naturally, most attractive to dramatists. A position at the royal household was likely to be lucrative, certainly prestigious; it also offered the possibility of increased exposure for a playwright's art, since the royal court entertained large audiences (often with international representatives), with greater frequency than the noble courts did. Henry VII retained William Cornish as a Gentleman of the Chapel, but Cornish also composed entertainments. Henry VIII paid Heywood, later a choirmaster at Paul's, as a virginals-player, and Heywood scripted *Four PP, Johan Johan, The Play of Love, The Play of the Weather, The Pardoner and The Friar,* and *Witty and Witless* between 1519 and 1533,[18] when lightness, farce, romance, and courtly *débat* had particular appeal for the King and, consequently, for his court. Nicholas Udall, trained at Winchester and Master at Eton, wrote *Rafe Roister Doister,* perhaps *Thersites* and *Respublica,* some of the verses for the pageantry that celebrated Anne Boleyn's coronation in 1532, and produced plays and Christmas entertainments for Queen Mary.[19]

Early Tudor dramatists also found places at the noble courts throughout England. By 1490, Henry Medwall, educated at Eton and Cambridge, was employed, probably as a lawyer or clerk, by Cardinal Morton. While fulfilling his

---

[18] Saunders *et al.*, xxi–xxv; hereafter referred to as *Revels*; Motter, 28.
[19] Withington, *English Pageantry*, 181–7; Chambers, *MS* 2, 451–2; Bevington, *Tudor Drama and Politics*, 121; Motter, 28.

bureaucratic function, Medwall also served as the Cardinal's household playwright, scripting *Nature* and *Fulgens and Lucrece*, the latter probably for a Christmas banquet honouring the Flemish and Spanish ambassadors in 1491.[20] Although there is no irrefutable evidence that Bale, Skelton, and Rastell were actually retained as members of noble households, they did establish close ties with noble patrons.

John Bale, for example, wrote plays for John de Vere, Earl of Oxford, and for Thomas Cromwell, both Protestants active in the reform movement under Henry VIII. In the early 1530s, Bale was converted to Protestantism, and perhaps patronized by Lord Wentworth, a cousin of the Seymours; shortly thereafter, he began composing what appears to be a Protestant cycle, including *God's Promises*, *Christ's Temptation in the Wilderness*, and other plays that have disappeared.[21] Later in the 1530s, Bale turned for patronage to de Vere, the first Protestant earl of Oxford and Henry VIII's Great Chamberlain, composing English comedies and tragedies in various metrical styles for the Earl. Bale's autobiographical *Anglorum Heliades* records that: 'Edidi etiam in idiomate vulgari diuersas Comedias atque Tragedias. Sub diuerso metrorum gerere, Presertim ad illustrissimum Dominum Ioannem Ver, Oxonie Comitem.'[22]

De Vere, who supported the King's divorce and Anne Boleyn's faction, found Bale's partisan political interludes attractive and useful. The texts of Bale's *Super Vtroque Regis Coniugio*, *De Sectis Papisticis*, *De Traditionibus Papistorum*, *Contra Corruptores Verbi Dei*, and *De Traditione Thomae Becketi* do not survive, but their titles alone indicate that Bale was writing precisely what the Earl and the King would wish to hear: plays supporting Henry VIII's second marriage and religious reforms, while attacking the papists and clergy who would resist him. Harris assumes that these plays were written expressly for the Earl's players about 1534, since Bale's own troupe was not formed until four years later. In

[20] Medwall, 1–19; *Revels*, 138. For a valuable biography and review of the life records, see Moeslein's introduction in *The Plays of Henry Medwall: A Critical Edition*.
[21] Fairfield, 33–4; Jesse W. Harris, 15–16, 21–2; *Revels*, 50–1; Bevington, *Tudor Drama and Politics*, 98.
[22] BL Harl. MS 3838, f. 112; see also Anglo's *Spectacle*, 268.

Playwrights and Players 119

addition, Harris postulates that Oxford kept the manuscripts, further evidence for the value of unprinted play texts, for in 1536 when Bale compiled *Anglorum Heliades*, he omitted the first lines of the plays, supposedly inserting them at a later date when Oxford had returned the texts.[23]

From the protection and support of the Earl of Oxford, Bale moved to an even more powerful patron, Thomas Cromwell, who was closer than de Vere to that ultimate target, the royal court. Bale composed *Three Laws* and *King Johan* for Cromwell, plays which spoke directly to both the Secretary's and the King's interests: *Three Laws* attacked papist abuses and urged Protestant reform; *King Johan* pointed out the insidiousness of Catholic control over and interference with secular power. Not only did Bale write the plays, he and his troupe also acted in them, probably under the name 'Lord Cromwell's Players'. Cromwell's accounts preserve payments to 'Bale and his ffelowes' for performances in September 1538 and January 1539 at Archbishop Cranmer's household at Canterbury; the January performance was almost certainly *King Johan*. Bale and his players continued to perform under Cromwell's patronage until the Secretary fell from power in 1540 in the wake of the King's rage over his fourth marriage.[24] De Vere died the same year and Bale, bereft of his two powerful patrons, was forced to flee to the Continent, there to await the accession of Edward VI and the return to power of the Protestant Seymour faction, among whom Bale had powerful friends.

Just as Bale provided appropriate scripts for Oxford's and Cromwell's players, John Skelton may have supplied texts for the Earl of Northumberland's players. Northumberland already had two playwrights in his employ, his almoner, who was a 'maker of interludes', and a family chaplain called William Peeris or Pyres, who was paid for the 'transposing' or 'alteration' of a Corpus Christi play at Beverley.[25] Either

---

[23] Jesse Harris, 72 n.
[24] Bale, xviii; Jesse Harris, 15; *L & P HVIII* xiv/2, 339. Fairfield, 190 n., quotes PRO SP 1/116 ff. 158–9 to show that in 1537 Cromwell was soliciting antipapal plays. A Suffolk vicar called Thomas Wylley offered the secretary plays against 'the Pope's counselors'; see also Bevington, *From 'Mankind' to Marlowe*, 52.
[25] NHB 61; Lancashire, 'Orders', 13 n. The connection between William Peeris and the drama is most intriguing, for this is one of the few indications that we have

could have supplied scripts for Northumberland's players. Although there is no evidence that Skelton's *Magnificence* was performed at Northumberland's household (Paula Neuss suggests auspices at a London guild-hall),[26] Skelton's list of his own works includes 'paiauntis that were played at Ioyows Garde'. 'Paiaunt' is noted in the *Oxford English Dictionary* as an early variant of 'pageant', a word that has a variety of meanings. Since Skelton specifies that his were 'played' and chose to include them among his literary accomplishments, it is likely that these were poetic scripts for dramatic scenes or poetic monologues designed to accompany tableaux vivants, like Lydgate's mummings. Malory assists us in identifying Skelton's allegorical reference to the Arthurian Joyous Garde by informing us that 'Somme men say it was Anwyk, | and somme men say it was Bamborow.' Both properties belonged to the Earl of Northumberland.[27] If this tracing of the allusion is correct, Skelton emerges as the author of Northumberland household pageants, such as those ordered to be presented as the Earl's Twelfth Night revels and on the occasion of his daughter's marriage.

Skelton's connection with the Percy earls of Northumberland is first shown in print by his elegy on the fourth Earl, dedicated to the young fifth Earl, and including verses to Dr William Ruckshaw, a priest in Percy's service. The Percy family, however, was not the only aristocratic family to note Skelton's talents, for Henry VII's Privy Purse expenses refer to Skelton as 'My Lady the Kinges moder poete'. Margaret Beaufort, Countess of Richmond, was a powerful patron to

to establish a connection between a member of a noble household, one of Percy's chaplains, and the civic cycle drama. Critics have suggested that such drama was scripted by the clergy, but with the expulsion of drama from the church, religious institutions seem to have bequeathed much of their responsibility to civic authorities and guilds. In Peeris we have a perfect compromise: a man fully trained in religious doctrine, a poet (he wrote a verse history of the Percy family), and a man in close contact with the laity through his position in Percy's household; Peeris would have had access to the Earl's library and the opportunity to view the latest in touring entertainment. Perhaps Percy and other noblemen like him were patrons of the civic drama, in its composition if not in its execution.

[26] Skelton, 42–3.
[27] Bean, 416; 1. 1383; Gerald Brenan, *A History of the House of Percy, from the Earliest Times down to the Present Century*, 2 vols. (London: Freemantle & Co., 1902), i. 145; Malory, vol. iii, 1685.

many artists, with obvious influence at the royal court. In addition, Skelton allied himself with the powerful Howard family, dukes of Norfolk and earls of Surrey. His 'Garlande of Laurell' compliments the Countess of Surrey, as his patroness, and he was close enough to the family to spend Christmas with them in 1522, perhaps again contributing pageants.[28] Even without considering Skelton's writings, which seem intended for an élite audience at court or school, his close connections with the Percys, the Norfolks, and with Margaret Beaufort indicate that Skelton wrote under the patronage of, and particularly for, a conservative faction of the nobility who could protect him, if need be, from powerful enemies.

Sir Thomas More, himself a literary artist, exerted influence over his sons-in-law John Heywood and John Rastell. Heywood already had a powerful patron in Henry VIII, and Rastell was probably financially secure through his careers as a lawyer and a printer, so neither had desperate need of More's money. More certainly would have seen their plays, perhaps performed within his own household. The extent of More's patronage of known dramatists is, however, not as important as his intimate connection with a printer.

Few of the interludes that must have been current in the first half of the sixteenth century survive in manuscript or printed form. Five plays, including 'a tragidie in anglishe of the vniust suprimacie of the bisshop of rome' and a copy of *Old Custome*, appear in an inventory of the effects of John Dudley, Lorde Lisle, *c.*1547–51,[29] but besides this notice, no other extant inventory records evidence of play texts in noble libraries. Early sixteenth-century printers' inventories are similarly unrepresentative of the number of contemporary scripts, which is hardly surprising since household players had neither the funds to have scripts printed nor the motivation, since widespread dissemination would destroy

[28] Pollet, 7, 9, 23, 119; Stone, 208; Carpenter, *John Skelton*, 138. Carpenter notes Skelton's musical knowledge (13). Combined with his close early connection with the Northumberland household, and with Dr Ruckshaw in particular, this knowledge suggests that Skelton may have been one of Percy's Chapel Children, sent to Cambridge where Alan Percy, the fifth Earl's brother, later served at St John's. See also William O. Harris, 15.

[29] Ian Lancashire, *Dramatic Texts and Records*, 47.

the effect of their art. Printers were businessmen, aware that the appeal of play texts was limited to a literate audience whose interests the plays served, and therefore questionable in terms of financial return. The influence of a noble patron could have provided the encouragement or even the subsidy that a printer required to publish and distribute a moral interlude.

Alan Nelson has suggested that More knew Medwall while both were at Cardinal Morton's household, that More may have acted B in *Fulgens and Lucrece*, and that More may have provided the connection between Medwall and the Rastells, who printed both *Fulgens and Lucrece* and *Nature*. De Worde was patronized by Margaret Beaufort, and his handlist of publications includes *Youth*, *Hick Scorner*, and *The World and the Child*, all plays with which she would have had sympathy, and all written for noblemen with whom she was acquainted. More concrete evidence of the relationship between noblemen and printers is provided by a Spanish diplomat about 1531 who reported that the Earl of Wiltshire had sponsored a farce depicting Cardinal Wolsey going to hell, and a duke, probably Norfolk, ordered that the play be printed.[30] These brief observations indicate that both playwrights and printers needed powerful protection for the stridently polemical works they were disseminating, and that the survival of many controversial interludes that ended up in print, such as the sharply critical *Godly Queen Hester*, may be directly attributable to noble patronage.

PLAYERS: DUTIES AND PRIVILEGES

Once a troupe received a script from its patron and performed it for his household, they set off to communicate it to the other audiences. For the players, this was a profit-making venture, but for the patron, a tour of his scripts could ensure that his political, economic, and artistic prominence was vividly represented throughout the land. Within this context, a nobleman's players did indeed become, as Hamlet informed Polonius, 'the abstracts and brief chronicles of the

---

[30] Medwall, ed. Nelson, 3, 17; see Lancashire, *Two Tudor Interludes* and 'The Auspices' for political interpretations of the interludes; *Spain*, iv/2, 40–1.

time; . . .'. In addition, the players formed a network for the circulation of news, rumour, and gossip from household to household, a fact that motivated Hamlet to continue, 'after your death you were better to have a bad epitaph than their ill report while you live'.

Many theatre historians, most notably E. K. Chambers, T. W. Craik, and Glynne Wickham, have devoted years and volumes to investigating the evolution of the patronized player troupes.[31] Rather than summarizing from their works, I should here like to consider the administrative and logistical details that delineated the relationship between professional troupes and the households in which they performed. Household regulations, financial accounts, and literary references to travelling players preserve some details that suggest answers to four important questions: what services did a patron expect from his retained troupe? what did the players do when not resident within the household? what procedures did troupes follow when they arrived at a household to play? and what options did a patron have in selecting dramatic entertainment?

The earliest reference that has come to light of a travelling troupe patronized by a nobleman occurs in the accounts of Henry VI in 1426, when he was entertained by four boys of the Duke of Exeter performing interludes. From the early fifteenth century on, references to such patronized itinerant troupes appear in civic, school, and private accounts, increasing in frequency throughout the Tudor reigns.[32] These accounts, however, are infuriatingly lacking in details crucial to the theatre historian, usually preserving only the amount paid to the players and the name of the troupe's patron.

As Giles Dawson notes in his introduction to the Kent records,[33] even notices of payments to players by civic authorities may be misleading because of inconsistent account-keeping which makes the payments difficult to date with precision. In addition, the absence of payment does not automatically connote the absence of players, for in times of

---

[31] T. W. Craik's chapter 'The Companies and the Repertory', in *Revels* provides the most recent historical overview, based primarily upon Chambers's *MS*.
[32] Wolffe, 37; *Revels*, 110–11.
[33] Dawson, xxvi–xxviii.

financial hardship, players may have depended upon the townspeople's donations rather than on municipal expenditure for their reward. Consequently, the accounts are helpful to some extent, but do not make it easy to trace touring patterns with any certainty. Similarly, household accounts communicate virtually nothing of the administrative details of player maintenance, travel, or performance, making it difficult to characterize the relationship between players and households. Yet significant omissions in household books and accounts, paradoxically, prove useful.

For example, Edward IV's *Black Book* clearly delineates the duties, rights, and responsibilities of the minstrels and the Chapel, but it makes absolutely no mention of players. Yet the King's brother, the Duke of Gloucester and future King Richard III, did retain a player troupe.[34] The fifth Earl of Northumberland also retained players, but his regulations mention them only briefly: 'ITEM My Lorde usith and accustometh to gif yerely to every of the iiij Parsons that his Lordschip admyted as his Players to com to his Lorschip yerly at Cristynmas Ande at all other such tymes as his Lordschip shall comande them for Playing of Playe[s] and Interludes affor his Lordship . . .'.[35] Although the notice mentions four players on a yearly salary, it does not record the amount of that salary. The accounts of Henry VII and Henry VIII are more helpful in determining paying mechanisms and amounts. A yearly wage of £3. 6s. 8d. (5 marks), was paid to each of Henry VII's players (four in 1494; five in 1503) from general household expenses through the Exchequer.[36] In addition, players could expect rewards from the King's personal funds, as noted in John Heron's Chamber accounts. On 3 November 1501, John English, head of the King's interluders, was paid £6. 13s. 4d. for 'his pagent'.[37] The exorbitant amount of this expenditure, English's salary for two years, suggests that rather than rewarding the player, Henry was reimbursing him for the costs of staging a court entertainment. The players were also granted a suit of livery yearly, and might

---

[34] *Revels*, 110; Chambers, *MS* 2, 186–7.
[35] NHB 262.
[36] Chambers, *ES* 2, 78–9; Wickham, *EES* 2, 116.
[37] Anglo, 'Court Festivals', 37.

expect rewards from visiting lords and ladies at important court occasions.

This system of payments varied little through the reigns of Henry VIII, Edward VI, and Mary. Wages paid by the Exchequer remained fairly consistent, although the rewards and special payments expended through the Chamber accounts did, of course, vary. When performing at Court, the interluders might also expect the Revels Office to defray certain costs for sets and properties, and to lend or sometimes donate costumes,[38] which naturally became valuable as touring stock.

The Earl of Northumberland's *Household Book* does not outline the specific duties and responsibilities of his troupe, nor does it specifically direct that they be provided with livery, food, or lodgings as other household servants were, although they probably did receive such amenities. On the contrary, this notice implies that the players, like their lord, generally operated outside the confines of the manor, returning to their patron only on particular and presumably pre-arranged occasions. Since Percy travelled a great deal, this is not particularly unusual. Because the players, unlike the Chapel and the minstrels, were not necessary or useful on a daily basis, this arrangement freed the patron from the financial burden of supporting idle retainers. Furthermore, the household accounts of noblemen rarely record rewards or payments to their own players, although they often reward visiting troupes patronized by others. All these omissions indicate that the players spent relatively little time with their patron, or also served the household in other capacities and were paid under other accounts.

Many players spent extensive time on tour. Household, school, monastic, and civic accounts rarely specify how many players compromised a troupe, but occasionally account keepers are unexpectedly specific. For example, of the eighty-two references to players in Selby Abbey accounts, thirty-five specify the number of men rewarded (see Appendix A). Most frequently, the reward was given to a single player, in three cases 'a player of the Duke of Gloucester', although Howard

---

[38] Chambers, *ES* 2, 81–3.

accounts specify Gloucester's troupe as four. It is difficult to imagine what one player acting independently might perform, unless he recited and mimed monologues; perhaps these men were minstrels rather than actors. On one occasion, the Abbey rewarded 'three players of the Duke of Gloucester, Lord Fitzhugh and Lord Lovell', so that on some occasions individual members of patronized troupes may have combined their resources to create a more versatile troupe for touring.[39] An alternate and more plausible explanation is that these rewards to one man represent moneys expended on the entire troupe via its leader, which would mean that the Abbey saw three plays by three troupes rather than one play by a combined troupe under the patronage of Gloucester, Fitzhugh, and Lovell.

Most frequently, however, Selby accounts specify rewards to troupes numbering three, four (the size dictated for Northumberland's troupe), or five members, numbers more consonant with what has come to be regarded as the typical troupe size. Other accounts support this assumption: Henry VII's Chamber accounts most frequently reward troupes of four; Maxstoke Priory, Winchester College, Shrewsbury Corporation, and Howard household accounts also rewarded troupes of four. Durham Priory, however, frequently mentions troupes of two, especially during earlier years; again, these may be minstrels. Although this *mélange* of numbers appears more confusing than helpful, it does demonstrate that although troupes differed considerably in size, troupes of four, like Percy's, one of the King's (the other numbered six), Gloucester's, and many others, seem the norm.

When a full troupe did not tour, what became of the non-touring members? Since they were not continuously supported at the expense of the household, they would have been forced to seek other employment if they chose not to tour, rather like their twentieth-century decendants who wait on tables as frequently as they wait in the wings. Some professional players served their patrons in other capacities when they were not called upon to act, which explains Richard Gibson's occupational metamorphosis from player to Yeoman of the

[39] Wickham, *EES 1*, app. C; Chambers, *MS 2*, app. E; Blackstone, 3.

Wardrobe under Henry VIII. According to Chambers, John English, one of Henry VII's players, also served as a tailor. Chambers also points out that two of Henry VIII's players followed trades; George Mallor was a tailor or glazier, and John Young was a mercer. When these men were not acting before the royal household, they were likely to return to these trades, occupations perhaps more lucrative, certainly more secure than the unpredictable rewards of touring. Although patronage offered professional performers legal and economic advantages, which I will explain in detail shortly, obviously acting has always been a shaky business.

Perhaps players in other households also acted before their lords at the required times and returned to other duties within the household when their dramatic services were not required. Such procedures would also have provided support for the player's family, who could also be employed by the household and could remain there when and if the actor travelled. This double duty could explain the lack of recorded privileges for players, since they were either non-resident, or else were provided for under other occupational titles. When a nobleman required that a player be resident for additional time, special financial arrangements would be made. This seems to be the case at Rutland's household in 1542, when Anthony Hall was provided with board for four weeks because he was 'lernyng a play to pley in Christemes'. Later the same year, Hall was paid for 'scowrying away the yerthe and stones in the tennys playe', which indicates that he, like Gibson, English, Mallor, and Young, had an alternate occupation within the household.[40]

Apparently some players travelled with their patrons. In 1503, when Henry VII sent his daughter Margaret north to marry James IV of Scotland, he sent his players, headed by John English, along with her. The players performed a morality after the wedding, and probably entertained at other times during the princess's grandiose journey. Similarly, when Henry VII welcomed the Earl of Northumberland's players on Twelfth Night in 1493, Northumberland was probably spending the holiday at the royal court. We know

[40] *Revels*, 36; Chambers, *ES* 2, 78 n., 80 n.; Chambers, *MS* 2, 187 n.; HMC 4, 322.

from the *Second Northumberland Household Book* that Twelfth Night was one of the most important, most lavishly celebrated occasions within Northumberland's household, a time at which an ordinance required that the household players perform an interlude. In 1493, therefore, Northumberland had either to depend upon an external troupe of players to execute the ordinance, or to be with his own troupe at the court of Henry VII. The latter is almost certainly the case, for in 1493 the Earl, a minor whose powerful father had been killed in 1490, was living at court as a ward of Margaret Beaufort, the King's mother, under the protection, and probably the watchful eye, of the King.[41]

PLAYERS AND HOUSEHOLD ADMINISTRATION

We know that players travelled, with or without their patrons, in groups varying in size from one to six or more. We know that they arrived at noble households, that they performed, and that they were paid for their services. We know very little, however, about the procedures which governed the arrival, performance, and departure of a troupe of patronized players.

If, as Northumberland's household book suggests, his players arrived at preordained times, the household would have been prepared to receive them, meals and lodging would have been previously arranged, the festivities would have been designed, and the role of the players within those designs decided upon. The players were customarily required on Twelfth Night, and the Twelfth Night celebration was prescribed by the ordinance, so both the players and the household officers knew exactly what to expect, exactly where they must be and what they must do at each particular moment. The only variable in the scheme was the text that the players would perform. Perhaps, like Rutland's Anthony Hall, Northumberland's players arrived at their lord's household early, to receive and rehearse a commissioned play, to prepare properly for the coming extravaganza. As the

[41] John Leland, *De Rebvs Britannicis Collectanea*, 4 vols. (London: J. Richardson, 1770), iv. 265–7; Chambers, *MS 2*, 187; Warton, i. 164; Mill, 320; Anglo, 'Court Festivals', 28; Lancashire, 'Orders'; for a biographical notice of the fifth Earl of Northumberland, Henry Algernon Percy, see Appendix D.

previous chapters have demonstrated, household revels attempted thematic unity, requiring that many types of entertainers and entertainments be integrated within one comprehensive design and intent. Consequently, it is unlikely that a player troupe, particularly at an important occasion, would perform an old familiar script and forcibly insert it into the revels, an action which would undermine the composite effect.

External troupes visiting a noble household would, therefore, have been unable to fit conveniently into planned revels. They would not be expected to. Although various households may have operated under similar rules, with similar patterns to the festivities, external troupes could arrive unexpectedly and unprovided for. In addition, the visiting troupes could be unfamiliar with the resources, both material and architectural, of a household they visited. How did the household administration accommodate such visitors?

No description of such procedures has as yet come to light in the historical records of the early Tudor period. Four literary references, however, provide some idea of the possibilities, including how visiting troupes were introduced into the household, how their dramatic offering was determined, and how their efforts were received by the audience and patron.

Act II of *Hamlet* contains one of the most famous imaginative accounts of the arrival and performance of a troupe of touring players. Although Rosencrantz and Guildenstern have already warned Prince Hamlet that the players have arrived and have explained why the players are forced to tour, it is Polonius, the Chamberlain of the royal household, who actually ushers the players into the presence of the Prince. The 'tragedians of the city' are well known to Hamlet; he immediately accepts their offering to play because he knows their quality and because it suits his purposes. After ordering Polonius to see that they are 'well bestowed', Hamlet, aware of this particular group's repertoire, makes specific requests about the play they shall enact, confident that they are adaptable enough to add his own verses to their text. In Act III, when *The Murder of Gonzago* is performed, the players must contend with interruptions from the audience, including Hamlet's critical commentary and Claudius's hasty retreat.

The Induction scene of *The Taming of the Shrew* also enacts a scene in which travelling players enter a noble household. Here, a servingman ushers the players into the Lord's presence. The troupe is unidentified, but the Lord is familiar with their expertise, so the players are welcomed, given food and lodging for the night, and warned to behave themselves. Like Hamlet, the Lord has a purpose in hiring the troupe, for their performance nicely fits into the jest he intends to play on Christopher Sly. Once again, players are welcomed because their quality is known and because they suit the purpose of the nobleman.

A Midsummmer Night's Dream presents a different situation for the player—household interaction, one almost as famous as that in *Hamlet*. In this case, Philostrate, Master of the Revels to Duke Theseus, presents to his lord a list of four entertainments from four different visiting groups. Theseus rejects three of the four for a variety of interesting reasons: he had told Hippolyta the harping eunuch's story of Hercules; he has seen the 'old device' of the tipsy Bacchanals; he suspects that the critical satire of the Muses is 'not sorting with a nuptial ceremony'. In spite of Philostrate's admonitions, the Duke selects the *Pyramus and Thisby* of the 'hard-handed men that work in Athens' believing that 'never anything can be amiss, / When simpleness and duty tender it'. In spite of his selection, the Duke, like Hamlet, leads his court in a lively critique of the play, interrupting it so thoroughly that at points the amateur players themselves break the illusion of the play to respond to the noble audience. Unlike Hamlet, however, Theseus does not request a particular text. In *Hamlet* and *The Taming of the Shrew*, the arrival of the players is an unexpected, albeit welcome, occurrence; in *A Midsummer Night's Dream* the arrival of the players is expected because of the occasion. Historically, the details of an entertainment as important as a royal wedding would have been arranged far in advance, yet Shakespeare shows us the process of that arrangement.

Although these references appear in the late rather than early sixteenth century, the same patterns emerge in an earlier play, the anonymous *Sir Thomas More*. Here, More's wife introduces the players into her husband's presence, but Sir Thomas will accept the players only after they have identified themselves as the Cardinal's men—after they have established their social degree, political persuasion, and artistic quality. As in *Hamlet*, the arrival of the players is unexpected, but happily coincides with a pre-arranged banquet for the mayor and aldermen of London, so More asks the players what texts they have prepared, then selects an appropriate play from their repertoire. During the performance of an unrecognizable *Marriage of Wit and Wisdom*, Sir Thomas, echoing Roper's apocryphal statement, steps into the play himself, assuming the role of an actor who has gone to fetch a forgotten beard. Further, More stops the play entirely when the banquet is served, requesting that the players begin again after supper. A marginal direction notes that the players are rewarded as their audience disappears to dinner.

Although *Hamlet*, *The Taming of the Shrew*, *A Midsummer Night's Dream*, and *Sir Thomas More* are artistic constructs rather than historical documents, they are remarkably consistent about some facets of the relationship between touring players and the households they visited. In all cases, an intermediary representing the household management makes the initial contact with the troupe. In all cases, the patron himself accepts the players and selects what shall be played. In addition, the visiting troupes are, in three of the four cases, carefully identified within the context of the play: *Hamlet*'s players are professionals under civic patronage; *Sir Thomas More*'s players are professionals under private patronage; *A Midsummer Night's Dream*'s players are amateur locals. The social identity of the troupe becomes a factor in the patron's decision to accept them. Once the play begins, however, none of the troupes can expect quiet, attentive audiences unless, like Sly after the Induction scene of *The Taming of the Shrew*, they are asleep. This is caustic comment upon Renaissance audience reception that is unfortunately frequently omitted in most modern productions—a further indication that we understand very little about the theoretical relationship between stage, actor, and audience in the sixteenth century.

If the touring troupes of Tudor England followed the

pattern of their literary analogues, then noble patrons took a far more active role in the selection of their household revels than has thus far been noted. Plays and players were not selected at random by subordinates and then presented to the household as a *fait accompli*. Based upon the identity of the players and upon the appropriateness of the text for the occasion, the patron's selection was far from capricious. Nothing about these arrangements was haphazard, even if the arrival of the troupe was unexpected.

The Northumberland Household Book demonstrates precisely how organized one of these arrangements—the financial outlay—could be. During the Christmas season, when the Earl was accustomed to receiving many and various entertainers, his household book dictates rewards to musicians and players, based upon the rank of the troupe's patron and upon the relationship between the Earl and the troupe's patron. Thus, an 'Erlis Players' received twenty shillings 'If he be his [Northumberland's] speciall Lorde and Frende ande Kynsman'. 'Lordis Players' received ten shillings. The rewards to minstrel troupes were dictated by still another criterion: whether they visited 'yerely' or 'seldome'. Annual visitors received three shillings four pence, whereas less frequent visitors received double that amount.[42] Like extant civic, monastic, and school accounts, Northumberland's precise schedule of rewards indicates special interest in the quality of the patron rather than the quality of the players or their texts. Furthermore, the schedule demonstrates that both player and Treasurer were aware of financial procedures beforehand, and could budget accordingly.

After a troupe of players requested admission to the household, after the patron had accepted them and selected an appropriate text, the players required space for playing and preparing. Richard Southern and David Bevington have thoroughly investigated extant texts, demonstrating that most are adaptable, suited to performance in various Tudor great halls that may have differed in size and design, but followed the same basic architectural patterns.[43] Visiting

---

[42] NHB 253–4.
[43] See *Revels*; Bevington, *Tudor Drama and Politics* and *From 'Mankind' to Marlowe*; Southern, *The Staging of Plays Before Shakespeare*.

players, then, also knew generally what facilities they could expect at any household they visited, but were prepared to adapt to specific surroundings.

This short-notice adaptability, combined with the close proximity of audience and player that both Southern and Bevington note, argues for a degree of unpredictability, what we might consider informality, in the dramatic offering. As we have seen in *Hamlet, The Taming of the Shrew, A Midsummer Night's Dream,* and *Sir Thomas More,* Tudor audiences, even if they were members of the aristocracy, were not the mute restrained types that we find in theatres today. The 'fourth wall' concept was non-existent, so audiences could and did interrupt and interact with players. Indeed, Shakespeare's comments may betray the irritation of a dramatist writing in a time when the aesthetics of response were beginning to change, when players were beginning to resent audience invasion of the stage space, when dramatists were attempting to close the stage, to encourage suspension of disbelief rather than the reverent and absolute identification of the liturgical forms. Playwrights were aware that congregations were becoming audiences, but household observers, considering themselves owners of the entertainment, might wish for an interruption from the sponsor. No matter how carefully arrangements for reward and selection had been made previously, the performance itself was subject to surprises.

The atmosphere of household plays is vividly communicated by Robert Armin in *Fool Upon Fool*. A troupe of players was dressing themselves in 'the Gentlemans kitchin' in preparation for an entrance 'through the Entry into the Hall'. A visiting fool, Jack Miller, was also waiting in the kitchen and noticed several freshly baked pies. The 'Players Boy ... in his Ladyes Gowne' persuaded the fool to purloin a few pies for them, whereupon Jack stuck his face into the oven, burning off all his hair. This ludicrous event affected the entire evening's performance: '... the Lady of the Play being ready to enter before the Gentiles to play her part, no sooner began but remembring Iack, laught out, and could goe no further: the Gentleman muzed at what hee laught . . .'.[44] The boy

[44] Armin, f. E2.ᵛ.

explained his mirth, and the fool was produced, entertaining the gentleman but effectively ending the play. Later that night, 'the Players drest them in another place', and tried again.

Armin's anecdote expresses not only the informality of the occasion, but also the adaptability of the players. The boy did not hesitate to filch a pie or to break character in order to share a jest; the whole troupe responded to the wishes of their host, postponing their play so that the 'Gentiles' could share in the laughter.

Thus far I have considered the noble patron in a somewhat passive role, as the receiver of players who begged admittance. Yet the patron could also serve an active function; at times he required a dramatic entertainment and had to seek one, as was the case when Lady Lisle directed a household official to find a play in 1538. Perhaps similar circumstances motivated John Rastell to adapt his *Four Elements*, to include a disguising and omit 'tedious' philosophy, for performance under private noble auspices.[45]

If a patron wanted to see a play, he had three options. First, he could, alone or in company, travel to attend one at a local church, school, or city. Richard II watched the Corpus Christi cycle at York in 1397, and Queen Margaret saw Coventry's in 1457. In 1536, Sir Humphrey Ferrers of Tamworth Castle suffered a broken shin venturing out to the local play.[46] Second, a nobleman could depend upon resident household members, such as his Chapel or minstrels, to provide dramatic entertainment. If some members of his player troupe remained within the household in capacities other than acting, the patron could perhaps call upon them to play. Third, he could hire a visiting troupe. With these options at his disposal, a patron could, if he wished, watch some sort of play at almost any time. What, then would motivate a nobleman to retain a troupe of players?

THE ADVANTAGES OF PATRONAGE

Civic and private accounts demonstrate that many players attached themselves to noble households. Since it appears

[45] Bevington, *From 'Mankind' to Marlowe*, 46.
[46] Chambers, *MS* 2, 115; Lancashire, 'Patrons and the English Moral Play'.

that they spent more time away from the household than within it, one wonders why they felt the need of a patron. The salaries and rewards given by the patrons were usually insufficient to support the players, nor do they appear to have been automatically entitled to food or lodging within the patron's household for extended periods of time, as other household servants were. Presumably they acquired livery at times, but few records besides the royal accounts note this, and patrons were not, in any case, excessively generous. Northumberland's *Household Book* implies that his players made a contract to appear at 'home' on only a few pre-arranged occasions. Were they unwelcome at others?

Besides giving players a local habitation and a name, noble patronage endowed them with a legal status and protection from the strict laws against masterless travellers. Wealthy patrons could also provide costumes and properties that were crucial to effective performance but too expensive for players to purchase for themselves. Any patron who permitted a group of men representing his household to set off with weary, stale, or flat accoutrements would be risking ridicule and loss of reputation. In addition, the social prestige of the patron gave his players a certain status, which ensured introduction to other households and to cities. Municipal officials and household officers would consider carefully before expelling or insulting the king's or the Duke of Norfolk's players, since such actions could have negative repercussions. Generous treatment, such as that extended by the Earl of Northumberland to the players of his friends and relations, was offered in proportion to the rank of the patron. Thus, the social hierarchy of the troupes reflected in microcosm the social hierarchy of the aristocracy. The more powerful the patron, the more welcome and lucratively rewarded his players.

The statutes enacted to control vagrancy were the most fundamental threats to the life and liberty of itinerant players. Masterless vagabonds at large in England had posed a threat to local control as early as 1285, when the Statute of Winchester addressed the problem. Henry VIII reactivated the statute by royal proclamation in 1527, and repeated it in 1531, including explicit directions to local authorities for the punishment of idle wanderers.[47] Throughout the Tudor reigns, those who could not claim masters or sufficient employment could be arrested, beaten until bloody and stocked in the public square, branded, forcibly returned to their original environs, or sold into slavery. Obviously, any player who wanted to keep body and soul together and stay at liberty, let alone make a profit through his itinerant art, had dire need of a patron whom he could claim as master. The frequent repetition of the statutes indicates that the central and local governments found them difficult to enforce, but it also indicates that the Crown meant business. Some players may have been able to slip through the tightening snares of the law, but most found it far more expedient to seek livery of some sort.

A second wave of regulations was directed towards controlling plays rather than players, but these regulations could nevertheless prevent players from practising their trade. Barely four years after he had taken the throne, Henry VII was concerned about the control of 'unlawful plays'.[48] His son and grandchildren, presiding over polemical battlegrounds that worried them considerably, were far more vigilant. Particularly after his break with Rome, Henry VIII found that the players' repertoires could be dangerous to his policies, and so he acted repeatedly to control and purge what he viewed as seditious sentiments. In 1537, angered at a May game that purported to advise him how to rule his realm, Henry ordered Suffolk justices to enforce his restrictions.[49] Under Edward VI and Mary, the violence of the Reformation and Counter-Reformation made the religious content of plays an issue of such sensitivity that the Crown forbade any play contrary to the sovereign's doctrinal position, and even went so far as to prohibit plays altogether.[50]

As with the laws against vagrants, the frequency of

[47] Great Britain Record Commission, *The Statutes of the Realm*, i. 97, iii. 328, hereafter, *SOR*; Hughes and Larkin, i. 172, hereafter *TRP*; Chambers, *ES 4*, app. D, 260.
[48] *TRP* i. 18–19.
[49] *L & P HVIII* 12/1, nos. 1212, 1284.
[50] *SOR 3*, 894–7; *SOR 4*, pt. 1, 38; *TRP 1*, 478–9, 514–18; Chambers, *ES 4*, app. C.

proclamations about seditious content implies that, while plays were perceived as potent, volatile threats that must be controlled, enforcement of control remained a serious problem. The protection of a patron gave many players an exaggerated view of their immunity, for many were willing to risk offence and gamble with their freedom for potential profit. The Earl of Oxford's players were impudent enough to plan to play at Southwark while Bishop Gardiner was conducting funeral services for Henry VIII. Gardiner, unable to control the players himself or through local authorities, went wailing to Protector Somerset for more powerful assistance.[51]

Players may or may not have been personally committed to the philosophies contained in their texts (some, like Bale and his troupe, undoubtedly were), but they knew that polemical plays could be particularly profit-making because they were topical, tinged with danger, and perhaps sensational in the potential for slander and scandal. Perhaps the Crown found it necessary to repeat its position continually because the players were protected by the public popularity of their texts. Noble patronage, however, could be far more protective than that of the proletariat. When public safety was not at risk, the local magistrate must have been perplexed indeed at his responsibility for enforcement of the regulations. Should he tolerate a local noble's troupe at the risk of offending the sovereign, who may, with luck, never hear of the transgression? Does he curtail the activities of a Protestant nobleman's troupe in an area of strong Protestant sentiment, risking insult and public outcry, simply because the Queen is Catholic? Although the arm of the sovereign was long, the arm of a troupe's patron might be closer and, in certain circumstances, more dangerous or helpful to the community. Such decisions put local authorities between Scylla and Charybdis. It is small wonder, therefore, that civic officials turned a blind eye to certain performances and that the Crown constantly attemped to restore their sight.

While some statutes actively forced players to seek patronage to protect themselves from the law, others

[51] Lemon, i, 5.

encouraged players to seek patronage so that they might be exempt from it. In 1463, Edward IV had exempted players from the regulations concerning array, which severely limited the cost and flamboyance of a commoner's clothing.[52] The implications of this exemption are twofold. First, since they were included with priests, judges, scholars, henchmen, heralds, pursuivants, sword-bearers, messengers, and minstrels in the exemption, players might easily get an inflated impression of their social standing. The public might also get this impression, for the Tudor social hierarchy depended heavily on conventional signification, particularly on external signs of affluence and power. Second, the exemption assumes that players needed to dress in highly decorated and costly garments in orders to practise their art. Players were repeatedly exempted from the statutes limiting array throughout the Tudor reigns,[53] a fact that raises a significant question about the financial resources of itinerant troupes: where did these garments come from?

Costumes were not cheap. If a player were acting a nobleman or king, he had to look the part, which meant finding a source for the appropriate garments. Since the visual aspects of a play are as important as the rhetorical ones, a player's art would inspire neither awe nor profit if it did not somehow impress the audience. Poorly dressed players could not properly represent their patron, who was concerned with impressing local populations. For all these reasons, the players' costume stocks must have met certain standards of design and expense.

A 1530 lawsuit regarding players' garments between John Rastell, printer and playwright, and Henry Walton illustrates just how valuable such costume stock could be. Rastell's description of the costumes is worth repeating here, for it demonstrates the visual richness of player garments:

... a players garment of green sarcenet lined with red tuke and with roman letters stitched upon it of blue and red sarcenet, and another garment paned with blue and green sarcenet lined with red buckram, and another garment paned likewise and lined as the other, with a cape furred with white cats, and another garment paned with yellow, green, blue, and red sarcenet, and lined with red

---

[52] SOR 2, 402. [53] SOR 3, 8–9, 179–82, 430–2.

buckram. Another garment for a priest to play in, of red Say, and a garment of red and green Say, paned and guarded with gold skins, and fustians of Naples black, and sleeved with red, green, yellow, and blue sarcenet. And another garment, spangled, of blue satin of Bruges, and lined with green sarcenet. Also two old short garments, paned of satin Bruges and of sarcenet of divers colours in the bodies. Also a woman's garment of green and blue sarcenet, chequered and lined with red buckram, also two caps of yellow and red sarcenet. . . .[54]

Rastell had also left two large curtains and about 100 yards of cloth, thirty yards of which had come from 'a box in my Lord Cardinal's great chamber', surely no ordinary homespun. Valued at twenty marks (one year's salary for King Henry VII's troupe of four interluders)[55] these costumes were no less elaborate than those described in the King's own Revels wardrobe.

A shrewd businessman, Walton saw an opportunity for profit, and rented Rastell's stock to players of 'stage-plays' at the rate of 40d. or 2s., and to interluders for 8d. The distinction between stage plays and interludes is not completely clear, but it appears that the former were enacted outdoors, the latter indoors. Presumably the cost of hiring costumes to be used outdoors was higher because the garments were in more serious risk from the weather and the crowd than they would be during indoor performance. In addition, it is possible that an outdoor performance, being potentially larger than an indoor one, could garner higher profits, in which Walton would wish to share. Depositions from George Birch and George Mallor, one of the King's players, testify that these men had seen various local players sporting Rastell's stock during Henry VIII's elaborate Greenwich revels in 1527. In order to be useful for this occasion, the costumes would have to be eye-catching and impressive.

It is clear from the documents of the Rastell–Walton suit that players needed appropriate costumes; that costumes were general enough in style to be used to clothe different types of characters; that many players who could not afford

---

[54] The documents of the suit are reprinted in Pollard, 307.
[55] Chambers records that the King expended 20 marks p.a. as salary to one entire troupe, *ES* 2, 78; Wickham, *EES* 2, 116.

to construct and maintain their own stock were forced to hire it; that even a limited stock of garments could be expensive; and that the owner of such stock could make a handsome profit. To whom would itinerant players turn for these basic tools of their trade? They cannot have hired them for each performance. Locating costumes for rent would have been difficult, time-consuming, and undependable, creating logistic problems that would make touring a nightmare of inefficiency. More important to the practical players, hiring costumes would have decimated their profits, defeating the chief purpose of touring. Patronized troupes no doubt travelled with their own small, versatile, easily transportable stock of costumes donated by their patron from his own cast-off finery and from expendable stock in the household revels wardrobe. In 1546/7, the King's interluders hired garments from the Wardrobe Office for their tour; this seems a bit stingy on the part of the patron, but it insured that the players would take care of the costumes, and that the Wardrobe would acquire money to repair and reconstruct garments.[56]

Besides providing players with the basic necessities for their trade such as costumes, properties, and protection from the law, patronage also allowed itinerant troupes an introduction to various playing opportunities. Rosemary Horrox draws on many detailed examples to demonstrate that the cities and towns of Tudor England actively cultivated the goodwill of many noblemen to ensure that civic authorities might have powerful friends to turn to when the need arose. Welcoming a nobleman's players and treating them well was dictated as much by politics as by a desire for entertainment. Giles Dawson's edition of Kent records confirms that towns were particularly generous to troupes from the royal household and from the Wardens of the Cinque Ports, whose influence in the region was considerable.[57]

TOURING

Reconstructing the touring patterns of itinerant players is an act that approaches the realm of historical fiction, which,

[56] Wickham, *EES* 2, 117; Chambers, *ES* 2, 81; *MS 1*, 183 n.
[57] Horrox, *The Crown and the Provinces*, 145–66; Dawson, xviii.

however well-researched and documented, still owes a considerable debt to the imagination. Several basic problems remain immovable stumbling-blocks in the way of predicting itineraries with any certainty. First, the primary evidence, records of payments to patronized troupes, is only now beginning to be systematically collected and catalogued in a form that will be useful to scholars. Second, the hundreds of references to patronized players that have been collected and edited are incomplete and notoriously difficult to date. Third, estate accounts, which may one day reveal the extent of itinerant performance in private households, remain virtually untouched and perhaps often undiscovered. The accounts of the royal courts indicate that households frequently received visiting players, but until the accounts of the lesser nobility are examined with similarly detailed attention, we can only suppose that the aristocracy followed the royal example. Fourth, in many areas of England records of the passage of player troupes may never have existed. Some villages may have kept no records, but may still have played host to players who depended on donations for their recompense. In towns where records were kept, the omission of rewards to players does not prove that players were never there, only that municipal funds were not expended on them.

In spite of these formidable difficulties, it is possible to discern general geographic patterns, but not specific troupe itineraries, by examining the movements of a nobleman's troupe.[58] For example, the players of Charles Brandon, Duke of Suffolk, appear at Southampton in 1529–30, at London in 1530, again at Southampton in 1530–1, and again at London in 1531. Although it is impossible to determine where the players stopped between Southampton and London (perhaps returning to their patron's seat at Suffolk Place, Southwark?), they had to stop somewhere on the seventy-mile journey. The most direct route to London would have taken them through Hampshire by Winchester, Basingstoke, Alton, Aldershot, and Farnham to Surrey, where at Guildford they could cross the river and proceed north to Woking, then follow the Thames through Kingston to London. There is, in the

---

[58] See Appendix C.

absence of municipal records, no way of proving that Suffolk's players actually performed at these locations, but it is unlikely that an itinerant troupe would bypass major population centres or resist the opportunity to earn a few shillings on a road they had to travel anyway (see map, p. 146).

As Suffolk's players travelled the forty miles between the royal court and Cambridge in 1538, they could have profited by stopping at Barnet, Hertford (where the Stafford family may have been home at Writtle), Ware, Saffron Walden, and Melbourn. The years 1539–40 generally found the troupe in the north, appearing at Louth, Lincolnshire, and at York; they also performed at Lydd in Kent the same year. In 1540–1 they travelled the breadth of England from Bristol to Lydd, and in 1541–2 they appear in Kent at Dover, Folkestone, and again at Lydd.

Sparse as these notices are, they suggest conjectural patterns, for the Duke's men seem to have concentrated their activities in limited geographic areas during each year. In 1529–31 they appear to be touring Hampshire and Surrey; in 1537–9 they cover Essex and Cambridgeshire; in 1540–1 they travel in Lincolnshire and Yorkshire, as well as covering the long route from Bristol to Kent, perhaps in two separate tours. In 1541–2, their performances are concentrated in Kent, quite a manageable tour.

The fourth Duke of Norfolk's players appear, at least from the available accounts, to have remained closer to home. Performing most frequently in Ipswich and Norwich, they capitalized upon the powerful influence exerted by their patron in his native Norfolk and Suffolk environs. Politics may also have encouraged the Norfolk players to remain near home. Since Somerset was the King's closest friend as well as his brother-in-law, a popular courtier, and frequent visitor to court, his players would be far more free to travel than most, or may have travelled extensively with their lord and his king. In marked contrast, Norfolk's relationship with the royal household had always been problematic, to say the least. The Duke's opposition to Wolsey, the disastrous marriages of his nieces Anne Boleyn and Katherine Howard, and the perceived threat of his son the Earl of Surrey to the royal succession surely encouraged Norfolk's players to steer clear of the

King. In addition, men like Norfolk and Northumberland were distanced geographically and ideologically from the royal court, and so tended to form strong independent courts of their own, more responsive to local styles and concerns.

Similarly, the troupes under Sir Thomas Cheney and George Nevill, Lord Abergavenny, appear most frequently in Kent, where these lords held office as Wardens of the Cinque Ports. The motivations for these touring patterns are not difficult to understand; profits were highest where patrons held most sway. Thus, Thomas Seymour's troupe appears to have concentrated its touring activities in coastal towns during its patron's tenure as Lord Admiral from 1546 to 1549, appearing on the Kent circuit at Dover in 1547–8, at Lyme Regis on the Dorset coast in 1548, and again at Dover and New Romney in Kent in 1548–9. A solitary payment at Cambridge in 1549 may imply an Essex tour.

While the Admiral's troupe was touring Kent in 1548–9, the players of his brother, Protector Somerset, were also appearing in Kent at Canterbury, Dover, and New Romney. During the same year, however, Somerset's troupe also appeared in Leicester, Norwich, Cambridge, and Lyme Regis. It is tempting to suggest an itinerary that followed the south coast to Kent, then through Cambridge to Leicester and Norfolk for this year, or perhaps a tour that reversed that sequence. Imprecise dating of records makes it impossible to determine the order of performance stops.

This examination of Suffolk, Norfolk, Cheney, Nevill, and Seymour troupes has of necessity been selective, attempting only to make suggestions about a handful of potential touring patterns, not to provide thorough and exhaustive analysis of player itineraries, which would require a full-length study dedicated solely to that purpose. Even the patterns suggested here may well be indicative more of surviving records than of actual touring patterns. Still, these observations suggest that itinerant troupes limited their activities to certain geographic regions during each year, and that the popular circuits included Kent, East Anglia, Bristol to Kent, Southampton to Kent or London, and Cambridge to Lincolnshire and York.

The more extensive (but still imprecise and insufficient)

accounts of Henry VIII and Edward VI seem to support these hypothetical circuits. The convenient Kent tour appears particularly popular, for Henry VIII's troupes appear in that area twenty-one times, as the Duke of York's and later the King's players, between 1494 and 1547. During four of these years, Henry's players also appeared at Bristol, following the proposed Bristol to Kent circuit. Four times they appear at Southampton, perhaps following the Southampton to Kent to London circuit. Three times they appear at Plymouth, a city that the Southampton to London route could also take in. Since Henry retained two troupes, his accounts could also indicate two different itineraries.

The Kent circuit was also popular with Edward VI's troupe, for they appeared almost yearly, first as the Prince's men and then as the King's, from 1538 to 1553. Like his father's troupes, Edward's also travelled the Plymouth to Southampton leg four times and the Bristol leg three tmes. Edward's players also undertook the Cambridge tour and the East Anglia route, appearing five times in Norwich. Henry VIII's troupe appeared only twice in Norwich in fifty-three years, perhaps because they found East Anglia, a Norfolk territory, less hospitable and therefore less generous than Kent. They also tended to avoid Cambridge, appearing there only three times. Henry VIII's troupes appear to have concentrated their activities in the south and around London, with occasional forays north. They may have wished to remain close to the court, where the King's influence was strongest and where they could hurry home to their patron if major entertainments were planned. The boy-king Edward needed his interluders far less frequently than did his dramatic father.

As more evidence about player and patron movements becomes available, scholars may be able to fill out these patterns and to make more solid deductions about the motivation and structure of player itineraries. For the present it may be valuable to consider the practical matters involved in touring in order to describe the day-to-day lives of the troupes.

Anyone with theatrical experience knows how complicated mounting a play can be. Moving the play, complete with actors, sets, and properties can be a stage manager's nightmare unless careful planning, efficient organization, and realistic budgeting of time and money predict and prevent the disasters that are likely to occur. Since the sixteenth-century interluders had no stage managers but themselves, these responsibilities fell upon the actors, who had to be their own directors, publicists, bookkeepers, and crew. The success or failure of the tour could easily depend not only on how well they performed, but also on how efficiently they did so.

The players' load, limited to one or two hampers containing few but sufficient costumes, properties, and personal belongings, would have to be light. Still, they would not have been overjoyed at the prospect of carrying it by hand through Kent, so they probably arranged for a horse and cart. Dawson's Kent records frequently mention expenditures for food for players' horses. Lydd records twice specify 'foote players', but these troupes do not appear to be in the service of noblemen.[59] Perhaps another advantage of noble patronage was that the troupe might beg a horse from the patron's stable. Players also hired horses, for in 1537 John Young, one of Queen Jane's four players, brought a suit against an ostler who rented them a dying horse to carry their costumes on a northern tour.[60] John English and his troupe probably rode mounted at the King's expense when they travelled north with Princess Margaret on her wedding progress. If players customarily hired their horses, it is unlikely that all rode, for much of their profit would be eaten up in rental and maintenance. Horse and cart was far more practical an arrangement.

As the players approached a town, regulations required that they apply to the mayor or town officials for permission to play. They would then concern themselves with finding the most profitable place or places to perform, either in a hall, street, inn, private home, or market square. Kent records show that players occasionally received municipal rewards 'over and above' what they collected from the people,[61]

[59] Dawson, 31, 94, 102–3.
[60] Stopes, *Shakespeare's Environment*, 235–7.
[61] Kent records refer to town and guild halls, market squares, and high streets as places of performance; Dawson, 10, 11, 41, 98, 135, 138.

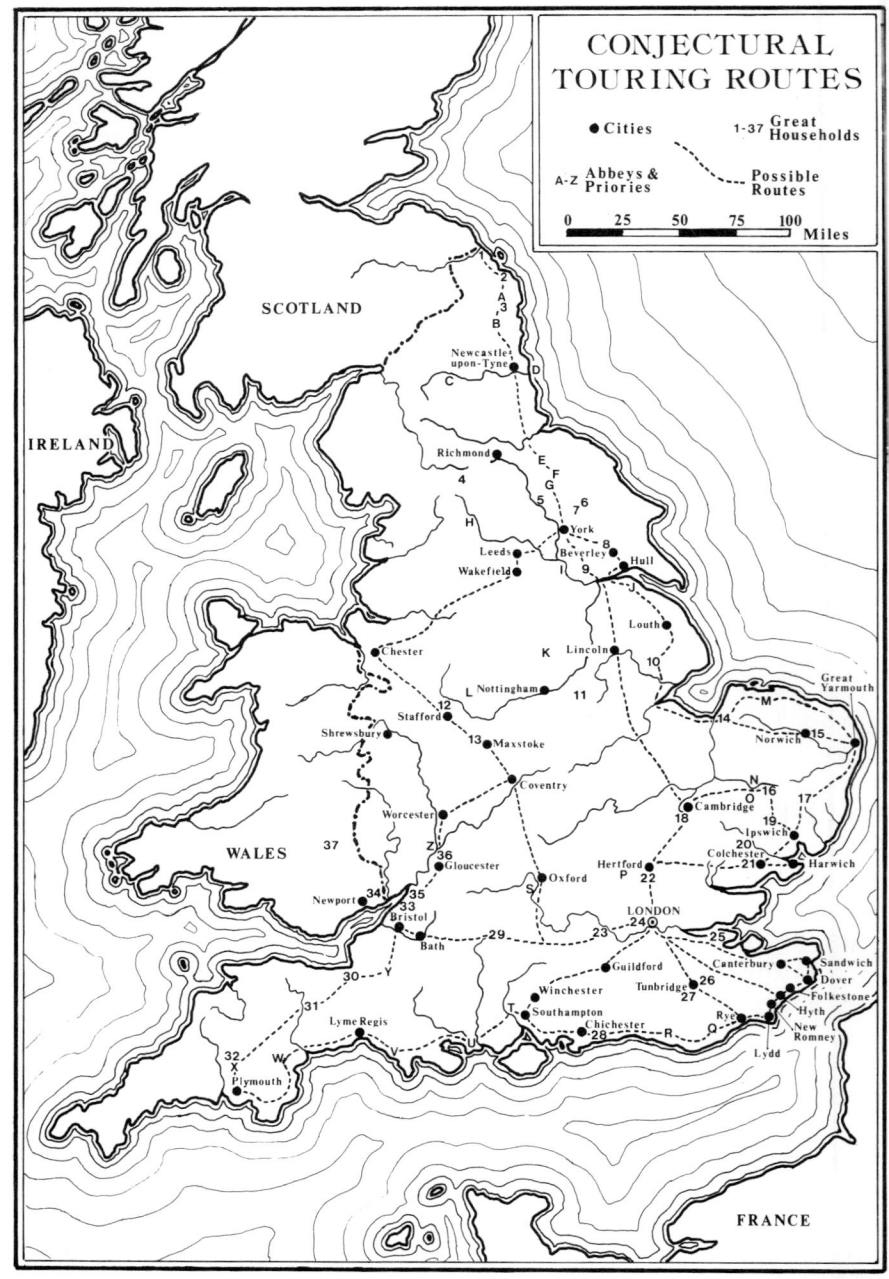

Fig. 10.

Map drawn by P. H. Miller

MAP OF CONJECTURAL TOURING ROUTES

Note: These routes were determined by observing where a troupe appeared during a limited time (confirmed by extant rewards in municipal and household accounts) and by consulting seventeenth- and eighteenth-century road maps to select the best (but not always the most direct) routes through the greatest number of cities, towns, and manors that might provide playing engagements.

Key
(a)   Principal Seats of Early Tudor Patrons

No.	Seat
1	Berwick (Percy, earls of Northumberland)
2	Bamburgh (Percy)
3	Alnwick (Percy)
4	Bolton Castle (Henry, Lord Scrope)
5	Topcliffe (Percy)
6	Castle Howard (Howard, dukes of Norfolk and earls of Surrey)
7	Sheriff Hutton (Howard)
8	Leconfield and house at Hull (Percy)
9	Wressle (Percy)
10	Tattershall (Brandon, Duke of Suffolk)
11	Belvoir Castle (Manners, earls of Rutland)
12	Stafford (Stafford, earls of Stafford and dukes of Buckingham)
13	Maxstoke (Stafford)
14	Castle Rising (Howard)
15	Mt Surrey (Howard)
16	Kenninghall (Howard)
17	Framlingham (Howard)
18	Castle Camps (de Vere, earls of Oxford)
19	Tendring Hall (Howard)
20	Hedingham (de Vere)
21	Earls Colne (de Vere)
22	Writtle (Stafford)
23	House at Windsor (William Parr, Earl of Essex)
24	Somerset House on Strand (Edward Seymour, Earl of Hertford and Duke of Somerset)
	Milk St London house (John Bourchier, Earl of Bath)
	Suffolk Place, Southwark (Brandon)
	Ely Place (John Dudley, Earl of Warwick)
25	Wulfhall (Edward Seymour)
	Cowling Castle (George Brooke, Lord Cobham)
26	Tonbridge (Stafford)
27	Penshurst (Stafford)
28	Arundel Castle (Thomas FitzAlan, Earl of Arundel)
29	Marlborough Castle (Seymour)
30	Bridgewater Castle (Henry Daubeney, Earl of Bridgewater)
31	Tiverton Castle (Henry Courtney, Earl of Devon)
32	Tavistock (Bourchier)
33	Thornbury (Stafford)
34	Newport (Stafford)
35	Berkeley Castle (Henry, Lord Berkeley)
36	Sudeley Castle (Thomas, Baron Seymour)
37	Brecon (Stafford)

(b)   Major Abbeys and Priories

Map Letter	Abbey or Priory Name	Map Letter	Abbey or Priory Name
A	Hulne	N	Thetford
B	Brinkburn	O	Bury St Edmunds
C	Hexham	P	St Albans
D	Tynemouth	Q	Battle
E	Mt Grace	R	Lewes
F	Rievaulx	S	Abington
G	Byland	T	Romsey
H	Bolton	U	Christchurch
I	Selby	V	Abbotsbury
J	Thornton	W	Widecombe
K	Welbeck	X	Tavistock
L	Croxton	Y	Glastonbury
M	Walsingham	Z	Tewkesbury

FIG. 11. From the title-page of William Haithorne's *Roman Comique*, itinerant players (c. 1676) arrive at an inn. The cart loaded with sets and costumes, the overdressed young man, and the minstrel bearing his instrument seem less than welcome. In the background, another player troupe performs on a platform stage. Both troupes are small, and indicate the frugality of the touring life.

Playwrights and Players 149

implying either two separate performances or one performance that incorporated a plea for donations or an admission charge. Although the rewards at these small towns cannot have been great, a clever or experienced player could design a tour that would at least pay expenses. Publicity would have to be cheap and efficient. Players would have to know how far people were willing to travel to see a play, and plan their stops at optimal distances, using word of mouth and crying banns along the road to attract the audiences. Seasoned troupes would also know where the pickings were best—which townspeople and innkeepers had been most generous; where their patron's name would wield some authority; where they had formed friendships over past years; where middle-class families might commission a private performance; which towns held fairs, and what nearby manors might welcome them. All these factors would influence their choice of stops. Even the few pence gathered at small towns might purchase meals that would have to be eaten and paid for at any rate.

Estimating the gross or net earnings of a sixteenth-century tour is difficult, since rewards varied depending on certain considerations, including the wealth of the hosts, the quality of the patron and performance, the time of year, and many other factors. For example, in 1540–1 the city of Dover rewarded the Duke of Suffolk's men 6s. 8d.[62] If they had collected this amount at each stop (which is unlikely), their receipts would have approached the salary of one of the King's interluders for a year. Rewards to the Duke's players during the same year and therefore presumably on the same tour at Folkestone (12d.) and Lydd (20d.) seem more typical.[63]

A 1528 suit between George Mallor, one of the King's players, and Thomas Arthur, his pupil, indicates how much a player might make on tour. Mallor was irate that Arthur, after spending only seven weeks learning plays, absconded with three other players to the provinces where he profited richly from his 'stolen' treasure of scripts. The renegade troups earned £30 'in sundry partiez of Englond in plainge of

[62] Dawson, 39.
[63] Dawson, 69.

many interludes',[64] effectively preventing Mallor from making money touring the same scripts in the same area, so Mallor wanted the profits. Again, the value of texts to players becomes apparent, for scripts were valuable commodities that merited as careful protection as did a tradesman's basic tools. Although there is no way of determining either the length or the route of Arthur's tour, the alleged profits were considerable, almost ten times a Royal interluder's yearly salary. The Mallor–Arthur dispute shows that players were careful to protect their privileges, their plays, and their earnings.

Between his salary and the profits of touring, a patronized player could earn a livelihood. He also had a home to return to where his family might find employment, and was perhaps given or lent the basic tools of his trade. Without some form of patronage, the itinerant players would have been a beggarly lot indeed, homeless, ill-prepared for their art, and forever vulnerable to harassment. A 1595 reference from Chester is enlightening about the desirability of patronage. A warrant for Edward Lord Dudley's players Francis Coffin and Richard Bradshaw directed that they be admitted to towns and provided with playing space. Apparently the players abused their privilege, for in 1602 the Mayor of Chester relieved them of the warrant, believing that Dudley had long since discharged them, and warned them to stop playing.[65]

Players needed to be retained by patrons, but did patrons need to retain players? Many noblemen could rely on other sources for dramatic entertainment and some who could not afford to retain Chapels or players were forced to. Even those who did retain troupes saw their own players infrequently. Since Tudor noblemen rarely took action without considering the financial or political advantages of it, players must have represented more than just an occasional diversion.

Just as a nobleman's name lent his players prestige, the maintenance of players contributed to a nobleman's status. Unlike priests and trumpeters, players were a luxury, not a necessity, whose expenses might well be beyond the resources

[64] Overend, 426.
[65] Clopper, 177–8.

of the poorer members of the aristocracy. Thus, the extravagance of retaining a private troupe demonstrated the patron's financial solvency, social prestige, and artistic sophistication. The value of such an impression cannot be underestimated during the period of transition from feudal to Renaissance economic and political systems. As noblemen lost vassals, they were forced to attract loyal servants. Although loyalty could be—and was—bought, it was also encouraged through vivid demonstrations of power, wealth, and prestige: extravagant wardrobes, conspicuous consumption of goods and services, and expensive architecture testify to this fact. Patronizing a player troupe provided good publicity.

Most important, a troupe of players provided its patron with lines of communication. The value of news and choice gossip to a society lacking newspapers and dependent upon political intrigue should not be underestimated. Player troupes were indeed the 'abstracts and brief chronicles of the times', for as they travelled, they gathered information to be communicated to their patrons upon their prearranged return. The information, however, could flow in two directions. When visiting cities, abbeys, schools, and noble households, troupes represented their patron, demonstrating his qualities through their praise, his philosophies through their texts. When a patron retained players, he also retained potential mouthpieces and spies; thus, his money was well invested.

Plays and players were, ironically, too important to be kept close within the households that retained them. The plays would have polemical value in households full of backbiting and gossip, but in order to achieve the maximum effect, words had to be spread, not endlessly repeated to the same group. Preaching to the converted has always been an exercise in the ridiculous, and noble patrons recognized this. Although the primary purpose of the players was to entertain, at home or abroad, retained troupes were also apostles, sent to spread the word of the lord in their allegorical parables.

4
Plays

MESS. Therefore they thought it good you hear a play
       And frame your mind to mirth and merriment
       Which bars a thousand harms and lengthens life.
SLY. Marry, I will, let them play it. Is not a commonty a Christmas gambol or a tumbling-trick?
PAGE. No, my good lord, it is more pleasing stuff.
SLY. What, household stuff?
PAGE. It is a kind of history.
SLY. Well, we'll see't. Come madam, wife, sit by my side and let the world slip: we shall ne'er be younger.
                    The Taming of the Shrew, Induction, ii. 131–40

A play sponsord by a nobleman and performed by a troupe of itinerant players is about to unfold before the sleepy eyes of a commoner, Christopher Sly, who is obviously unaccustomed to watching such revels. In marked contrast, the household servants display their familiarity with the occasion; even the messenger knows that plays are meant to be therapeutic diversions, and the young page calmly explains the nature of the entertainment. The Lord who hired the players shows even more knowledge, for he, like Hamlet, recognizes the troupe and compliments one of their number on a previous performance.

What is the source of the comedy here? Is Shakespeare using Sly's naïvety to comment upon social class, or is he merely observing that members of great households, regardless of class, were more experienced playgoers than their unretained comrades? If Shakespeare's unidentified 'lord' were a simple knight, his household servants would probably be commoners, their theatrical expertise acquired during their service. The central jest of the Induction scene of *The Taming of the Shrew* is founded on the confusion of the outsider, Sly, thrust into the centre of the household structure, where his ignorance of courtly behaviour and of the customary activities of a great household becomes comic.

This is not to say that the commoners of England never saw plays. Thousands attended the craft cycles, church plays, folk plays, and moralities, which were designed to communicate important concepts about the Christian religion or, in the case of folk drama, the mythic (and therefore 'pagan') patterns of death and rebirth, order and chaos, so crucial to agrarian cultures. The early Tudor interludes (often called moral plays or moral interludes),[1] current from the accession of Henry VII in 1485 to the accession of Elizabeth in 1558, represent a change, a different social sensibility both in style and in content, that separates them from the miracle, mystery, and morality plays, and looks forward to the plays of the public theatre.

Up to this point, I have been concerned chiefly with presenting historical materials that begin to define the relationships between entertainers and the households they served. In the absence of memoirs, eyewitness accounts, or scripts, it has been difficult to contemplate the effect of the Chapel and minstrel performances, but in the case of the players we are fortunate that a number of texts have survived. Now I would like to discuss specifically the early Tudor interludes as texts, to analyse their conventions, structures, and ideas in order to determine how and why patrons and playwrights exploited the dramatic form, and how this affected audience response.

One of the most basic changes between the folk or religious forms and the interludes was the identity of the producer. Whereas the mystery and miracle plays were generally executed through co-operative efforts of parish and civic organizations, and the folk plays were generally produced by the local population or small groups of wandering players, most of the interludes current from 1485 to 1558 were produced under scholarly or noble auspices. David Bevington's *Tudor Drama and Politics* and Sydney Anglo's

---

[1] Alan Dessen cogently discusses the problems of terminology, 10–16. I have discussed the problem in the forthcoming edition of *The Princeton Encyclopedia of Poetry and Poetics* under the entries 'interlude' and 'morality'.

Spectacle, Pageantry, and Early Tudor Policy demonstrate that dramatic entertainments could and did serve specific social and political goals, a theory that Glynne Wickham extends to his investigation of the later Elizabethan plays in volume 3 of his *Early English Stages*. Implicit in Richard Southern's *The Staging of Plays before Shakespeare* is the assumption that many early interludes were designed to be staged in the great halls of ecclesiastical or noble households, schools, colleges, and Inns of Court, rather than in public squares, streets, or churches, although the interludes might appear on tour in such locations.

Once the producer changes, naturally the purpose of the play changes. This is perhaps most obvious when we look at the protagonists of these interludes, no longer the plebeian Christians of *Mankind*, *Everyman*, or *The Castle of Perseverance*, nor the saints of the miracles, nor the biblical personages of the mysteries, nor even the Robin Hoods and St Georges of the folk drama. Rather, the characters who populate the early Tudor interludes are noblemen, allegorically named but nevertheless identifiable by their preoccupation with specifically aristocratic concerns and practices. Plebeian characters are often relegated to the sub-plot, itself a new direction in the structure of the plays that indicates an acute class-consciousness. The only earth the meek inherit in the interludes is the soil that they work, and even that is only at the pleasure of an aristocrat.

Perhaps the most significant change is a shift in concern, from the moral health of the human being and the theological history of English culture to the social, political, and economic ideologies of the ruling class. Again, the message reflects the producer and the intended audience. Whereas in the religious plays, designed to be viewed chiefly by the common citizens, exalted social position is irrelevant or even detrimental to moral health, in the interludes social position is equivalent to or reflective of moral health, almost in prediction of the Calvinist doctrine of the 'elect'. Such a philosophy was certainly sweet music to the ears of the patrons when the plays were performed within their households, for it reinforced the appropriateness of the existing hierarchy. In schools and universities, filled with young men who would soon be employed by such households, the interludes acted as primers for the propaganda of power.

All of these changes required that writers adapt systems of signification to communicate their perceptions visually and aurally, and manipulate conventional structures to express these messages. No longer would the paper crown signify a powerful villain, but rather a beleaguered nobleman who was trying to rule well. No longer would the simply garbed early Christians and their Old Testament prefigurations play the pious heroes, but instead they had become the simple peasantry who served and were ruled by characters that closely resembled contemporary power figures. Time and space, paradoxically, became more specific as they became more generalized; as the plays moved from the Holy Land to every land, from biblical time to any time, audiences were more free to unravel the allegories by applying them directly to personal and contemporary experience in addition to absorbing timeless moral lessons.

Playwrights began to establish the nobility of their characters by selecting particular historical details that were intimate facets of noble life-styles, then manipulating these signs for their own purposes; thus the ranting vice, Herod, becomes the boastful noble, Youth. These new signs contribute to the creation of subtle cultural codes that form the structures of the plays, for many years labelled 'simplistic' because of alleged physical and artistic limitations. Rather, the accusation reflects the chasm between historicities, for the early interludes reflect historical patterns of retention, precedence, and ceremony, all matters of utmost concern to the original audiences, who understood the 'rules', and could easily receive the messages.

In contrast, modern audiences frequently react in two ways: either they accept the naïve 'morality' of the plays, utterly oblivious to their complex politics; or they are left baffled, without the key to the iconographic indicators, the visual or rhetorical referents for the allusions, or the immediate applicability to their own life-styles. Many consider the interludes dated, and in a sense they are, for like any political drama, they reflect specific polemics that may or may not have universal application. Yet those who dismiss these plays are ignoring the revolutionary achievement that permitted playwrights like Shakespeare and Marlowe to exist; by redefining signs from the religious drama, by manipulating structures to express social and political ideas rather than religious didacticism, the interlude makers created a new form of allegory, and taught audiences to interpret it and to apply it to their own times. Such a development made it possible much later for *King Lear* to warn about the dangers of dividing the kingdom, for *Henry V* to glorify sixteenth-century England, for Queen Elizabeth to see herself in *Richard II*.[2]

Just as the conventions and structures of the religious drama could be adapted for secular purposes, so could the themes. Early Tudor playwrights, many of them clerics, were quick to recognize that forms which had for centuries programmed their audience with the Church's ideology could be appropriated and adapted to perform the same service on behalf of the secular power structure. During the consolidation of Tudor power, when the role and even the definition of nobility were undergoing cataclysmic revision, the interludes provided effective opportunities for the noble patron to express his philosophical and political views, in an attempt to reinforce his particular perception of the social order.

Modern readers are frequently bored or confused by the Tudor interludes chiefly because they are *readers* rather than members of an *audience*. In order to fully understand and appreciate the complexity and richness of these plays we must, to a certain extent, learn not to stress the dramatic text (which was, at any rate, unavailable to virtually all the audiences) and to read the performance text. For example, allegorical names, which bother so many readers and seem to reduce the plays to simple moral propaganda, would not be so obtrusive to fifteenth-century audiences, first because their response was already trained to unravel and apply the allegory, and second because they were not constantly reminded of the characters' names through rubrics, as modern readers are. We may *read* 'Youth' or 'Lechery', but the Tudor audience would *see* the well-dressed young earl and the lewdly dressed local bawd.

[2] Neale, 386.

Although theatre is primarily a mimetic form, it is a cruel irony that many readers receive it as diegesis, and many critics treat it as such. Readers tend not to hear the music of the words or the instruments, nor to see the physical comedy, the pageantry, the processions, the horizontal and vertical movements of characters, the actions unsignalled by written stage directions, that express in proxemics the subtle messages of the plays. For example, while reading *Wit and Science* many completely miss the crucial and humorous fact that Wit defeats the monster Tediousness simply by going to sleep, an action rather than a rhetorical announcement of intention. Some lines and allegorical shifts of meaning are baffling, and therefore pronounced primitive and unprofessional by readers who cannot see and hear beyond the dramatic texts. Only by examining their historicity, by recreating contemporary audience responses, by learning to 'read' the performance texts as early Tudor viewers might, may we completely appreciate the complexity of these interludes.

It is my primary purpose here to examine the qualities that differentiate the early Tudor interludes from the religious plays. Without tracing direct debts and connections, I will also briefly point out new dramatic structures and techniques that the Elizabethans developed into the masterworks of Renaissance art. By changing the nature of the protagonists, by teaching the audiences to interpret familiar conventions and structures in economic, social, and political contexts rather than strictly as spiritual lessons and theological truths, and by presenting specific aristocratic ideologies in propagandistic forms, the early Tudor playwrights began to enlarge the *raison d'être* of theatre from tableau-vivant sermons to powerful social documents designed to influence hearts and minds. Each of the changes, in characters, signs, structures, and ideological purposes, will be discussed in detail in the pages that follow.

CHARACTERIZATIONS

If the early Tudor interludes were directed primarily toward socially and educationally élite audiences, their characters would naturally reflect the interests of those who were or wished to be in power. Indeed, almost without exception the interludes are peopled with noble characters who express their stations by the same methods that the historical nobility used, but without the negative sub-text common to the religious or folk plays. Early Tudor dramatists taught their audiences new ways to interpret traditional signs by continually exploiting the observable social hierarchy, expressed through genealogy, courtly language, life-style, and extravagant dress to identify, often in a neutral or positive context, their characters as noble types. As Patricia Barry has noted: 'Kings and kinglike characters are present in at least one hundred of the extant plays that may be regarded as current from 1485 to 1603, a fact which shows that king plays were important to the whole Tudor period.'[3]

Characters who are neither kings nor kinglike, those drawn from the merchant and agrarian classes, are, as often as not, comical or condescending portraits, reflecting the snobbery of the aristocratic and the educated, and reinforcing the divisions between classes. As early as 1430, Lydgate introduced the peasantry and their petty problems as a comic diversion for the royal court in *The Mumming at Hertford*. Heywood's lower-class characters, particularly in *The Play of the Weather*, *Johan Johan*, and *The Four PP*, are generally considered to be creations for farce. Even the boys' plays reflect this sensibility. For example, the character People in *Respublica* (attributed to the schoolmaster Nicholas Udall for the court of Queen Mary), is well-intentioned and moral, but nevertheless becomes comic as the simple-minded, dialect-speaking butt of the action. From A and B in *Fulgens and Lucrece*, the male and female households of Rafe and Christian Custance in *Rafe Roister Doister*, and the entire casts of *Jack Juggler* and *Gammer Gurton's Needle* to the rude mechanicals of *A Midsummer Night's Dream*, lower-class characters were definitely, albeit gently, ridiculed, and most frequently relegated to the sub-plot, itself perhaps a reflection of the parodic nature of carnival folk forms.[4] Early

---

[3] Barry, 7.
[4] A recent and thorough consideration of the theories of Bakhtin and Foucault as they apply to Renaissance drama appears in Michael Bristol's fine study *Carnival and Theater: Plebeian Culture and the Structure of Authority in Renaissance England*.

Tudor playwrights were discovering, as the Greek comic playwrights had, that the carnival represents a healthy release from the tensions produced by the constant effort of imposing an arbitrary order. While the satiric bite and the threat of danger may not rival that of Aristophanes or Marlowe, the problems of the main plot are reflected in the more superficial levels of the sub-plot, thus signifying not only the triviality of the plebeian concerns but also the foolishness of the protagonist's behaviour. Nevertheless, the central characters, those whose fates actually concern the playwrights and therefore the audience, are invariably kingly or noble, regardless of whether they are used for comic, tragic, or melodramatic purposes.

These noble characters are not always heroic; indeed, sometimes they are not even good. For example, the character Pride in Medwall's *Nature* is, as Bevington has noted, a 'courtly type' and not an 'abstraction',[5] in spite of his allegorical name (which, as I have mentioned, would not be continuously highlighted in performance). At his entrance Pride complains that none can recognize nobility, and proceeds to give the audience a lesson in signification by expounding on his ancestry, estates, and fashionable dress. Bedecked in gilt spurs, scarlet wool, with hair, gown, and sleeves of the latest cut, retaining a bastard son to serve him at board and to carry his weapons, Pride is an easily recognizable portrait of the less enviable qualities of the nobleman. Later, when Envy tells Pride that his office has been given to another, Pride's lament is typical of the situation in which many of the nobility found themselves:

> For thexpense of myne apparell
> Towardys this vyage,
> What in horses and other aray,
> Hath compelled me for to lay
> All my land to morgage   (1. 866–70).[6]

Financial ruin forces Pride to retire to the country for a year, a charge that was levelled at the Earl of Northumberland,

---

[5] Bevington, *Tudor Drama and Politics*, 51.
[6] References to Medwall's plays are drawn from Nelson's edition.

and which he used to excuse himself from court activities.[7] About 1508 the Earl of Kent found himself in similar straits.[8] These realistic details signal the audience to respond more specifically to 'abstractions' such as Pride, in contrast to the way that they respond to Pride in a play like *The Castle of Perseverance*, where the character is not identifiable by action as a particular person or of a particular class.

The portrait of Pride is negative, but more in social than in moral terms, even though he is, after all, one of the seven deadly sins. Thus Medwall's allegory employs the attributes of both the sin and the aristocrat to convey the particular decadence of the upper class, not the generalized evil of Pride, the vice. This shift in dramatic portraiture, and therefore in audience response, represents a significant change in characterization from the religious forms to the early interludes. Abstract spiritual deficiencies become concrete character flaws. The name in the rubrics may signal to a reader that Pride is the same old medieval vice, but the action on stage indicates to a member of an audience that the characters are far different.

Medwall also casts World as a nobleman, but his purpose here is more subtle than a simple portrait of aristocratic excess. World is a monarch, enthroned, able to bestow 'auctoryte and power' to make man 'lord of every regyon', and to provide servants 'Accordyng to a man of your degre!' (1. 472, 475, 526–9). It is particularly in this last aspect—the provision of servants—that the portrait of World becomes insidious, for he influences Man to banish Innocency and Reason and to accept Worldly Affection and Sensuality in their places. In World, Medwall has chosen to criticize not the superficial signs of noble degeneracy, such as boasting and extravagant dress, but the deeper, more philosophical problem of the nobleman as a temporal creature, politically and materialistically motivated.

In the character Man, Medwall provides another, still more complex portrait of noble character. Unlike the static

---

[7] Brenan, i. 141, 168–9. Two months after Northumberland escorted Princess Margaret to Scotland, he was fined £10,000, probably for too much ostentation. Leland's account describes the Earl's costumes and activities in detail.

[8] Lancashire, 'Auspices', 101.

noble characters Pride and World, Man is dynamic. To the manner born, his social birthright cannot change, but his moral qualities will develop to match that birthright, as the audience had been trained by the morality tradition to expect. Although at the beginning of *Nature*, at Man's allegorical 'birth', the signs associated with him are those of every man, by the time he enters World's court, he has gathered the icons of the noble man. Man must '... folow the gyse that now a day goth | As far as hys estate may yt mayntayne' (1. 451–2). Under World's influence, that estate is considerable, 'Worth a thousand that ye were beforne!' (1. 469). Pride tells us that Man 'is borne to great fortunes' (1. 836), and asks to be taken into Man's service. Since Pride is himself a gentleman with 'great estatys', Man must represent Pride's social and economic superior.

Nature begins with a neutral portrait of the uncorrupted nobleman, then proceeds to demonstrate how the superficial attributes of noble life lead the noble spirit into degeneracy. By Part II of *Nature*, man has succumbed, through the influence of Pride, Worldly Affection, Sensuality, and their crew, to the influences of temporal life; these influences are reflected in his clothing in the 'new guyse' (a gown sewn with lace, a doublet open at the back, a silken shirt, and striped hose: 1. 1058–81) and his 'retynue' of the seven deadly sins (1. 1196–200), a wonderful blend of secular and sacred signification, of the morality and interlude traditions. The morally corrupt aristocrat must rescue himself by accepting the spiritual guidance of Meekness, Charity, Patience, Good Occupation, Liberality, Abstinence, and Chastity, a plot development which would, incidentally, have held great appeal for an ecclesiastical household like Cardinal Morton's. Rather than converting Man from noble sinner to common saint, the virtues counsel him to enjoy his temporal gifts in moderation; they never attack his nobility, merely his abuse of that station. Thus Medwall manipulates traditional signs to promote an ideology that the privileged classes wished reinforced, drawing clear and irrevocable class distinctions and demonstrating that aristocrats, like the traditional abstraction 'Man', may stumble, but will ultimately (perhaps with the aid of the local clergy?) regain the divine moral, social, and economic grace that made them noble in the first place. Common audiences might sympathize, but could not as easily identify with such noble protagonists. In fact, since the lower classes were retainers, they are subtly and insidiously associated with the vices, and thus warned to serve their masters properly or be damned, another clever blending of social and religious conventions.

The dynamic character, drawn from the psychomachia but overlaid with aristocratic qualities, was exploited by many other Tudor dramatists. In the anonymous *The World and the Child*, as Lancashire has noted '... Manhood's titled rank (239, 241) and preoccupation with courtly love (135–39), estate administration (162–63), chivalric enterprise (208) and warfare (243–66) point to the aristocracy'.[9] Like Man in *Nature*, Child must learn to use his intrinsic gifts and talents properly. Similarly, the title character in *Youth* is clearly noble, perhaps even a portrait of the future sixth Earl of Northumberland, for the dialogue of the play closely echoes verses inscribed on the young man's rooms at Wressle.

> I am goodly of person;
> I am peerless wherever I come.
> My name is Youth, I tell thee.
> I flourish as the vine tree.
> Who may be likened unto me
> In my youth and jollity?
> My hair is royal and bushed thick,
> ... I am the heir of all my father's land, ...   (42–57).[10]

Youth's initial statement of nobility is supported later by Pride's testimony that Youth 'is come of a noble stock' (489), and by Youth's own claim that

> ... I am promoted to high degree.
> By right I am king eternal—
> Neither duke ne lord, baron ne knight,
> That may be likened unto me;
> They be subdued to me by right,
> As servants to their masters should be   (591–6).

---

[9] Lancashire, 'Auspices' 100.
[10] Lancashire, *The Tudor Interludes*, points out many detailed references that link the character Youth directly to Henry VIII; 54–8.

Youth must be cured of the pride and profligacy signified by his attitude toward his own nobility and the ignobility of others, by his dress, by his spendthrift habits, and by his dalliance with Lechery.

The dynamic protagonist of Skelton's *Magnificence* follows the same pattern. Magnificence is unquestionably aristocratic, in fact a 'prince of might' (166) who confers knighthood, lives in a palace, and keeps a counsel of nobles. Like Man, Child, and Youth, he must learn to resist pride and profligacy in order to become a good ruler. Clearly Skelton was capitalizing on accepted conventions when he has Magnificence compare himself to historical and mythological heroes such as Alexander, Cyrus, Caesar, Cato, Darius, Hercules, and Charlemagne; using the familiar icons of civic pageantry not only conjured up vivid and spectacular visual and aural images, it also stressed Magnificence's royalty in Tudor terms by likening him to the royalty such heroes greeted in the civic processions for coronations, weddings, victory celebrations, and visitations.

Adversity robs Magnificence of his 'goods and Raiment' (1876A), reducing him from a figure of splendour to a drab penitent; while the action is familiar from the religious drama (namely, Everyman's penitential garb and Mankind's progressively shortened robe), the visual shift from *haute couture* to rags transmits a social as well as a theological message. Just as Man retains Pride in *Nature*, so Magnificence retains, among others, Courtly Abusion, a courtier concerned only with the cost of his clothing and the newest fashion from France (828–910). Rather than generalized morality, *Magnificence* represents specific actions, so specific in fact that Wolsey read himself into the performance text and became a life-long enemy of the poet, once even clapping him into prison.[11] Even the 'vice' characters represent temporal events or flaws in the mind and character rather than spiritual pitfalls.

The significant feature, in terms of this particular study, of

---

[11] Skelton, ll. 1467–515. All references to the play are drawn from Neuss's edition; see 31–42 for the parallel to Cardinal Wolsey. See Withington, *English Pageantry*, and Anglo, *Spectacle*, for detailed analysis of civic pageantry's use of historical and mythological heroes to compliment the aristocracy.

the dynamic protagonists of *Nature, Youth, The World and the Child*, and *Magnificence* is that they are noblemen, unlike Mankind, who is a farmer, or Humanum Genus in *The Castle of Perseverance*, whose nobility is never mentioned, or the protagonists of the folk, saints', and cycle plays, where noblemen are rarely mentioned in a positive context. If this change was not actually caused by new audience types and demands, it would certainly trigger a change in audience response, or perhaps even in audience type. In these egalitarian times, with humanism and Marxism firmly represented in our world-view, it is possible for us to identify with Hamlet and forget that he is a prince of Denmark, but early Tudor audiences did not have the luxury of these philosophies. They could identify with the sinful but redeemable Mankind or Humanus Genus; they might even identify with the humanity of Christ, his apostles, and the saints, although these figures were clearly the spiritual superiors of the audience, and as such were models rather than representatives.

But what is the relationship between the audience and the noble protagonist? If the spectators were aristocrats, both identification and emulation were possible. If, on the other hand, they were commoners, unable by birth to ascend the social hierarchy and therefore to identify or emulate, the effect of the play changes utterly. While plebeian audiences might be comforted by the fact that their economic and social superiors were as vulnerable as they to Fortune and temptation, the primary exemplum communicates that the seriousness of the transgression increases in direct proportion to social class. Common audiences would see that their rulers had to struggle to achieve perfection.

Although the moral interlude echoes the omnipresent mythic pattern of fall and redemption (expressed as psychomachia in the religious plays), once again the playwrights have adjusted the sequences to make the purposes and themes of these early interludes decidedly different. The situations that the dynamic noble characters find themselves in, their expressions of social and political power and wealth, and even the lessons they must learn are particularly applicable to the temporal welfare of the early Tudor aristocracy and their retainers, are frequently acquired powers of the mind and lessons in judgement, rather than innate strengths and weaknesses of the soul.

Characters may still be allegorized, but the allegory must be interpreted differently now, and the purpose of the allegory, which included protection for the playwright, differs significantly from its use in the religious and folk plays, in which allegory provides a vocabulary to express the ineffable. As Wickham has clearly demonstrated in his *Early English Stages*, these changes in dramatic strategy and purpose continued to develop during the Elizabethan period, until playwrights eventually learned to further adjust the allegory, lessening their dependence on the early Renaissance models and protecting themselves by distancing their presentations of contemporary figures and situations in time and space, or by surrounding snippets of contemporary allusion with disarming plots drawn from folklore, legend, or foreign tales. We all know well where the forest of Arden lies, but is Queen Elizabeth really Richard II?

This technique of setting contemporary criticism in 'safe' times and spaces is clear in *Fulgens and Lucrece*, one of the earliest extant interludes whose auspices have been firmly defined as Archbishop Morton's. Here, playwright Henry Medwall is concerned with static portraits of the nobility, expressed in imitation of classical drama rather than in moral allegory, reflective perhaps of Medwall's years of reading Greek and Latin at Eton and Cambridge. In addition, the play provides a marvellous example of how the various signs of nobility may be employed to provoke positive and negative audience responses.

The 'Roman' senator Fulgens announces his nobility in his first speech, noting his prosperity, his 'place in the cenate [*sic*]' and 'honorable degre', his 'riche apparell', and his 'wyfe of gode condicyon' (1. 234, 240, 244). All these could be attributes of either the degenerate or virtuous nobility, but by mixing theology from the religious plays with the class-consciousness of the interludes, Fulgens establishes himself almost literally on the side of the angels, as a positive portrait of the aristocrat who does not abuse his privilege. The manner in which he speaks of his station reinforces the concept of the ruler's divine rights and superior morality since he thanks God for his gifts and further notes that

> ... who so doth take
> The larger benefite, he hath the more nede
> The larger recompense and thank therfor to make (1. 217–19).

Similarly, Fulgens's daughter Lucrece, a beautiful maid of 'clere understanding', is 'discrete' and 'full of honest and verteous counsell / Of here owne mynd, ...' (1. 263–70). Although Fulgens is easily swayed by the suit of Publius, whose nobility is illustrated by the same signs, manipulated so as to communicate negativity, the senator never abandons his natural virtue. Lucrece is portrayed in even more positive fashion, for she uses her moral and intellectual nobility to advantage, properly judging the honour, and therefore the true nobility, of her suitors.

Publius and Gayus are Roman to the same degree that Bottom is Greek. In Publius and Gayus, Medwall allows us two opposing views of the Tudor nobleman, the former representative of the old nobility of 'grete birth' and 'substaunce' far higher than that of the title characters, as Fulgens notes when he says that his daughter 'is full unworthy' | Of birth and goodis to loke so hye, ...' (1. 309–10). Publius appears initially to be a neutral portrait of the aristocrat, yet as the play progresses, it becomes clear that his nobility is only superficial.

One of the strategies Medwall uses to turn neutral aristocratic characteristics into negative moral flaws is to allow the negative model to elaborate rhetorically. Whereas positive characters in the religious plays often pronounce long soliloquies to communicate scripture, in the interludes such verbosity is more likely to be read as boasting. For example, God may with impunity speak at length about his virtues and powers in order to demonstrate to the public the basic elements of their spiritual history, but Fulgens and Gayus must skip lightly, and therefore humbly, over their blessings, thus demonstrating their virtues mimetically rather than diegetically. In contrast, Publius dedicates a full fifty lines to such conventional negative signs as self-praise of his largess, the price of his hose, and the fashion of his noble raiment (1. 698–778). This rhetorical concentration upon Publius's ostentation and its wastefulness is, as is customary in early Tudor interludes, a sign to the audience that the character is a satiric and critical view of noble behaviour. Similar moments are memorable later, in Shakespeare's plays, as when in *Henry IV Pt. I* Hotspur complains about a 'certain lord' who came perfumed and overdressed to the battlefield; or when Hamlet sneers at Osric; or when Lafew dresses down Parolles in *All's Well that Ends Well*. Such criticism of overdressing would have been a trifle easier under the sombre Henry VII than it would under his son and granddaughter, who were not known for their subdued taste. There was, and still is, a thin line between the fop and the fashionable.

Medwall attacks the traditional nobility on the basis of its three most obvious *hamartia*: pride in ancestry, unnecessary ostentation, and profligacy, qualities that characterize the aristocracy and at the same time constitute its primary faults. Medwall never questions the validity of their social position in the hierarchy, nor does he suggest revolution, but rather presents Gayus, the newly created nobleman who, through work, good deeds, and service to his country, has risen 'Unto grete honoure fro low degre, . . .' (679–87). Gayus may not boast the ancient lineage and great wealth of Publius, but Gayus's moderate behaviour and careful husbandry will allow him, at least in the fictive confines of the play, to live a morally noble life, free from ostentation, profligacy, and pride. This dialectic of the virtuous new versus the decadent old is hardly surprising, since Archbishop Morton owed his position completely to the new King, Henry VII, and continually harassed the surviving Plantagenet nobility through his economic policies. Thus, the playwright presents the ideology of his patron.

Other early Tudor dramatists draw similarly static models to set the positive and negative styles of aristocratic behaviour by manipulating audience response to conventional signs and by distancing their plays in myth and history, taking their cues from the civic pageantry. For example, Heywood uses the very same qualities that Medwall uses to compliment rather than criticize his patron Henry VIII through the mythic character Jupiter in *The Play of the Weather*, who begins the play by discussing his position and ancestry in celestial terms before withdrawing to his dais. Similarly, the virtuous but misled King Assuerus in *Godly Queen Hester*, who differs significantly from his biblical model, begins the play with a discussion of virtue, nobility, and justice, establishing himself as a positive model; yet he is also inordinately interested in ancestry, questioning everyone, from the evil Aman to the virtuous Mardocheus, about their family backgrounds before withdrawing to his closet. Both royal figures, curiously, withdraw from the action of the plays immediately after their soliloquies, perhaps to ensure protection for the playwright from potential offence to the living monarch.

Audience response to ostentation in dress may also be manipulated by playwrights to impress rather than disgust. For example Nemesis, the goddess-queen of *Respublica*, and Imperial Majesty, the god-king of *King Johan*, are dressed in blindingly magnificent costumes to emphasize their spiritual and moral superiority over the other characters. Wisdom in *Wisdom Who is Christ* appears in 'ryche purpull clothe of golde' with 'ryall hood furred with ermyn' crowned and bearing sceptre and orb.[12] In these plays, the presence of royal rather than simply flamboyant colours and fabric ensures that the same noble attributes of costume, ancestry, and wealth could be exploited not to ridicule nobility but rather to establish instantly and vividly, in visual and rhetorical terms, the unquestioned regality of positive models.

In a wonderful example of this paradox of cultural contexts, the same qualities could also be manipulated to create negative models. Well before the Tudor period, Rex Vivus in the fragmentary *Pride of Life* (c.1350) speaks of his kingship in terms of power and influence rather than of duty and justice, thereby establishing himself as a representation of the vainglorious nobleman.[13] Parody is employed in *Rafe Roister Doister*, making Rafe the antithesis of Magnificence, by Merrygreek's comic comparison of Rafe to Launcelot, Hercules, and Hector, and his comments upon Rafe's 'face... for ladies of high and noble parages', which are

[12] Eccles, 114. All references to the play are drawn from this text.
[13] Happe, 43–62.

deflated by mocking lists of Rafe's military exploits over spiders and elephants. Rafe retains minstrels, insists upon the respect due to his station and possesses 'movables, householde stuff and lande'.[14] Udall manipulates all these conventions of noble behaviour to establish Rafe as a figure of ridicule, and therefore a negative model.

At the same time as early Tudor playwrights were cementing the identification between dramatic art and political reality, early Tudor observers were beginning to notice that those in power were creating images for themselves, often using theatrical techniques and based on dramatic figures familiar to the popular culture. Barry theorizes that all kings were considered actor-kings, that an aristocrat had to 'act the part' if he expected to establish or enlarge his sphere of influence. Sir Thomas More vividly articulates this thought when he writes of the coronation of King Richard: '... these matters bee Kynges games, as it were stage playes, and for the more part plaied vpon scafoldes'.[15]

The complex fugue of the actor-king is further emphasized by a comment in *The Great Chronicle*. During Henry VI's progress in 1470, he appeared poorly, without appropriate kingly ceremony, prompting the observation that he appeared 'more lyke a play than the shewyng of a prynce to wynne mennys hertys ...'.[16] In marked contrast to poor Henry VI, the Tudors, most notably Henry VIII and Elizabeth, mastered theatrical effects and succeeded in blurring the line between artifice and actuality to recreate at their courts the pageantry and splendour of whatever heroic model they chose. England had rarely seen rulers with the theatrical talents of Henry and Elizabeth (who succeeded in the supreme double-think of speaking of herself as a male), and had rarely seen courts of such consciously fashioned theatricality. The emblems became more real than the ideas they represented, as the populace expected life to imitate art and the aristocrats enacted the machiavellian truth that one *is* what one appears to be, that facade becomes identity, and that such facades must be carefully constructed and maintained.

[14] Udall, I. ii. 137; I. iv. 63–4; I. iv. 51.
[15] Barry, 257; More, ii. 81.
[16] Thomas and Thornley, 215.

STRUCTURES

Early Tudor dramatists did not stop their experiments at the level of these emblems, but went on to revolutionize the very fabric of the plays as well, by employing the political constructs of maintenance, hierarchy, and ceremony as structural motifs for their plays. These abstract concepts and patterns were crucial to the aristocracy, both as reinforcements of their own social certitude and as messages to those below them in the 'great chain' of the correctness of the divinely ordained hierarchy. In the drama, use of these patterns formed systems that audiences recognized as reflections of their experience.

The practice of maintenance received a great deal of attention and criticism during the early Tudor period. The more retainers a nobleman gathered around him, the more dazzling a spectacle he created in his household and on progress, transmitting a message of wealth and power to his audience. Maintenance was also a political necessity, for the nobility facilitated communication and exercised control over their far-flung estates through a complex system of retainers and officers. Quite naturally, Henry VII and his son viewed this practice as a threat to the throne, for no Crown could rest easily while a potentially troublesome aristocrat, possibly with a justifiable claim to the throne, was lurking about with a large and loyal private army. Consequently, Henry VII undertook, through laws and fines, to limit the number of retainers a nobleman might employ. Henry VIII continued his father's 'reform', for the *Letters and Papers* record that 'The King's solicitor told him that the Lord Marquis, the Lord Hastings, Sir Richard Sacherverel, Lord Abergavenny and Sir Edward Guilford, by information put into the King's Bench, are likely to be in great danger "for retaining of servants".'[17]

Although the Tudor kings persisted in their attempts to control maintenance, the aristocrats persisted in counting their wealth by how many liveried servants and retainers they directly controlled.

[17] *L & P HVIII* ii/1, 595.

This practice defined the nobility; it was as important an indication of their station as was their extravagance in dress, and as such, was immediately and extensively exploited by early Tudor dramatists as a theatrical convention, providing a second, deeper level of ideological persuasion. Good, neutral, and occasionally central characters all take service with other characters in the plays, the most common occurrence being that the 'vice' character ingratiates himself into the court of an impressionable nobleman as a retainer. Rarely do the 'virtues', whose moral and, by extension, social position is too high to allow them to take service with any man, appear as retainers, the lower orders, both social and moral, take service frequently to degrade the noble character or to provide comic action. Thus what appear to be strictly moral allegories and spiritual dilemmas are used to provoke consideration of economic, social, and political debates. The practice of maintenance is, like ostentation and ancestry, criticized diplomatically; nobles are warned to take care in choosing the number and character of their retainers, but are themselves reprimanded only for their lack of good judgement. Besides delineating the perils of playing the hierarchical game, depicting the system of maintenance provides early Tudor dramatists with a structure, easily deciphered by the audience since it is so familiar from life, on which to build the ebb and flow pattern that accurately reflects their experience.

Good retainers are few in early Tudor drama. In *Godly Queen Hester*, Mardocheus is taken into the King's service and a ring and seal bestowed upon him for his virtue only after the evil retainer, Aman, is exposed.[18] Magnificence's good counsel, Measure, is quickly exiled from court. The most obviously useful retainers appear in Redford's school play *Wit and Science*, where Wit's mother Nature and Reason supply Study, Diligence, Instruction, and Confidence as servants. Wit's misuse of these positive forces results in his fall, an appropriate lesson for retainers in training. Similarly, Nature supplies Man with Reason and Innocency in Medwall's *Nature*, but these positive retainers are quickly banished at the advice of World, to be replaced by Sensuality, Pride, Worldly Affection, and their evil associates.

[18] Farmer, 284. All references to the play are drawn from this edition.

The sole example of the protagonist becoming a retainer to vice figures occurs in *The World and the Child*, where the relationship between the World and the Child mirrors in detail that of a nobleman and his retainer. At the beginning of the play, Child asks World for clothing and meat in return for his service. Later Child says

> This vij yere I haue serued you in hall and in boure
> With all my trewe entent (121–2).

Throughout the play, Child serves his master, and in return World advances him in temporal terms, clothing him, renaming him, and eventually dubbing him a knight, all typical of the system of maintenance in the real world. In addition, the seven deadly sins are characterized as kings, and Child chooses to serve the King of Pride, thus attaching himself to two patrons at once, a practice not uncommon in Tudor England. Child can be likened to the henchmen at the court of the fifth Earl of Northumberland, raised and 'educated' by the patron and dependent upon him for their physical and social needs. Child is also noble enough to be considered for knighthood, to be called 'son' by his patron, and to be dressed gaudily in gold and purple, royal colours reminding the audience that, in spite of his errors, Child is nevertheless noble. Thus, the idea of maintenance becomes a structuring motif from the beginning of the play.

Generally the negative characters take service with the protagonists. In *Godly Queen Hester*, for example, the King takes the initially anonymous Aman into his service as Chancellor. Aman, in turn, returns with 'many men awaiting on him', a signal to the audience that this character is proud and pretentious. During the play, Aman is advanced to the rank of lieutenant to rule Israel, with the robes and gold wand of the office.[19] Similarly, the vice figures of Clergy, Nobility, and Civil Order become King Johan's high council in Bale's play, and a ceremony of fealty is actually enacted upon the stage (515–16). In both plays, the vice figures can only begin corrupting the protagonists after they are retained as trusted officers. The same technique is used in *Respublica*; the vices determine to bring down the country by taking service with

[19] Farmer, 253, 270.

Respublica, who in turn promises them a 'large preferment' (559). Youth agrees to take Riot and Pride into his service in *Youth*, saying

> And thou wilt my servant be,
> I shall give thee gold and fee (329–30).

Youth, as the centre of the action, is once again cast in the double role of the patron; he pays Riot and Pride both to entertain and to corrupt him. The character Man in *Nature* retains Worldly Affection, the architect of his downfall, as well as Pride, who resorts to offering Sensuality a bribe to ensure his preferment (1. 834), undoubtedly common practice in royal and noble court life. Magnificence is similarly ill-treated by his retainer Felicity, although the latter is balanced by a good retainer in the character of Measure.

In most Tudor plays, the process of maintenance forms the plot and encourages the linear structure so common to the art and the life of the period. Maintenance, as a type of patronage, was one of the few accepted methods of social ascendancy; anyone not connected to a nobleman had little hope of social or economic success in the Tudor hierarchy, unless he was fortunate enough to advance himself through civil service, as Sir Thomas More did, or through the Church, as Wolsey did. The best way for a vice figure to corrupt and degrade the secular protagonists with whom the interludes are primarily concerned was to use the system of patronage for his own ends. These types of plots warned both the patron and the patronized to use their powers properly. Thus, the dramatic structures, which realistically reflected the social systems, reinforced the status quo by repeatedly illustrating the dangers of abusing the existing hierarchy.

When neutral or comic figures become retainers to the protagonists, the plays frequently sprout a subplot, a structure not common in the religious or folk plays, nor in the classical examples studied in the schools. Besides the *Secunda Pastorum* Mak sub-plot (which seems further evidence for private auspices), one of the earliest examples of such a situation is possibly the messenger's role in the mid-fourteenth-century fragment *The Pride of Life*. A 'bachelere' or squire, who is given power and land through the king's largess, Solas, or Mirth as he is called, serves as a diversion rather than a vice, taking no significant part in the unfolding of the action. Similarly, A and B in *Fulgens and Lucrece* take service with Lucrece's two suitors, and proceed to provide the comic sub-plot of the play. Merrygreek in *Rafe Roister Doister* is a retainer cut from the same cloth, a parasite who encourages Rafe in his ridiculous shenanigans, to create amusement rather than to corrupt. Skelton makes the best use of this type of the comic retainer in the character of Fancy, who takes service with Magnificence, changes his name to Largess, and claims to have been made a knight (521). Although Fancy contributes to the downfall of the protagonist, his primary function in the play is to provide comic relief.

The origin of the sub-plot in early English drama is a subject that certainly bears further investigation. The religious plays, even the gargantuan *Castle of Perseverance*, flow smoothly along in episodic fashion rather than splitting the structure into parallel units. From Aristotle to Dryden, the ongoing (and often misguided) stress on the three unities reminds us that Graeco-Roman drama was understood to be single-minded in its plot development, though the complications of the Roman comedy sometimes provide such contrapuntal diversions. Perhaps the impulse toward sub-plot sprang from observation of the carnival festivals like the Feast of Fools within the solemn Christmas feast, or from the tripartite structure of household celebrations, in which one entertainment is embedded in another, or from the double occupations of most patronized poets, clerics, and schoolmasters who must also function in a social and political world. At any rate, in early Tudor interludes such as *Fulgrens and Lucrece* we may trace the beginnings of the conscious double strand, as playwrights attempt to weave the same theme on two different social levels, thus ensuring its reception while once again stressing class distinctions. By the age of Shakespeare, such structures, with the lower classes banished almost exclusively to the comic sub-plot, had become the rule.

Equally important to the early Tudor nobility, and interrelated with the concept of maintenance, was the system of social hierarchy, the 'great chain' that dictated precedence on all public occasions, and the overwhelming concern of scores of chamberlains, pursuivants, and the whole College of Heralds. This complex order is encoded in the plays, either as a device for character delineation or as a structural motif, another pattern of logical progression that encourages linear development. Thus in *Weather* the plaintiffs appear in descending order of rank, beginning with the gentleman and the merchant, to the lower-class millers, who are followed by the women and the boy. As Bevington states, the 'chief function . . . is to observe precedence . . .'.[20]

Social order is also the chief structuring device in *The Mumming at Hertford*, in which the men speak first, explaining their complaints, and then the wives are permitted their answers. As in *Weather*, the King sits in judgement at the end of the proceedings. The plot of *The Four PP* concerns the question of 'maistry' and proper order, as it attempts to ascertain which character has the best connection with heaven. The achievement of social superiority forms the structure of the *débat* in *Gentleness and Nobility* and in *Fulgens and Lucrece*, as the characters strive to delineate the qualities of the truly noble. Even goddesses and abstractions are subject to the system: Nemesis is of a higher status than even the ruler, Respublica; Imperial Majesty outranks King Johan.

The social order and the moral order need not be identical. In fact, the lower classes are often thrown the leftover medieval bone reflected in the proverb 'It is easier for a camel to pass through the eye of a needle than for a rich man to enter heaven'. For example, in *Respublica* People is at the bottom of the social hierarchy, but morally he is superior to the vices, who occupy offices at court, communicating to the commoners the aristocracy's message that it is far better to remain a poor but loyal subject than to risk life and liberty by machiavellian manipulation of court politics.

This close attention to social order and proper observation of rank is a recurring motif in early Tudor life and art, as a means of concretely reinforcing an abstract ideal of order. In

---

[20] Bevington, *Tudor Drama and Politics*, 68.

life, this attention may reflect tension during the dawning years of humanism, as Renaissance concepts began to clash with the medieval world-view—a crisis perhaps most clearly reflected by Marlowe's *Dr. Faustus*, a play of Renaissance ideas in a medieval form. As a dramatic structure, hierarchy often forces the dramatists into the same linear patterns of *débat* and precedence that appear in plays concerned with maintenance.

Critics of the early Tudor interlude have long assumed that the linear structure peculiar to these plays is a result of their moral didacticism, their casting limitations, or their aesthetic simplicity: yet it is the dramatist's interest in portraying the social hierarchy that creates this structural effect. Since the Tudor nobleman was concerned with his social standing at least as much as he was concerned with his spiritual state, the plays direct their attention to questions of hierarchy. Indeed, moral progression and regression is often explored in terms of social advancement or descent. Vices begin without standing at court, achieve their goals through social ascendancy and retention, and are expelled when they are exposed. When protagonists fall from social heights, a fall from spiritual heights is implied or indicated.

The early Tudor interludes express moral health by reflecting social hierarchy, in contrast to the religious drama. Miracle and mystery plays concern themselves with biblical characters who are rarely aristocrats, and when noble characters enter the plays, they are generally portrayed in negative terms, as are Pharaoh, Herod, Pilate, and Pilate's wife. The hierarchy of the religious plays is dictated strictly by spiritual, not temporal, superiority. Thus the peasant-apostles are elevated above the villainous priests, knights, and kings in a 'great chain' whose pinnacle is spiritual, not social. Conversion, or moral ascendancy, was not expressed by altering the character's social position.

The early Tudor aristocracy expressed social hierarchy in many ways. As I have maintained in previous chapters, rank within the household was dictated by a strict organization of the duties and privileges of the retainers. Position at table, in processions, and in ceremonies all served to remind people of their social standing, both in the noble and in the royal courts. The inclusion or exclusion of a noble in royal court functions could have far-reaching repercussions; places of honour in state ceremonies could form the basis for quarrels and feuds. The Duke of Buckingham, for example, was insulted and irate when he was forced to serve the lowly born Cardinal Wolsey at the Field of the Cloth of Gold.[21] In the Earl of Northumberland's ordinance for Twelfth Night, which continually demonstrates strict observation of precedence, the Earl and his Countess walked in the centre of the opening procession, with the highest ranking household members nearest them, the lowest further away. The order further stipulates that a few of the highest rank were permitted to sit at tables, and even dictates the specific location of those tables in relation to the dais where the Earl and Countess were seated. The service of the banquet following the dramatic and musical entertainments concentrates solely upon the Earl as the central figure of the ceremony;[22] this concentration is so exclusive that it is difficult to determine when and how the rest of the household was fed.

Anthropologists have stressed that ceremonies and rituals are the means whereby a culture displays and reinforces, through visual and aural terms, its most basic structures. Consequently, it is hardly surprising that ceremonies that validate Tudor notions of hierarchy appear in early Tudor drama. The use of ceremony further reinforces the tendency toward linear plot development, for a ceremony is unified by established theme, not by suspenseful action, just as many of the interludes concern themselves with static action in order to explore or debate a particular theme. The interlude structure, linear, episodic, and progressive in nature, is analogous to the structure of the ceremony, which was an important and frequent ingredient in the pageantry of the royal court entertainments.

Many plays, like *Fulgens and Lucrece*, reveal their plots during the exposition, placing emphasis on the manner of development rather than on the denouement, again similar to the emphasis intrinsic in ceremonial activity, where purpose

---

[21] Russell, 169–74; *Venice* iii. 56.
[22] Lancashire, 'Orders', 25–7, 32–3, 36–42.

is preordained and execution is the crucial factor. In addition, doubling requirements often force the playwright to present a character and remove him, so that the actor may assume a new character. The structure resulting from this technique is processional, as the protagonist confronts a stream of characters who continually enter and leave the action, rather like the omnipresent medieval image of the dance of life and death. Processions of good and evil characters, with man in the centre, are common in early Renaissance drama and such processions are similar to ceremonies. Everyman, for example, seems to move, as in civic pageantry, from station to station as he confronts his various unreliable friends. Again and again, protagonists meet with virtues and vices who fade in and out of the action, almost as though the characters are journeying through a labyrinth of people and places.

While noble characteristics and the social hierarchy provided structure and content for the plays, ceremonies indicated blocking and properties, for proxemics, physical movement, and the use of ritual objects are integral to the form. As with maintenance, the imitation of ceremony could be used either to reflect or to parody, depending upon the context and the tone of the author. Ceremonial effects, which are mimetic rather than diegetic, establish mood and rank in plays such as *Weather*, where Jupiter enters in pomp, retires to his dais, and the suitors are admitted one by one in descending order of social rank. Proper actions are expected of all. Merry Report cries to the audience:

> By your faith, have ye, nother cap nor kne?
> Not one of you that will make curt'sy
> To me, that am squire for goddes precious body? (189–91)

The decorum established at Jupiter's court is similar to that of World in Medwall's *Nature*, where the character enters the stage in a procession composed of Worldly Affection (who bears the gown, cap, and girdle for Man), Nature, Reason, and Innocency. World sits silently on a dais, the image of a nobleman in his court. Even references to ceremonies are allusive, as in *Youth*, where the ceremony for creating Knights of the Collar is mentioned. Ceremony is used when the vices are introduced to Respublica, and at the entrance of

Nemesis. More often, however, ceremony is parodied in the dramatic action.

Such is the case in *King Johan*, where religious and courtly ceremonies are used again and again with biting irony. Throughout the play, church and civil ceremonies become the actions through which the vice characters degrade the King. For example, in a mock ceremony that concerns precedence (758–71), the vice characters arrange themselves in proper social order for presentation to the King. Usurped Power and Private Wealth enter singing and are placed at the rear of the playing space. Dissimulation leads forth Private Wealth, who says

> Of me private welth, cam fyrst usurpyd power
> Ye may perseyve yt, in pagent here this hower   (781–2).

Thus begins a complex and comic back and forth procession to determine in precisely what manner Usurped Power shall enter the court. First, Sedition says he must go back and be carried in by Usurped Power, forming a visual metaphor. Eventually, Private Wealth, Dissimulation, and Usurped Power all carry Sedition into court. This mock ceremony provides comic action, delineates social structure, and develops the moral allegory; the irony of the moral allegory tints the comedy with an aura of degeneracy. Similarly, in Act II, Dissimulation cries 'wassayle' and enters with the poisoned cup (2038), calling to the minds of the audience not only the celebratory mood of Christmas but also the ceremonies that accompanied the feast and the presentation of the wassail in the aristocratic households on Twelfth Night.[23] The allusion makes the action even more darkly ironic.

Bale's parody becomes more vicious when he paraphrases and imitates actual ceremonies. Bevington has called the excommunication scene in Act I a 'lampoon of the ritual',[24] which indeed it is. Bearing the cross, bell, book, and candle, the vices perform the ceremony, complete with responses and songs. In Act II, the ceremony of confession is similarly

---

[23] For a realistic view of the wassail ceremony practices in the noble courts, see Lancashire, 'Orders', 12, 39.
[24] Bevington, *Tudor Drama and Politics*, 103.

treated. Throughout the act, Bale has inserted grotesque parodies of Latin and of church services to reinforce the degradation of the King, who is deposed and reinstated in a fashion that combines civil and religious ceremony to reiterate Bale's point that the church wields complete power over the state (1648–1755).

Ceremony is used to the same effect in *Respublica*. In II. iii the vices are presented to the ruler in ceremonial fashion, yet the soberness of the ceremony is undercut with a song. In III. iii this presentation is echoed by the entrance of People, who is ceremoniously presented with Adulation looking on. Ceremony is used in *The World and the Child* (196–203) when Child is arrayed in new robes and dubbed a knight, an action that reinforces World's power over Child. Imitation of the actual ceremony equates the play world with the real world.

Early Tudor playwrights might also use ceremonial activities for strictly comic rather than insidious effects, particularly when lower-class characters ape their superiors. *Fulgens and Lucrece* enacts a parodic courtly joust, complete with the lady as judge. Ignorant imitation of noble actions provides a diversion from the main plot of the play at the same time as it gently satirizes the actions. Similarly, the parody of the Service for the Dead in *Rafe Roister Doister* (III. iii) is primarily a comic or satiric device, for Rafe's melancholy is reduced to the ridiculous through his use of serious religious ceremony to express so light and so temporal a problem.

IDEOLOGIES

Up to this point, I have concentrated on delineating the specific conventions by which the early Tudor dramatists held their mirrors up to nature in order to create the visual, rhetorical, and structural languages whereby their themes could be communicated. These themes have formed the subject for thousands of pages of critical attention, and it would be impossible and pointless for this study to attempt to summarize various interpretations, or to comment upon them all. Similarly, detailed investigation of the themes of each extant interlude is a herculean task far beyond the scope and intention of this chapter. It would be redundant to recapitulate, for example, Bevington's full-length study *Tudor Drama and Politics*, or Wickham's thorough treatment of the Elizabethan interludes in volume iii of his *Early English Stages*.

The themes of the extant early interludes address noble interests and express noble ideologies, a point particularly crucial to a study of great household entertainments. These themes may be divided into three categories: first, the definition of nobility; second, the social and moral education of the nobleman; and third, the proper use of aristocratic power to promote political harmony. Like any categorization, this division is, to a certain extent, an imposed structure to facilitate discussion; but it is far from arbitrary, for these three themes represent the essential concerns of noble life: the very existence of a superior class, and the temporal function of that class. The three themes are also interrelated, for it is impossible to discuss the aristocratic use of power without understanding what an aristocrat is or what his powers are. Rather than forming pigeon-holes into which plays may be stuffed, these three categories provide a guide to the focal, but not the sole, themes of the interludes they govern. In order to investigate this complex problem efficiently, I intend to determine which plays address which themes, then to examine one of the plays in each category in detail in order to delineate the salient features of the thematic division—which can then be applied to other interludes that address the same themes. This structure will provide an overview of the early Tudor interludes while considering their similarities and differences.

Plays that attempt to define the nature of nobility were particularly vital to the early Tudor aristocracy, for the entire class was undergoing redefinition. When Henry VII took the role of *deus ex machina* in ending the War of the Roses, he was quite naturally suspicious of the incumbent nobility and partial to the noblemen whom he had created or who had clearly demonstrated their loyalty to the Tudor cause. In addition, the social revolution that accompanied the slow death of feudalism as a viable economic system eroded the once unquestioned power base of the aristocracy: land, wealth, and military power. More than ever, political shrewdness and economic acumen became talents that a nobleman required to achieve and maintain his position. Unfortunately for the aristocracy, these talents were not determined by heredity alone; such skills could be acquired by the middle class, and as that class developed, its members could also acquire the land and wealth that had previously been controlled solely by noble hands.[25] Consequently, it was crucial to the aristocracy that clear distinctions be drawn to divide noble from ignoble.

As I have stressed above, the question of what constitutes true nobility provides the focus for Medwall's *Fulgens and Lucrece*, in which the rival suitors, Publius and Gayus, represent the two sides of the pitched battle between old and new aristocracy.[26] By selecting traditional and feudal practices as negative character indications for Publius, and contrasting these with the new humanist and capitalist attitudes of men such as Morton and Henry VII, Medwall is critical of the type of nobleman he characterizes in Publius, but is careful never to attack the idea of nobility.

For example, the methods Publius uses for his courtship, taken together with his personality, show that his nobility, in Tudor terms, is superficial. First, he approaches the lady's father, bargaining, perhaps unconsciously, for her as if she were a feudal chattel. In contrast, Gayus approaches the lady herself, demonstrating that he is not socially bound by traditional mores, and that he considers Lucrece to be guardian of her own fate, as he has proven himself to be. Publius resorts to the expensive entertainments of disguisers and minstrels to impress Lucrece, whereas Gayus simply talks with her. Further, during the crucial debate that determines the outcome of the rivalry, Publius resorts to *ad hominem* arguments, including insult, snobbery, and boasting of the past achievements of his family, since he is patently unable to recommend himself on his own virtues. Gayus is clever enough to point this out (626), to extol his own virtues, and

---

[25] For an extended discussion of the ideas that have been summarized here, see Stone and Macfarlane. Bevington also discusses the influence of these economic and political movements in ch. 3 of *Tudor Drama and Politics*.

[26] Bevington, *Tudor Drama and Politics*, 42–50.

to speak of present and future accomplishments. Through their actions, the two noblemen express Medwall's critique of the degeneracy of the incumbent nobility and his praise for the virtuous example that the new nobility provide.

The comic sub-plot also explores this dichotomy by satirizing the traditional forms of courtship. A and B, as messengers sent with romantic love-tokens, botch their tasks completely. In order to court Jone, they employ chivalric techniques; 'courtly' song competition and the joust are parodied to show the ridiculousness of such superficial methods. Direct dialogue, without ostentation or interference, proves to be the most successful technique for courtship.

As an exemplum of the interlude that addresses the theme of the true nobility, *Fulgens and Lucrece* utilizes several techniques that provide a guide for categorizing this type of play. First, Medwall provides positive and negative role models that are static in characterization. Second, the concept of social class is never questioned, but specific attributes of the nobility are attacked. Third, the negative role model is not a vice figure or active corrupter but rather represents ignorance and abuse of privilege. Fourth, the theme is explored through language, by means of dialogue and *débat*, and through action, by means of plot and often through satire. Interludes that address the same theme with similar methodology include *Gentleness and Nobility*, *Calisto and Melebea*, *Jacob and Esau*, and *Rafe Roister Doister*.

Gentleness and Nobility (which Bevington attributes to John Rastell, with possible influence from Heywood, about 1523–9)[27] communicates even through its title that Rastell, concerned with the same theme Medwall explored in *Fulgrens and Lucrece*, pursued it through the same methods. Since he was a member of the More circle, humanist in inclination, and firmly allied with the Tudor guard, this attitude is hardly surprising. The virtuous, intellectual, but ignoble Plowman provides the positive model, the decadent Knight the negative; both are static characters. Although the Plowman is supposed to be a member of the lower class, his characterization is far from realistic. His philosophical

[27] Bevington, *Tudor Drama and Politics*, 76–7. Norman Saunders seems convinced that it is Rastell's work, dating it about 1527–30: see *Revels*, 14.

language shows him to be an educated man whom Rastell has cast as a peasant in order to make a point about natural virtue. The Knight's decadent and idle character is indeed assassinated, but his class is not. In fact, the denouement of the play reaffirms the solidity of the social order:

> We can not help it, then syth it so is,
> I wyll let the world wagg . . . (1009–10).

Further, the desire of the Merchant to aspire to the noble class indicates that the aristocracy, for good or ill, was firmly entrenched. Rastell, through the Philosopher, simply argues that it reform itself. The Knight is not admirable, but neither is he actively evil. The language of the play, through the *débat* form, explores the history and nature of aristocratic abuse, and the fisticuffs provide action that expresses the frustration of the victims of aristocratic abuse of power, as well as the immaturity of men who must resort to physical violence to settle their differences.

The anonymous *Calisto and Melebea* was issued in 1527 by Rastell's press. Melebea and the virtuous servant Parmeno provide the positive models, Callisto and the procuress Celestina the negative. Callisto, idle and lecherous, is the representative of the decadent aristocracy, who is defeated at the close of the play, but not obviously reformed. Unlike the Knight in *Gentleness and Nobility*, or Publius in *Fulgens and Lucrece*, Callisto acts as a corrupter on the rhetorical level, but leaves the role of active corrupter to Celestina. Similarly, Melebea wavers in character, is tempted, but does not significantly change. The behaviour of individual noblemen is criticized, but once again the class is never directly attacked.

Jacob and Esau, probably composed during the reign of Edward VI, is a complex play that is open to interpretation on various political and religious levels,[28] a revolutionary and radical play that clearly sets itself against the status quo. As sons of Isaac, both Jacob and Esau are typological prefigurements of the nobility; the highest of the Old Testament religious class is meant to represent the highest of

---

[28] Bevington, *Tudor Drama and Politics*, 110–12; *Revels*, 19, 57. Bevington discusses the political interpretation of the play and the religious polemics in detail. References to the play are drawn from Crow; Wickham, *EES 3*, 86.

the Tudor social class. Once again, we find static positive and negative models of nobility. Esau wastes his time hunting, abuses his servants, and sneers at his neighbours and parents (38; 65–9). His servant Ragan admits:

> ... I serue an ill husband and a waster.
> That neither profite regardeth nor honestie— ...   (702–3).

In contrast, Jacob is virtuous:

> He lyueth no looce life, he doth God love and feare.
> He keepeth here in the Tentes, lyke a quiete man:
> He geueth not hymselfe to wildnesse any when   (157–9).

Once again, both characters are static representations and there is no implication that the nobility is inherently evil, merely that certain members, through their 'owne evil inclination', not through 'education', are 'looce and leue' (164–8). Esau serves as negative exemplum, not as vicious corrupter. Ironically, it is the positive character, Jacob, who executes the central stratagem of the play, cheating his elder brother of his birthright. This usurpation, however, occurs within the class; no outsider supplants an aristocrat. Rebecca's 'voyce ... from the Lorde' makes it clear that the new aristocracy is to gain control over the old:

> Rebecca, in thy wombe are now two nations,
> Of unlike natures and contrary fashions
> The one shal be a mightier people elect:
> And the elder to the younger shall be subiect   (228–31).

Jacob is virtuous enough to feel a twinge of guilt about the usurpation, but politic enough to co-operate with God's will. While *Jacob and Esau* addresses the issue of the virtuous noble and the degenerate, it is chiefly concerned with validating the power shift from the traditional nobility to the new Protestant nobility. Through his own virtue and through God's wishes, Jacob usurps Esau, just as the new Protestant nobility wished to think itself the moral superior of the old during Edward VI's reign.

Udall's *Rafe Roister Doister* is not concerned with new nobility replacing old, since it was probably performed by boys for Queen Mary.[29] It does, however, draw one of the finest caricatures of the idle man. As has been previously demonstrated, Rafe is a comic representation of all that is undesirable in a noble character: pomposity, profligacy, and foolishness. Positive examples of behaviour are provided by Christian Custance, Tristram Trusty, and Gawyn Goodlucke, all members of the wealthy merchant class who would, like the merchants in *Weather* and *Gentleness and Nobility*, like to be members of the aristocracy. All are static; the good remain good and the foolish remain foolish. Udall does not in any way advocate social revolution, yet he does ridicule the idle rich while complimenting the industrious rich. Rafe cannot be viewed as a corrupter, for his attempts to win the affections of Christian Custance are so ridiculous that they are obviously destined for failure; thus, any threat or menace that may be inherent in the situation is disarmed. What follows is a critique, through satire and parody, of the 'miles gloriosus' (another feudal characteristic), and pomposity in certain noblemen.

Udall uses language and action to satirize the idle rich. Rafe damns himself through his own dialogue, playing the vain love-sick courtier to the amusement of the audience. Christian Custance makes her disdain for him quite clear from the beginning. Like *Fulgens and Lucrece*, *Rafe Roister Doister* uses the motif of courtship to expose the positive and negative aspects of character. In both, comic servants parody and interfere with the courtship of the main plot. Like A and B, Merrygreek cannot properly deliver a love-token. The joust of *Fulgens and Lucrece* becomes a full-scale battle in *Rafe Roister Doister*, similarly comic in form and in result.

Although they differ stylistically, all the plays discussed above address the same theme through similar methodology. By providing criticism of particular types of noblemen without attacking the ideology supporting that concept of class, these playwrights strove to produce change in their élite audiences. Although the characters are static, the audience should be dynamic. By observing the foolishness and failure of the negative models, and the virtue and success of the positive models, the audience was encouraged to reform itself.

[29] Bevington, *Tudor Drama and Politics*, 121.

Other playwrights chose a different focus for their themes, concentrating upon the possibility of a preventive social and moral education of the aristocrat. Many of these plays are critical of aristocratic character, but rather than simply portraying aristocratic excess, they attempt to assign reasons for noble degeneracy. It should hardly be surprising that many of these plays, in contrast to those just discussed, speak for the traditional conservative nobility. Through these plays, the entrenched nobility defended itself, maintaining that those of its faction who behaved badly did so through ignorance, ill judgement, and evil counsel, not because of degeneracy resulting from long-standing wealth and ancient title. The plays admit noble abuses, warn against them, explore their motivations, and provide advice about how to avoid them. Rather than pleading for reform, these plays suggest prevention of abuse through a return to traditional values.

Skelton's *Magnificence* falls within this group of interludes. Skelton, a traditionalist allied with leaders of the old guard, espouses the values and attitudes of the conservatives. Skelton's position appears so vehement that many have interpreted *Magnificence* as a political allegory with Wolsey as its villain and Norfolk as its hero.[30] Although I do not wish to enter into that particular fray, its very existence indicates that *Magnificence* does address a significant social issue: what type of adviser should hold sway over the developing aristocratic mind?

Skelton draws Magnificence as an arrogant, ignorant noblemen, but the character does not remain static. At the start of the play, Magnificence is a good character, who becomes increasingly better (until his fall) by accepting the counsel of trusted and moderate men:

> Wealth with Liberty, with me both dwell ye shall,
> To the guiding of my Measure you both committing:
> That Measure be master us seemeth it is sitting   (174–6).

---

[30] Bevington, *Tudor Drama and Politics*, ch. 4; Skelton, 31–42; Nelson, 'Skelton's Quarrel with Wolsey', 377–98; William O. Harris, 99–122; see also the introduction to the play in Ramsey's edition of *Magnyfycence*.

Immediately thereafter, however, Magnificence retains and ennobles Fancy, who is masquerading as Largess, purely on the grounds of a suspicious letter of recommendation from Sad Circumspection (311–12, 390, 521). From that moment, Magnificence's moral fall is steadily enacted. One after another, evil counsellors masquerading as good are foolishly retained: Crafty Conveyance becomes Sure Surveyance and attaches himself to Magnificence's household (643); Counterfeit Countenance becomes Good Demeanance (674); Cloaked Collusion becomes Sober Sadness (681); Courtly Abusion becomes Pleasure (963). All represent 'new' men, seeking honours and wages while corrupting their lord. Skelton's authorial voice speaks clearly of this concern:

> A knave will counterfeit now a knight
> A lurden like a lord to fight,
> A minstrel like a man of might, . . .   (417–19).

In marked contrast to the attitudes of the anonymous author of *Jacob and Esau*, Skelton finds the shifting social order matter for concern, not for celebration. By appealing to Magnificence's baser instincts, the disguised vices convince him to abandon Liberty and Measure, and to devote himself to lechery and profligacy. It is not, however, through his own evil character that Magnificence falls, but rather through misplaced trust and poor judgement:

MAG. And is this the credence that I gave to the letter?
FANCY. Why, could not your wit serve you no better?
MAG. Why, who would have thought in you such guile?

   (1868–70).

Adversity strikes Magnificence, both literally and figuratively, and Poverty, Despair, and Mischief tempt him to suicide. Magnificence, however, recognizes his error:

> Alas, mine own servants to show me such reproach
> Thus to rebuke me and have me in despite;
> So shamefully to me their master to approach,
> That sometime was a noble prince of might! . . . (2278–81).

Through Good Hope, Redress, Sad Circumspection, and Perseverance, Magnificence is redeemed. At first glance, these four seem to be the traditional virtues of the morality play, but Magnificence's downfall is drawn in economic and social terms rather than strictly in spiritual terms, and his redemption also has social overtones. Good Hope points out that prosperity and adversity are intended to teach man 'to beware withal', to mend his economic errors before it is too late (2377). Redress promises to 'amend' Magnificence's 'fame' if he will amend his 'wanton excess'; again, economic terms are used:

> Redress should be at the reckoning in every account (2414).

Magnificence tells Perserverance that

> ... Good Hope and Redress hath mended mine estate,
> And Sad Circumspection to me they have annexed
> (2463–4).

The retention of proper counsel corrects Magnificence's initial error. Their advice is also economic. Redress urges Magnificence that

> ... of nobleness the chief point is to be liberal;
> So that your largess be not too prodigal (2484–5).

Circumspection tells him

> In your rewards use such moderation
> That nothing be given without consideration (2491–2).

Thus is magnificence restored 'home' to his 'palace with joy and royalty' (2563) in a psychomachia that suggests temporal transition in the guise of spiritual descent and ascent. Unlike Humanus Genus in *The Castle of Perseverance*, who saves his soul through repentance, Magnificence saves his kingdom as well as himself from economic and political chaos.

Magnificence, an example of the interlude that examines the educational process of the young nobleman, warns the audience to heed the advice of moderate counsellors, to beware of untried retainers who could be negative influences. Since the untried retainers, the newly enobled, are the active corrupters, the play also attacks the ease of social ascendancy. Borrowing techniques from the traditional morality structure,

Skelton implies that the wise nobleman observes the traditional values personified by the character Measure.

Dynamic protagonists, the retention of newly ennobled vice characters who corrupt that protagonist, the presence of trustworthy advisers who redeem the protagonist in moral and social terms, and use of an adapted psychomachia structure are devices common to plays such as *Wit and Science*, *The Nature of the Four Elements*, *The World and the Child*, *Youth*, and *Lusty Juventus*. Not all these were written to reinforce the claims of the old nobility against the new, although *Youth* and *The World and the Child* seem to do this.[31] They are, however, all concerned with various theories of pedagogy; all attempt to delineate the process a foolish nobleman goes through in order to learn good governance, a theme which makes these plays particularly appropriate for households with young heirs and henchmen to educate, or for schools that would produce their servitors.

Although *Youth* follows the traditional pattern of the morality play (the protagonist falls into sin through the vice characters Pride, Riot, and Lechery, then is redeemed through the virtues Charity and Humility), it 'can be understood as prudent advice to a landed heir of noble blood and class [343, 487, 489] about how to choose reliable counsellors for his estates'.[32] As such, it addresses the themes of proper education, abuse of maintenance, and the evils of facile social ascendancy in basically the same terms as *Magnificence* does. Riot hopes to be dubbed a 'knight of the collar' (270–2), and recommends Pride as a new retainer for his lord (323–30).Youth is redeemed by his return to the good counsel of Charity and Humility, representing traditional Christian values. Thus the playwright supports the concept of a just nobility, blaming the corrupters for the errors of the young.

The dynamic protagonist of *The World and the Child* undergoes a transformation similar to that of Youth, with slight variations. Although maintenance is once again used as a structuring motif, it is the protagonist who is retained by

---

[31] Lancashire, 'Auspices'; *Two Tudor Interludes*.
[32] For a detailed discussion of *Youth* see Lancashire, *Two Tudor Interludes*; pp. 49–58 discuss the characters as the equivalents of household figures.

World. Again a political point of great interest to the nobility is stressed: not only must one choose counsellors carefully, one must also select alliances carefully, for serving the wrong master is as dangerous as employing the wrong servants.[33] Once again, the young nobleman is saved by placing his allegiance in proper Christian virtues; Conscience, rather than Folly, must guide the nobleman through life. Adherence to traditional mores produces a virtuous ruling class.

Wit and Science, a boys' play, explores this theme more in terms of intellectual than political development, yet the protagonist, Wit, is dynamic, undergoing a process analogous to Magnificence's. Affianced to Lady Science, Wit is a young nobleman who is given trusted advisers in the person of Confidence, Instruction, Study, and Diligence. But Wit abandons good counsel in favour of Ignorance and Idleness, and is overcome by the monster Tediousness. Only when Wit regains the valued counsellors and uses them wisely can he overcome the monster, win the lady, and live an organized, proper life.

Hick Scorner also concentrates on a moral educational process, but uses two protagonists, Free Will and Imagination, and one enigmatic vice, Hick Scorner, to illustrate the evolution of moral character. Interpretation of this play has troubled many scholars, perhaps because of its inordinate dependence upon a specific political situation.[34] In technique, however, the anonymous author of *Hick Scorner* follows the same pattern as the author of *Youth* does: evil influences corrupt the protagonists, who are saved through the influence of spiritual advisers. Free Will and Imagination are salvageable representations of human behaviour; through good influences, they may become valuable members of society.

Rastell exploited a methodology similar to those discussed above to stress the education of a nobleman in humanistic terms in *The Nature of the Four Elements*. Using dynamic characters, the structural motif of maintenance, and an adapted morality form, Rastell produced, as Bevington puts it, 'a humanist manifesto extolling new learning at the

---

[33] For political interpretations, see Lancashire, 'Auspices.'
[34] Lancashire, *Two Tudor Interludes*, 32–4.

expense of scholasticism, and a glorification of the intellectual rather than the decadent aristocrat as reformer of society'.[35] Earlier, Medwall had used the same technique to explore similar ideas in *Nature*. Like *Magnificence*, *Youth*, and *The World and the Child*, composed and produced on behalf of the entrenched nobility, *Wit and Science*, *Nature*, and *The Nature of the Four Elements* stress that a young aristocrat must be trained to become a good ruler, and seem particularly appropriate to school audiences and performers. The two groups differ only in their conceptions of the specific nature of the education a young nobleman should receive. Much later, the Edwardian interlude *Lusty Juventus* uses in addition religious polemic and straightforward condemnation of traditional and parental values to explore the education of the young Protestant nobleman.[36]

Whereas the plays in the first category attempt to delineate the nature of true nobility, presenting contrasts and allowing the audience to think and judge, the plays in the second category attempt to describe the process of creating a true nobleman, offering vivid impressions of the moral and political progress of the protagonists, along with pointed authorial advice to the audience on how to educate themselves and their heirs. A third group of interludes focuses more specifically on the actions of the nobility in order to explore the proper use of aristocratic power.

Political antagonisms and religious polemics lurk close to the surface in the plays in this third category. This study, however, is concerned chiefly with the advice offered to the nobility about the dangers and responsibilities of rulership. Taking the themes of the nature of true nobility and the proper education for a nobleman one step further, these plays employ protagonists who are already fully developed as characters, yet fall victim to the manipulation and machinations of political representations of evil. Here, rather than observing negative models of nobility or charting the degeneration and redemption of the arrogant young aristocrat, the audience focuses upon the state of the kingdom, and the

[35] Bevington, *Tudor Drama and Politics*, 83.
[36] Bevington, *Tudor Drama and Politics*, 86–95. Craik, 'The Political Interpretation of Two Tudor Interludes', 98–108.

social chaos created by the evil retainers of unwary rulers. In a sense, the playwrights suggest that the aristocracy should increase its power by assuming rather than delegating responsibility and control, advice that would appeal to the nobility but anger the monarch, whose Royal Proclamations had long sought to control such centralization.

For example, the anonymous *Godly Queen Hester* has been examined as a specific political allegory.[37] In more general terms, however, it offers warnings and advice that are widely applicable to any nobleman in a position of power. The King and Queen are static characterizations of the virtuous nobility. King Assuerus's royalty is established through dialogue that discusses his ancestry, wealth, and wisdom (250–2). Queen Hester, however, is constituted noble on the basis of her inherent virtues rather than her lineage or possessions. She is

> Sober, sad, gentle, meek, and demure;
> In learning and literture, profoundly seen; . . . (258).

The King, conveniently absent for most of the play, errs in the trust he places in Aman, a counsellor who achieves power and wealth through the generosity of his King, then proceeds to abuse that power, attempting to destroy the Queen and her people.

King Assuerus errs only through a positive quality—trust—enabling the playwright to make the lesson clear without defaming the noble character:

> All noble princes by me may beware
> Whom they shall trust and put in authority;
> Eke whom they shall promote to riches and dignity (281).

Mardocheus, the virtuous uncle of Hester, represents the trustworthy counsellor:

> We be right glad we know his lineage;
> His truth to us before was known well.
> We will him advance according his parage (284).

Thus, the playwright urges noblemen to retain counsellors of good ancestry whose loyalty has been demonstrated rather than the recently ennobled men of glib tongue.

---

[37] Bevington, *Tudor Drama and Politics*, 87–93.

Aman, as the representation of the eloquent but ignoble courtier, is thoroughly condemned. In one of the finest scenes of comic irony in all the early Tudor interludes, the vices complain that Aman has made them powerless, not through exercise of virtue, but by assuming all their tasks. Pride complains:

> And since Aman reigned, no man him retained
> Almost in any place.
> For Aman, that elf, would no man but himself
> Should be proud indeed (262).

Adulation is also out of business:

> And as for Adulation, must change his occupation,
> It is not worth a pease...
> For my lord Aman doeth all that he can—
> I assure you without doubt—
> To take up all flatte[r]s, and all crafty clatterers
> That dwell forty mile about (262).

Even Ambition is powerless:

> ...—I was wont to be a great clerk;
> But sin Aman bare rule neither horse nor mule
> But is as wise as I (264).

Ambition cannot 'get promotion' because Aman grabs 'every office and fee', leaving the under-employed Ambition to 'dwell among fools' (265–6). The testimony of the vices doubly damns Aman in brilliantly satiric terms, for while they rehearse his abuses, describing in detail how Aman has ruined the kingdom, they complain that the high counsellor is far more evil than they.

Plays such as *Godly Queen Hester* that address the theme of noble power and responsibility were doubly careful not to offend their noble, perhaps royal, audiences. The burden of guilt falls thoroughly and exclusively upon evil retainers. The ruler, on the other hand, makes an excusable error, trusting those who are unworthy of his trust; this allows the playwright to criticize the irresponsible delegation of authority rather than the authority figure itself.

The Marian interlude *Respublica*, like *Godly Queen*

Hester, is concerned with the use and abuses of power, using similar techniques to explore the theme. Respublica, the character who represents the sovereign, is static and good, endeavouring to set chaos in her kingdom to rights:

> ... what mervaile then y^f I wanting a perfecte staigh
> From mooste flourishing welth bee falen in decaye?
> But lyke as by default quicke ruine dothe befalle
> So maie good governemente att ons recover all (457–60).

The key concept here, as in *Godly Queen Hester*, is good governance, and it is the responsibility of the ruler to provide it.

Unfortunately, Respublica chooses the wrong counsellors to assist her in reconstructing her kingdom. Once again, it is trust that proves to be the fatal flaw, for Avarice, disguised as Policy, tells Respublica 'I durste put miself to you of truste' (496), and Respublica agrees that she will place herself, her treasure, goods, and lands 'whollye into y*our* handes' (II. ii. 39–40), thus abdicating control and responsibility. Adulation, Oppression, and Insolence, masquerading as Honesty, Reformation, and Authority, seek service with Respublica and are accepted:

> I thanke youe *and* I truste youe for my maintenance
> To bee adminster for y*our* goode governaunce (584–5).

Although Respublica's trust is misplaced, her motives are admirable, which prevents the audience from viewing her as a negative model. As in *Godly Queen Hester*, the blame for the ensuing chaos falls solely upon the recently acquired and hypocritical retainers. Respublica requires no prompting to accept assistance from Peace, Justice, Truth, and Mercy, the four daughters of God, for she has not sinned. As Truth states:

> Ah, good Respublica, thow haste been abused,
> Whom thowe chosest are vices to be refused ... (1369–70).

Once her error is pointed out, Respublica, like King Assuerus, purges the vicious retainers to heal her kingdom.

Respublica feels the effects of the vices' rampage of injustice, but People, the characterisation of the State, truly suffers as he is physically abused by the disguised vices in a clear allegory:

> Thei shaked me vp, chwas ner zo rattled avore.
> Theye vell all vppon me catche awoorde *that* might catche,
> Well was hym that at me people might geat a snatche
>
> (1586–8).

The beating People receives is symbolic of the ravages the State has endured at the hands of self-serving officials, as the State, not the sovereign, bears the brunt of the error.

Although Respublica begins to correct the abuses of her retainers as soon as she discovers them, it is Nemesis, the symbol of divine retribution, who actually sets things to rights. As a goddess, the character Nemesis reminds the audience that noble power is of divine origin. At the close of the play Nemesis, the archetype of order and justice, delivers the kingdom once again into Respublica's hands, confident that the purgation of vice, rather than the reformation of the sovereign, will result in political harmony and health.

Thematic and structural patterns similar to those found in *Godly Queen Hester* and *Respublica* are used in other early interludes that examine politics and power. The fragmentary *Albion Knight* includes the static representation of the ruler, the critique of maintenance, the condemnation of recently advanced untrustworthy and ignoble retainers, the suffering of the State as well as the sovereign, and the implication that irresponsible delegation of authority is a serious error, caused by naïve trust rather than by degeneracy.

Bale's adamantly Protestant *King Johan*, staged by Cromwell's players,[38] also addresses the theme of temporal power. Bale, like Udall in *Respublica*, employs disguised vices who abuse the King's trust to create chaos in the kingdom. Bale also includes a character similar in type and function to Nemesis; Imperial Majesty, the symbol of good governance and justice, enters at the end of the play to purge evil retainers, to re-establish order, and to reinforce the divine right and power of the monarch. The widow England, like People in *Respublica*, suffers the abuses of misappropriated power.

---

[38] Bevington, *Tudor Drama and Politics*, 98–105; see also Jesse Harris and Fairfield.

The character King Johan is a static model of the good ruler who, like the other rulers in these plays, is betrayed by disguised vices whom he, in trust, retains. Unlike *Respublica* and *King Assuerus*, however, King Johan himself suffers the consequences of his error. There is no happy ending for the ruling nobleman here, which is completely appropriate considering Bale's politics. His invective, his damning characterization of Catholic vice, would have been weakened, the facts of history would have had to have been changed, had King Johan survived the persecution. In addition, royal power had not purged Catholic abuse in Bale's time or in the historical King John's time. Consequently, a character like Imperial Majesty is more crucial to *King Johan* than it was to *Respublica*. Without divine intervention, Bale implies, there is no vehicle for the restitution of royal power or the administration of justice.

The interludes in this third group that address the uses and abuses of power are significantly different in their ideologies from the others, for they are directed primarily toward the monarch rather than toward the aristocracy. As such, the danger to the playwright increases, and consequently the royal figures are treated with great care, either by absenting them or by excusing them. Kings err; noblemen sin; people suffer.

The plays of John Heywood are tangentially related to *Godly Queen Hester*, *Respublica*, *Albion Knight*, and *King Johan*. Lois Potter believes that Heywood's compositions are more capricious *débats* than plays,[39] but David Bevington clearly points out that even Heywood's frothy plays argue for social harmony.[40] *The Four PP*, *Weather*, and *The Pardoner and the Friar* in particular stage arguments that represent various religious and social perspectives. *Love*, *Witty and Witless*, and *Johan Johan* are more concerned with folly and its spirited exposure. Yet the denouements of all Heywood's plays are similar; the situations are either left unresolved, preserving the status quo, or the plays beg for tolerance and co-operation to preserve the status quo. Heywood does not

---

[39] *Revels*, 167–72.
[40] Bevington, *Tudor Drama and Politics*, 64–74.

criticize the aristocracy, the practice of maintenance, or noble error, in delegation of authority. His characters are static, but they are rarely completely positive or negative models. Yet he is definitely concerned with human behaviour, and particularly with social harmony. In *Weather* Heywood implies that rulers should exercise authority to reconcile factions, not to set one against or above another. As Henry VIII's virginalist, Heywood wisely trod carefully when offering political advice, choosing themes that could offend none of the King's guests of various political and religious persuasions, of various classes and origins, who might view his plays.

Virtually all early Tudor interludes address themes of vital interest to the aristocracy in language and through structures that reflected life in the great households. The playwrights were careful writers, who aspired to call attention to abuses, to reform degenerate behaviour, and to advise those in power without offending their audiences or their noble patrons. Early Tudor plays continually demonstrate that their authors had detailed and complex knowledge of the social class about which they were writing. Household and school audiences would be quick to detect and appreciate satire that operated on situations familiar to them and to absorb lessons about their proper duties and responsibilities. Noble patrons could identify themselves with positive characters while ascribing negative characteristics to their rivals and enemies. If itinerant troupes took the plays to towns, the common people were provided not only with a view of the splendid and sophisticated life-styles of their social betters, but also with insight into the potential tragedy inherent in the problems of noble life. The early Tudor interlude, therefore, reaffirmed the existing social structure to all classes at the same time as it subtly manipulated audience response to accept the more specific political persuasions of the authors and their patrons.

The plays themselves reflect noble auspices and audiences; often there are direct parallels between play and specific political situation. In more general terms, noble concerns and life-styles inspired character portrayal, affected language and action, provided structural patterns, and suggested themes. Although writers certainly took artistic liberties, their plays animate, perhaps more vividly than could any history, letter, or painting, a way of life long disappeared. Through their rhetoric and their actions, characters in the early Tudor interludes preserve for us sketches of personalities and explorations of problems that were, to our sixteenth-century forebears, realistic and pertinent.

Conclusion

The study and appreciation of early Tudor household revels have languished far too long, but for several very good reasons. Critics cannot assess performance styles or their influence without sufficient primary source materials, which have yet to be properly collected, transcribed, and edited. The revels, ephemeral and usually unscripted, do not yield easily to reconstruction, understanding, or analysis; consequently, it is difficult for scholars to reassemble the shards of seemingly irrelevant information that might one day be carefully pieced together to form the total picture. Meanwhile, the revels are often neglected, overshadowed as they are by the prodigious civic drama, the great works of the public stage in the age of Shakespeare, and the more thoroughly documented later court revels of Jones and Jonson.

The difficulties that scholars have in understanding early Tudor household revels are, however, minuscule in comparison to the difficulties that modern readers and audiences have. Many of the religious, social, and theatrical influences that affected the revels have been forgotten, or perhaps even lost, in our modern world. No longer is our society organized into residential alliances like great households; no longer are patrons recognizable human beings with whom we live and for whom we work. Few will ever watch entertainments remotely resembling household revels produced specifically for them, with themes applicable to them, within their own communities. Thus, on even the most general level, household revels have become difficult to comprehend and impossible to integrate into our theatrical lives.

On more specific levels, the techniques of early Tudor performers and performances have changed so drastically that they seem to have disappeared altogether from contemporary theatrical theory. Amateur choirs often perform in local pageants, but, with the exception of the Vienna Boys' Choir, what professional church choir can today be considered a theatrical troupe? Such groups rarely perform the liturgical or scriptural plays for which their early Tudor counterparts were known, and never venture to produce secular disguisings. Vatican II sounded the death-knell for the Latin high mass, considered in early times the epitome of artistic beauty. Our perception of musicians has also changed. Audiences listen with polite attention to symphonies, chamber groups, and consorts, but never view the artists as early Tudor audiences did, as servants of a household who contributed their music to larger artistic and social concerns. We go to plays, plays do not come to us, except as flat electronic images emanating from small boxes, no substitute for live theatre or the company of an audience of friends and colleagues.

Yet not all these influences have been totally lost. Multimedia effects continue to be exploited in the contemporary musical theatre, where designers, dancers, actors, and musicians co-operate to achieve extravagant effects. Ballet preserves the marriage of minstrel and disguiser, opera the marriage of minstrel and singer-actor. Ticket prices reflect the huge costs of such efforts, which are no longer non-profit ventures, as great household revels were. Patronage is still with us, exercised by wealthy individuals and corporate donors, although its influence is far more subtle and, perhaps, far more insidious.

Even the style of great household disguisings may be creeping its way back into contemporary theatrical theory. Semiology has renewed critical interest in iconography and the interpretation of signs and allegory; this movement is now producing new artistic structures that will challenge the entrenched traditions of naturalism and realism. The success of shows like *Cats* in London and on Broadway demonstrates that the disguising may still be a viable art-form. T. S. Eliot's poetry set to Lloyd Webber's music combines with a junk-yard set and a score of dancer/singer cats with human qualities to create an allegory complete with anti-masque and apotheosis. Not so very different from Henry VIII's Turks and Wildmen or Jonson's classical ladies and grotesques. 'Performance art', the latest rage of the avant-garde theatre, combines music, poetry, dance and audio-visual effects to create mood and image rather than straightforward linear plot.

Conclusion

Today's audiences, like Polonius, may insist on categorizing and labelling theatrical performances, but early Tudor audiences did not perceive these theoretical divisions. The Chapels, minstrels, and players each commanded specific talents and expertise, but they blended various influences and effects, to bridge aesthetic gaps rather than to create them.

Great household Chapels, protected from dissolution and ecclesiastical censorship, flourished under the patronage of the aristocracy and developed into formidable performing groups. Within the walls of family chapels and great halls, liturgical and scriptural plays, often under attack from all sides, could be performed and developed with relative impunity. The Chapel's unique position—a religious organization operating within a secular institution—encouraged well-educated clerics to experiment with non-religious forms of entertainment, both in their own plays and in the disguisings to which they contributed. A dozen boys and men, trained in music and rhetoric, and able to assume roles varying in age and sex, were constantly at the disposal of the great households, a fact that enabled patrons to request elaborate performance specific to an occasion at almost any time, for which the household would provide sets, costumes, and playing space.

Like Chapel singers, minstrels were also necessary to their patrons on a day-to-day basis. The elaborate fanfares that marked the entrances, progresses, and meals of the Tudor aristocracy were certainly theatrical, but they were not theatre. Minstrels were expected to provide solo concerts, consort performances, and dance accompaniment whenever requested, but these entertainments, pleasant as they might be, were not theatre either. In disguisings and plays, however, minstrels did become actors. At times they may have spoken lines in their own plays or in other plays when interluders or Chapel Children required their services. In the disguisings, thematic music often replaced rhetorical description, and in these the minstrels were definitely integrated with the *mise en scène*. Appropriately costumed, with specific blocking and position, the minstrels differed from players only in that they communicated in musical notes rather than in words.

Players were different from Chapels and minstrels because

Conclusion 203

their services were not in such constant demand. Free (and perhaps encouraged) to travel, players were responsible for exporting great household drama to the population at large, thereby familiarizing the commoners of England with the theatrical styles and political sentiments of the aristocracy. Plays may have been initially commissioned by patrons for performance before their friends and retainers from resident almoners or talented poets, but the full value of the text was realized only after these 'brief chronicles' had been communicated abroad in cities, towns, and other households.

The extant plays conform wonderfully to the Renaissance ideal of mixing profit with pleasure, of delighting while teaching. Audiences, élite or common, could marvel at beautiful costumes, laugh at the farces enacted by comic servants, sigh at the trials of the protagonists, and celebrate the inevitable restoration of order at the denouement. At the same time, however, the audiences were being subtly and painlessly propagandized; the attitudes of playwrights and patrons toward social and religious problems were biased editorials, not objective news. Household audiences might recognize pointed topical references to people and situations more easily than the general public did, but both could understand the dialectic. Common audiences, like film and television viewers today, were allowed to eavesdrop on the life-styles of the rich and powerful, whose troubles were purportedly far more interesting and significant than their own mundane worries. Even on a structural level, the plays reflect the concepts of hierarchy and maintenance so central to noble life and so crucial to the preservation of the existing social order.

In great household revels, Chapels, minstrels, players, and writers interacted under one roof, learning from each other and blending their talents so that the sum could be greater than its parts. On significant religious feasts or secular festivals, these talented men experimented with forms and created art they could never afford, either financially or politically, to produce themselves. At Christmas, Twelfth Night, Shrovetide, weddings, and christenings, the entire household received a gift of theatre from their patron. Eyes, ears, and palates were fed with music, dances, plays, and

FIG. 12. 'Sir Henry Unton's Wedding' (c.1597), courtesy of the National Portrait Gallery. Perhaps the only painting of a Tudor great household revel, 'Sir Henry Unton's Wedding' makes economic and descriptive accounts visible to us for the first time. The minstrels are stationed in two areas, at the centre, and to the left. The viol players to the left are hatted and dressed differently; perhaps they were visitors. At the centre, the household consort plays flute, lute, viol, and fiddle to accompany a disguising of ten black and white cupids (perhaps Chapel Children?) accompanied by a drummer and eight people in disguising garb. Behind the wedding party, who are painted larger than the guests or entertainers to reflect their importance, lurk the household retainers. To the right, a cupboard, such as is called for in the Northumberland Household Book, displays the valuable plate. At the lower left, a figure in a cope may suggest the religious ceremony that had previously been celebrated.

courses of delicacies, all ceremoniously presented to insure unity of theme and composite effect.

Noble patrons nurtured the artists who composed music and drama as well as those who performed them. Although their motives were not totally unselfish or exclusively philanthropic, the aristocracy did provide their entertainers with several basic necessities. Chapels received vestments and 'civilian' clothing, minstrels and players received livery and sometimes costumes and instruments. Household Books record rations of food and fuel for Chapels and minstrels. Resident artists had rooms in their patron's manors, and travelling performers were lodged when they returned from their tours. As important as these physical necessities were, the legal and social advantages of patronage were perhaps even more valuable to the entertainers. Protection from the law and opportunity for socio-economic advancement were benefits that could not be measured merely in pounds. In return, patrons expected their artists to secure and enlarge the power and prestige of the noble household through their loyalty and expert performance, for noble patrons were quick to realize that theatre could become a powerful tool for those who wished to win influence. For perhaps the last time in western theatre history, subsidized theatre was an unquestioned asset and success.

Each chapter of this study has considered a specific performing group within the great households, showing how each contributed to the creation of a distinctive household form of theatre. With this overview, it becomes possible to suggest six qualities that make this form unique: the household as the source of the entertainment; the stylistic techniques of household performance; the occasions for household performance; the performance space itself; the financial arrangements; and the motives.

First, household entertainments were intended for a known audience and could therefore be specifically geared towards the group's knowledge and interests. This factor could inspire performers to direct their entertainment to particular events, ideas, personalities, or issues, localizing content, and to perform in styles native to a geographical region in that region's dialect, localizing form. In addition, household performers knew the level of sophistication and education of their audiences, which could dictate whether classical and foreign languages and allusions would be understood. For example, a reference to the Scots might work far better at Percy's Northumberland court than at Buckingham's Kentish one, where a reference to the French might be more appropriate. Rarely does a modern company have the luxury of so controllable an audience response.

Second, the presence of a myriad of entertainers within one household created the opportunity for multimedia performances that were too complex and expensive to be moved about. Freedom from the constraints of touring enabled the designers of household entertainments to use large casts varied in age and gender, to use complex sets and pageant devices, to blend music, dance, rhetoric, and visual art into one whole, unified thematically and stylistically. Household audiences also watched smaller, more individual entertainment from resident and itinerant troupes; thus, a household retainer had the opportunity to view virtually every type of theatrical art except the Corpus Christi play and the tournament without leaving home.

Third, household revels were generally intended to celebrate an occasion. At significant religious feasts and secular festivals, households could expect the holiday atmosphere to be created or embellished by theatre. A holy day was not just a time for extra religious services; it was also a time for plays, disguisings, and banquets. A holiday was not just a day free from work; it was also a time when retainers could indulge in games, sports, tears, laughter, and marvels. Thus, theatre became, within great households, identified with social, liturgical, and political events, and was perhaps imbued with the significance of those events.

Fourth, space within the manors and castles of the aristocracy provided convenient and familiar stages. The great hall, the chapel, the dining chamber, and even the courtyard could be decorated, arranged, and used for rehearsal well in advance of a performance; perhaps the process even contributed to the rising interest and excitement of the resident audience. Performers could exploit architectural features unique to their environment to create staging effects that would not be possible in other spaces. The household had only to assemble, not to plan or travel, in order to be entertained.

Fifth, household revels were strictly non-profit ventures; in fact, they lost money. Retainers not only watched sophisticated entertainment designed never to be repeated, they also watched it gratis. The household absorbed the cost of the hire and maintenance of entertainers, and underwrote the expenses of production, freeing the artists from the constraints of tight budgets and from producing texts of general appeal. These factors could easily have led resident artists to experiment with unique effects that can never be traced or recovered, since it is a sad fact that virtually no great house revel has been described in any detail.

The sixth quality of great household revels—motivation—grows out of and governs the other five. Noble patrons had several reasons for providing theatre for their retainers: to impress, to educate, to entertain, to communicate, and ultimately to control. The quality of an aristocrat's entertainment was a mark of his prestige; every nobleman produced the best that his financial means and political position would allow. The extravagance of the entertainment was directly proportional to the wealth and power of the patron. As the crown on the player's head signified kingship, the quality of art signified social and economic superiority.

The themes of household revels communicated the attitudes of the patron, thus allowing the nobleman to educate and influence those within earshot in the ideas he considered proper. Such propaganda strengthened the household alliance; some retainers were persuaded to be loyal to their patron's position, others were warned that divergence from his law could have severe repercussions. All who watched the revels were subliminally programmed, through content and form, to absorb the social codes and systems that created and maintained the power structure. These lessons were sweetened because they were entertaining. It is perhaps no accident that many household playwrights were almoners, those religious functionaries responsible within the household for the distribution of food, clothing, and money to the poor as charity. Charity is, however, complex. It is a virtue in the giver, and certainly a necessity for the receiver, but it is also a tool of power, for it creates dependence and obligation. Like every action in the early Tudor theatre of politics, drama served a dual purpose, one obvious, one more subtle and insidious.

When retained entertainers, particularly players, left their household, they signified all these values to external populations. The quality of their performance and accoutrements reinforced the people's impression of the patron. The plots and structures of their texts familiarized the people with the aristocrat's ideas, perhaps winning a few converts and igniting a few dissidents in the process. The returning players brought the household and its patron news and gossip from abroad; the players' reports of where they had been well and ill received could alert their patron to potential allies and enemies.

At the foundation of all the patron's motives was the desire for control. Control translated into a solid and loyal household structure, a firm political base. Within and without the household, this control reaffirmed the existing social order, even while it debated specific issues that concerned that order. In a period of social, political, religious, and economic upheaval like the early Tudor era, the battle for power may be fought on many fronts, and the theatre was certainly one of those battlegrounds. As the aristocracy gradually lost feudal power, it changed tactics; one way to retain influence was to manipulate thought, to control entertainers and their costumes, properties, stages, and texts. When playwrights and players like Rastell and Shakespeare gained control over stages, costumes, and particularly texts, noble patrons lost a measure of the power that could be gained by the manipulation of public opinion, and the public stage developed.

Shakespeare did not, like Pallas Athene, spring fully costumed with quill in hand from the forehead of Queen Elizabeth to rescue contemporary readers from allegedly dreary mystery, miracle, and morality plays. Rather, the Elizabethan drama must be seen as a natural development from previous traditions, with debts to the medieval dramatic structures, to the Corpus Christi plays, and to civic pageantry. To this list of influences must be added the great household revels, rich in allegory, classical and European influences, native English traditions, and multimedia effects.

Shakespeare's plays continually offer audiences a view of great household revels and patronized performers: Timon is surprised by a disguising during his banquet; Henry VIII performs a masque of shepherds; Romeo and Juliet meet at the Capulets' masked ball; Orsino commands that his minstrels and singers console him, while Olivia's steward Malvolio stands guard over the cakes and ale in the fool's wooing of *Twelfth Night*. Even the beleaguered Macbeths manage a banquet for their noble guests. The stylistic influence of the disguising may be seen in the magical feast and show of marvels of *The Tempest* and in the transfiguration of Hermione from statue to woman at the end of *The Winter's Tale*. The bear chasing Antigonus in *The Winter's Tale* and the wrestling match of *As You Like It* recall the bear-baitings and sports of household games. Oberon's poetic description of the origin of the flower 'love-in-idleness' is practically a recreation of Lord Leicester's Kenilworth revels for Elizabeth. Essex was able to use a performancer of *Richard II* to attempt to gain sympathy for his rebellion. Music (including fanfare to mark aristocratic entrances and exits), dance, and song continually find room on Shakespeare's stage. In the absence of detailed descriptions of great household revels, these literary analogues not only recreate the events, but also demonstrate that the techniques of early Tudor great household performance were inextricably woven into the later structure of Elizabethan drama.

Although the revels have long ended, and their patrons and performers have become the dust of history, these unique entertainments remain a remarkable testimony to the practical relationship of life and art. Artists became an integral part of the household structure, crucial to the social position of their patron, and patrons became preservers and promoters of culture. As Renaissance values superseded medieval values in England, as audiences changed from serfs to be commanded to upwardly mobile citizens to be influenced, noble household entertainments became more frequent and more complex, representing the change in the role of the nobility from warlord and landlord to businessman and politician.

APPENDIX A

Size of Itinerant Player Troupes

Municipal and household accounts seldom specify the number of actors in a troupe. The following tables extract references from selected accounts, recorded in Wickham's *Early English Stages*, Chambers' *Mediaeval Stage*, Anglo's 'Court Festivals', and Lancashire's *Texts and Records*, that do specify the number of players in a given troupe. This information allows us to estimate the size of an average troupe.

I. *Selby Abbey Accounts 1431–1532* (Wickham, *EES 1*, app. C)

No. of players	Frequency of references	% of total references
1	15	42.8
2	2	5.7
3	5*	14.3
4	4	11.4
5	7	20.0
6	1	2.9
7	1	2.9

* In one of these, the reward is for '3 players of the Duke of Gloucester, Lord Fitzhugh, and Lord Lovell,' perhaps an amalgamated troupe.

II. *Henry VII's Chamber Accounts 1491–1509* (Anglo, 'Court Festivals')

No. of players	Frequency of references	% of total references
1	1	11.1
2	1	11.1
3	1	11.1
4	5	55.5
5	1	11.1

Appendix A 211

III. *Durham Priory Accounts 1278–1555* (Chambers, *MS 2*, app. E)

No. of players	Frequency of references	% of total references
1	1	10
2	7	70
3	1	10
4	1	10

IV. *Maxstoke Priory Accounts 1422–1461* (Chambers, *MS 2*, app. E)
1 troupe of 4 players specified

V. *Winchester College Accounts 1400–1573* (Chambers, *MS 2*, app. E)
2 troupes of 4 specified

VI. *Shrewsbury Corporation Accounts 1400–1573* (Chambers, *MS 2*, app. E)
2 troupes of 4 specified
1 troupe of 6 specified

VII. *Howard Household Accounts 1465–1466; 1481–1492* (Chambers, *MS 2*, app. E)
2 troupes of 4 specified

VIII. Following is a list of other patrons whose troupe size is specified in various accounts (Lancashire, *Guide*, section B, 25–54).

Patron	Troupe Size	Date
Anne Boleyn	4	1534
Edward Belknap	4	1519
	4	1520
Henry Bourchier	4	1526–7
Charles Brandon	4	1525
	2	1531
Catherine of Aragon	4	1534
Edward VI	4	1538–9
	6	1547–52

VIII. (cont.)

Patron	Troupe Size	Date
Thomas FitzAlan	4	1519
Henry VII	4	1503–4
	4	1507
Henry VIII	4	1527
(two troupes)	6	1527
	4	1529
	1	1531
	4	1535
	4	1537
Thomas Howard	2	1530
Jane Seymour	4	1536–7
Francis Leek	6–7	1556
Queen Mary	4	1531
Henry Percy	4	1508
Richard III	4	1482–3
Edward Stanley	1	1532
	4	1532–3

IX. *Average Troupe Size*

Total of all troupe sizes in I–VIII	285
Total number of troupes in I–VIII	88
Average troupe size	3.39

APPENDIX B
Solo Instrumentalists

Harpers: BL Add. MS 24459 records rewards for twenty-six harpers, all attached to royal or noble households (*MM* 10–11). The first Duke of Norfolk retained a harper called Thomas (Collier, 139–40). Henry VI retained a Welsh harper and rewarded others (Anglo, 'Court Festivals', 30, 35–6). Edward Stafford, Duke of Buckingham, who had been raised at Henry VII's court, inherited his King's fondness for harpers. Within a two-month period, he rewarded William Estgate, who was perhaps his own harper, three times (*L & P HVIII* iii/1. 497) There is no record that Northumberland retained a harper, but Henry VIII retained two blind harpers (*L & P HVIII* ii/2. 1465, 1469, 1473). Shrewsbury Corporation accounts describe one, More, as 'minstrel of our Lord King . . . and the principal harper in England' (Chambers, *MS* 2, 252).

Psaltry: The psaltry (a stringed instrument that was plucked like a dulcimer) does not appear to have been a popular instrument in the fifteenth and sixteenth centuries. At Edward I's 1306 feast, two private psaltry-players entertained, one retained by Sir Henry de Percy, and one by the Queen. William Le Sautreour was psaltry-player for three queens, and travelled with his patroness (*MM* 10–11, 98).

Lute: References to luters occur in the records of households in the sixteenth century, but are rare in records of previous centuries. However, Edward I retained a lute player, so they did exist (*MM* 11). As references to harpers decrease in frequency, references to luters increase, implying that the lute was replacing the harp as the most popular solo stringed instrument. Luters, lutes, and strings are frequently noted in household accounts during the reign of Henry VIII, when noble amateurs began taking an active interest in making music, particularly on the lute; see Page, 11–21.

Henry VII's accounts record rewards to luters retained by Prince Arthur and Prince Henry; another called 'Master Gyles' may have been his own luter (Anglo, 'Court Festivals', 27, 29, 43; BL Add. MS 7099, f. 71). Another luter called Andolf received wages at 40s. per month (BL Add. MS 7099, f. 72). A luter called Watt 'pleyed the fole' before Henry VII on 4 October 1504. His act was, perhaps unfortunately, quite successful, for by November of that year he was called 'Watt the fole' (Anglo, 'Court Festivals', 39).

Henry VIII's 1544–5 accounts record monthly wages to two luters, Phillip and Peter Welder (BL Add. MS 59900); he retained larger numbers in other years and as occasional musicians. The name of Anne Boleyn's luter, Mark Smeton, has survived for historical rather than purely musical reasons.

Many noble households also retained luters. Lady Percy's visited Lord John Howard at Stoke in 1481 (Collier, 84). A sixteenth-century Earl of Rutland paid to have his lady's page taught to play the lute (HMC 4: 4, 381, 432, 532). Sir John Petre owned a lute, and presumably employed someone to play or teach it (Emmison, 70–1). Sir Thomas Challoner retained a lute player called 'hewme' and paid another household musician, Appleby, for lute strings (BL Harl. MS 9, ff. 13ᵛ, 18). The Paston letters depict a family avidly interested in lute music.

Organ: Since the organ was the chief instrument of the Chapel, all households that kept resident Chapels record payments for instruments, for repairs, and to organ-players. Because household accounts often lack details, it is usually impossible to distinguish between payments made for organ-playing within the context of divine services and organ-playing as secular entertainment. For examples of references to organs, see NHB 62 (Northumberland); Collier, 170 (Norfolk); Anglo, 'Court Festivals' 30, 33, 34, 38, 39; and BL Add. MS 7099 f. 82 (Henry VII); *L & P HVIII* ii/2, 1441 (Henry VIII).

Virginals: Virginals appear more often in household accounts during the reign of Henry VIII than they do before. One reason for this is the increase in the number of amateur musicians; the virginals, like the lute, was a favourite instrument for noble musicians. Sir John Petre owned virginals (Emmison, 70–1). Sir Thomas Chaloner paid to have virginals repaired and tuned (BL Harl. MS 69, f. 12). Henry VIII paid John Heywood as a player of virginals (BL Add. MS 59900, f. 59). The Norfolk, Northumberland, and Buckingham accounts do not mention the instrument or players of it.

Many factors could affect the amount given in reward to entertainers. Particularly good performers, unusual performers, and performers from a favoured patron or city could inspire superior rewards. Conversely, performers that were inferior, mundane, or from less consequential environs received smaller amounts. Unfortunately, Heron's accounts are brief and unspecific, making these inconsistencies puzzling. Yet some patterns can be discerned and these patterns show that soloists often received higher rewards than other performers. For example, the most common reward to minstrel troupes retained by noblemen was 20*s*.

Significant exceptions to this were: the 40s. given to the Queen's minstrels on New Year's Day on eight occasions; the 40s. given to Princess Katherine's minstrels; and 100s. given to two Spanish minstrels during the wedding celebrations. These were special rewards for special occasions. Retained troupes of players often received either 20s. or 13s. 4d., with the notable exception of the King's own players, who four times received 40s. All these rewards would have to be divided among the men who composed the troupes, but rewards to soloists were, of course, for the individual alone. The following examples show that the soloists frequently received higher rewards:

1492	Mar. 4	Item to the childe that pleyeth on the records	xx^s
	Apr. 29	Item to one that pleyed on the lute in rewarde	vj^s viij^d
	Jun. 11	Item to one that pleyed on the drone	vj^s viij^d
1494	Nov. 29	Item to my Lorde Prince luter in rewarde	xx^s
1495	Feb. 13	Item to hym that pleyeth upon the bagpipe	x^s
1496	May 10	Item to an harper of Fraunce	vj^{li} xiij^s iiij^d
1497	Feb. 17	Item to the Quenes fideler in rewarde	xxvj^s viij^d
	May 24	Item to Arnold my Lorde Prince mynystrell	xx^s
1498	Apr. 9–12	Item to Arnold, pleyer at recorders	xx^s
	May 23	Item to his [Prince Henry's] luter in rewarde	xx^s
1499	Jun. 15	Item to the organpleyer in rewarde	xl^s
1500	Oct. 23	Item to Weston for ij singers in rewarde	iiij^{li}
1505	May 31	Item to Piers Barbor for him that played at thorgans in the galery at Richemount	x^s

(Anglo, 'Court Festivals', 27–39).

APPENDIX C
Recorded Movements of Patronized Troupes

This examination of patronized troupes is based upon the most recently compiled lists in Ian Lancashire's *Dramatic Texts*. For the convenience of the reader, the pertinent records are reproduced here.

Charles Brandon, Duke of Suffolk (1484–1545)

1525	Shrewsbury	1529–30	Southampton
1530	London	1530–1	Southampton
1531	London	1538	Court
1538	Cambridge	1539	Cambridge
1539–40	Louth	1539–40	Lydd
1540	York	1540–1	Bristol
1540–1	Lydd	1541	Court
1541–2	Dover	1541–2	Folkestone
1541–2	Lydd		

Sir Thomas Cheney, Warden of the Cinque Ports (in office 1542–58)

1542–3	Canterbury	1542–3	Dover
1542–3	Folkestone	1543	London
1543–4	Folkestone	1544–5	New Romney

DUKES OF NORFOLK

Thomas Howard (1473–1554)

1529	London	1529–30	Thetford
1530	Oxford	1530–1	Bury St Edmunds
1535–6	Norwich	1535–6	Thetford
1543	Cambridge	1543–4	Canterbury

Thomas Howard (1538–72)

1556–7	Exeter	1556–7	Ipswich
1556–7	Norwich	1557	Cambridge
1557	Harwich	1557–8	Ipswich
1558	Lewes		

Appendix C 217

George Nevill, Lord Abergavenny, Warden of the Cinque Ports
(in office 1492–1535)

1509–10	Dover	1510–11	Sandwich
1513–14	Dover	1516–17	Sandwich
1517–18	Lydd	1517–18	Sandwich

Edward Seymour, Duke of Somerset (1500–52)

c.1536–44	Wulfhall	1545	London
1547–8	Cambridge	1547–8	Canterbury
1547–8	Dover	1548	Cambridge
1548–9	Canterbury	1548–9	Dover
1548–9	Leicester	1548–9	Lyme Regis
1548–9	New Romney	1548–9	Norwich
1550–1	Bristol	1551	Cambridge

Thomas Seymour (1508–49), Lord Admiral (1546–9)

1547–8	Dover	1548	Lyme Regis
1548–9	Dover	1548–9	New Romney
1549	Cambridge		

Edward VI (1537–53)

1537–44	Wulfhall	1537	Shrewsbury
1537–8	Canterbury	1537–8	Court
1537–8	Leicester	1537–8	Plymouth
1537–8	Southampton	1538	Cambridge
1538–9	Canterbury	1538–9	Plymouth
1538–9	Sandwich	1539	Cambridge
1539	London	1539–40	Bristol
1539–40	Faversham	1539–40	Plymouth
1539–40	Southampton	1540	Cambridge
1540	Court	1540	Ditton Park
1540	Shrewsbury	1540–1	Bristol
1540–1	Faversham	1540–1	Lydd
1540–1	New Romney	1541	Beverley
1541	Court	1541–2	Norwich
1542	Belvoir Castle	1542–3	Dover
1542–3	Folkestone	1543–4	Canterbury
1543–4	Folkestone	1543–4	Norwich
1544	Cambridge	1544–5	Canterbury
1544–5	Dover	1544–5	New Romney
1544–5	Norwich	1544–5	Plymouth
1546–7	Canterbury	1546–7	Norwich
1547	Court	1547	Dover

Appendix C

1547–8	Cambridge		1547–8	Canterbury
1547–8	Dover		c.1547–53	Grimsby
1548	Bristol		1548	Cambridge
1548	Court		1548–9	Court
1548–9	Faversham		1548–9	New Romney
1548–9	Southampton		1549	Court
1549–50	Norwich		1550	Cambridge
1550	Maldon		1550–1	Canterbury
1550–1	Dover		1550–1	Lydd
1551–2	Court		c.1551–6	Hoxton
1552	Court		1552	Lyme Regis
1552–3	Court		1552–3	Dover
1552–3	Lydd		1553–4	New Romney

Henry VIII (1491–1547)

1494–5	Dover		1505	Court
1505–6	Wells		1506–7	Thetford
1510	Court		1512	Court
1513	Calais		1515	Court
1515	London		1515–16	Plymouth
1516	London		1516–17	New Romney
1517	London		1517–18	Sandwich
1517–18	Shrewsbury		1518	Ely Priory
1518–19	Dover		1519	Court
1519	Coventry		1519	London
1520	Court		1520	London
1520–1	Canterbury		1520–1	Lydd
1520–1	Plymouth		1521	Court
1523–4	Plymouth		1523–4	Southampton
1524	Grimley		1524	Mettingham College
1524	Tiverton		1525	London
1525–6	Boston		1525–6	Dover
1525–6	Southampton		1526	Eltham
1526	London		1526–7	Lydd
1526–7	Mettingham College		1526–7	New Romney
1526–7	Plymouth		1526–7	Thetford
1526–8	Dartmouth		[1527]	Crowle
[1527]	London		[1527]	Shrewsbury
1527–8	Canterbury		1527–8	Selby
1527–8	Thetford		1528	Cambridge
[1528]	Grimley		1528–9	London
1528–9	Southampton		1529	Court
[1529]	Grimley		1529–30	Canterbury
1530	Court		1530	Hunstanton

1530–1	Belvoir Castle	1530–1	Bury St Edmunds
1530–1	Canterbury	1530–1	Faversham
1530–1	Lydd	1530–1	Southampton
1530–2	Southampton	1531	Court
1531	Dunheved	1531–2	Canterbury
1531–2	Great Yarmouth	1531–2	Oxford
1531–2	Leicester	1531–2	Thetford
1532	Shrewsbury	1532–3	Canterbury
1532–3	Durham	1532–3	Great Yarmouth
1532–3	Thetford	1533	Battenhall
1533	London	1533–4	Canterbury
1533–4	Dover	1533–4	Great Yarmouth
1533–4	Southampton	1533–4	Thetford
1534	Dunmow	1534	London
1534–5	Bristol	1534–5	Canterbury
1534–5	Norwich	1534–5	Oxford
1535	Worcester	1535–6	Bristol
1535–6	Dover	1535–6	Thetford
1536–7	Bristol	1536–7	Canterbury
1536–7	Dover	1536–7	Lydd
1536–7	Oxford	1536–7	Sandwich
c.1536–44	Wulfhall	1537	Court
1537–8	Sandwich	1537–8	Thetford
1538	Cambridge	1538	Court
1538–9	Canterbury	1538–9	Lydd
1538–9	Sandwich	1538–9	Windsor
1539	Court	1539–40	Canterbury
1539–40	Faversham	1539–40	Lydd
1539–40	New Romney	1539–40	Southampton
1539–40	Thetford	1540	Court
1540	London	1540	Shrewsbury
1540	York	1540–1	Bristol
1540–1	Canterbury	1540–1	Faversham
1540–1	Lydd	1540–1	New Romney
1541	Beverley	1541	Cambridge
1541	Court	1541–2	Dover
1541–2	Faversham	1541–2	Lydd
1542	Court	1542	York
1542–3	Canterbury	1544	Ditton Park
1545	Court	1545–6	Folkestone
1546	Court	1546–7	Canterbury
1546–7	Norwich	1547	Maldon

APPENDIX D
Biographical Notes

For the convenience of the reader unfamiliar with sixteenth-century biography, these brief entries note the families, major titles, seats, and characters of the early Tudor patrons referred to most frequently in this study. Drawn from the *Dictionary of National Biography, The Complete Peerage*, and various biographies noted in the bibliography, these notes are arranged both alphabetically by family name and chronologically by head of household to preserve the sense of historical flow.

Charles Brandon, Duke of Suffolk (?1484–1545)

Family
  I. Son of Sir William Brandon, standard-bearer to Henry VII, killed by Richard III at Bosworth.
 II. Married (1?) Margaret Mortymer; (2?) Ann Brown; (3) Mary Tudor, daughter of Henry VII (1514); (4) Katherine Willoughby.
III. Children by Ann Brown (?): Mary. Children by Catherine Willoughby: Henry, and Charles; all died young.

Titles

1509 Esquire of the Body
1510 Marshal of the King's Bench
1511 Marshal of the Household
1512 Knight of the Body
1513 Viscount Lisle
1514 Duke of Suffolk
1522 Warden of the Scottish Marches
1544 Steward of the Household

Seats
Suffolk Place, Southwark; Tattershall, Lincs.; Westhorpe Hall

Character
Charles Brandon, Duke of Suffolk, was probably best known for marrying the King's sister without royal permission and getting away with it. A particular favourite of the King's from his youth,

Brandon is conspicuous in Henry VIII's French campaign in 1513, and at virtually all important court occasions. In 1514, Henry sent Brandon to attend his sister Mary at her marriage to Louis XII, where he jousted at her coronation tournament. After Louis's death that year, Mary and Charles were secretly married in Paris, in spite of the rumour that Brandon already had two wives, Margaret Mortymer (whose marriage was annulled) and Ann Brown, who supposedly bore him a daughter, Mary. The couple returned to heavy fines and Henry's ire, but the King's anger passed quickly, and Brandon continued to receive titles, grants, and stewardships in abundance. In 1520 he was present at Henry's magnificent Field of the Cloth of Gold, and the Duke entertained Henry and Charles V with banquets and hunting at Suffolk Place in 1522. Considered an upstart by the traditional nobility, Brandon was ambitious and acquisitive, but he was, above all, the King's man. He supported the royal divorce, the prosecution of Wolsey and Catherine Howard, and served as High Steward for Anne Boleyn's coronation; he also figured prominently in the christenings of Elizabeth and Edward VI. As a special mark of his love, Henry buried Brandon at Windsor rather than Tattershall, as the Duke's will had stipulated.

HOWARD DUKES OF NORFOLK

John Howard, First Duke of Norfolk, of the Howard creation (?1430–85)

Family

I. Son of Sir Robert Howard and Margaret Mowbray, daughter of Thomas Mowbray, Duke of Norfolk.
II. Married (1) Catherine Moleyns; (2) Margaret Chedworth.
III. Children by Catherine Moleyns: Thomas, Earl of Surrey and second Duke of Norfolk; Anne, married Sir Edward Gorges; Isabel, married Sir Robert Mortimer; Jane, married Sir John Timperley; Margaret, married Sir John Syndam. Children by Margaret Chedworth: Catherine, married (1) John Bourchier, Lord Berners; (2) John Norreys.

Titles

1461	Knight; Constable of Colchester; Sheriff of Norfolk and Suffolk; King's Carver
1466	Vice Admiral for Norfolk and Suffolk
1466	Lord Howard
1466–74	Treasurer of the Household
1470	Baron Howard

1471	Deputy Governor of Calais
1483	Member of the Privy Council
1483	Duke of Norfolk; Earl Marshal of England
1483	Admiral of England

Seats

Stoke Neyland

Character

At about 13, John Howard took service as a henchman at the court of his kinsman the Duke of Norfolk, where he learned the skills that were to make him a formidable soldier and general. Strongly allied with the Yorkist cause, he was the first to proclaim Edward IV king in Suffolk in 1471. Howard became one of Edward's most trusted councillors, rewarded with huge land grants and martial commissions. At Edward's death, Howard smoothly switched his alliance to Richard III, acting as High Steward at the coronation; as marshal, he rode mounted into Westminster to clear the hall. He remained loyal to Richard, even though he was supposedly warned by the rhyme: 'Jack of Norffolke be not to bolde, | For Dykon thy maister is bought and solde'. Slain at Bosworth, the Duke was buried at Thetford and attainted immediately after Henry VII's accession.

Thomas Howard, Second Duke of Norfolk (1443–1524)

Family

I. Only son of John, first Duke of Norfolk, and Catherine Moleyns.

II. Married (1) Elizabeth, daughter of Sir Frederick Tilney, widow of Humphrey, Lord Berners; (2) Agnes, daughter of Sir Philip Tilney.

III. Children by Elizabeth: eight sons (five died young) including Thomas, the third Duke, and Edward, and three daughters. Children by Agnes: three sons, including William, Lord Howard of Effingham, and four daughters.

Titles

1473	Esquire of the Body to Edward IV
1478	Knight
1483	Earl of Surrey, Knight of the Garter, Privy Councillor, Lord Steward
1489	Lieutenant of the North
1501	Privy Councillor

1510 Earl Marshal
1513 Lieutenant of the North
1514 Duke of Norfolk
1520 Guardian of England
1521 Lord High Steward

Seats

Framlingham; Ashwellthorpe Hall

Character

Like his father, the second Duke was primarily known for his military prowess, although his political acumen made him a superlative statesman as well. He was supposedly educated at Thetford Priory, then served as a henchman to Edward IV. Transferring his loyalty to Richard III, he bore the sword of state at the coronation, was taken prisoner at Bosworth, was attainted, and served three-and-a-half years in the Tower for his pains. During his imprisonment, he set out to convince Henry VII of his loyalty; popular tradition credits him with defending his alliance with Richard III by claiming that he was bound to serve the annointed king, whoever he might be. He is reputed to have said that if the crown were placed on a post, he would fight for that post. Although these sentiments are apocryphal, Howard proved his loyalty by refusing to escape when he had the invitation in 1487. The demonstration apparently worked, for in 1489 Howard was released and restored to his earldom of Surrey, although the King kept most of his land.

After releasing him from the Tower, Henry VII continued to test his powerful vassal, chiefly with military commissions in the north, far from court. Howard was sent to quell the northern rebels who had murdered the Earl of Northumberland in 1489, and was kept busy fighting the Scots, becoming in the process the most important and successful general in England. By 1503 Howard was apparently secure in the King's good graces, for he headed the escort of Princess Margaret on her wedding progress to Scotland, was made executor of the King's will, and was present at all significant court occasions. Henry did not restore Howard's lands, however, until just before his death in 1507; no doubt the king wished to maintain some control over such a powerful nobleman.

In spite of his conservatism and his hatred for and feud with Cardinal Wolsey, Howard remained an influential councillor and respected general under Henry VIII. Howard's stupendous victory over the Scots at Flodden Field (at the age of 70) earned him the restoration of the family dukedom the following year, and the privilege of escorting Princess Mary to France for her wedding, where he offended Mary by dismissing all her English attendants and making himself generally disagreeable because he resented Wolsey's rising power. Still, he continued to be a prominent member of Henry VIII's court; in 1516, his wife served as godmother to the Princess Mary, and in 1520 Howard was left Guardian of the kingdom while Henry sported at the Field of the Cloth of Gold. Howard was politic enough to preside over the trial of the Duke of Buckingham in 1521; although he reportedly wept as he sentenced his friend and kinsman (with whose conservative sentiments he surely sympathized), his sorrow did not prevent him from accepting grants of the former Duke's lands as payment for his demonstration of loyalty to the King. Howard died peacefully in 1524 (an amazing achievement considering his decades of battle, his early alliance with the Yorkists, and his potentially threatening wealth and power), and was buried, like his father, at Thetford.

Thomas Howard II, Earl of Surrey and Third Duke of Norfolk (1473–1554)

Family

I. Son of Thomas, second Duke of Norfolk and Elizabeth Tilney.
II. Married (1) Lady Anne, daughter of Edward IV; (2) Elizabeth Stafford, daughter of Edward Stafford, third Duke of Buckingham, and Eleanor Percy, daughter of the fourth Earl of Northumberland.
III. Children by Anne: four who died young. Children by Elizabeth: Henry, Earl of Surrey; Thomas, Viscount Howard; Mary, who married Henry Fitzroy, Duke of Richmond and natural son of Henry VIII.

Titles

1497	Knight
1510	Knight of the Garter
1513–25	Lord Admiral
1514	Earl of Surrey
1516	Privy Councillor
1520–2	Lord-Lieutenant of Ireland
1522–47	Lord High Treasurer
1524	Duke of Norfolk
1533	Earl Marshal
1537–8	President of the Council of the North
1553	Privy Councillor (1547 attainted; 1553 restored)

Seats

Kenninghall; Tendring Hall; Ashwellthorpe Hall; Framlingham

Character

Thomas Howard continued the family tradition of formidable warriors and canny politicians. The earliest evidence of the latter talent is his marriage to Lady Anne, the King's sister-in-law and third daughter to Edward IV, to whom he had been betrothed by Richard III. During his father's lifetime, the Earl supported him both in war and in politics; he fought at Flodden field, opposed Wolsey's policies, and accompanied the royal wedding party to France in 1514. During the trial of his father-in-law, the Duke of Buckingham, Surrey was safely out of the country, serving in Ireland. On his return, he resumed his military career on the Scottish border; Skelton composed 'How the Duke of Albany, like a cowardly knight, ran away' as a tribute to the Earl's 1523 victory in the north.

Although the second Duke had never defeated Wolsey, his powerful enemy, the third Duke avenged his father by actively supporting the King's divorce, intriguing against the Cardinal, and promoting the King's marriage to his niece, Anne Boleyn. Henry rewarded the Duke with grants from the dissolved monasteries. In return, Howard demonstrated that his loyalty to his family was secondary to his loyalty to the king by presiding over the trial and execution of Anne Boleyn.

Howard had no more love for the King's second secretary, Cromwell, than he had had for the first. Taking advantage of the King's displeasure with Anne of Cleves, Howard was instrumental in Cromwell's fall, maintaining that '... it was merry in England before the new learning came up.' Howard's last court victory was arranging the marriage of Henry VIII to another of his nieces, Catherine Howard. After Catherine's brief and inglorious career, Howard's maltreatment of his family rebounded against him. Betrayed by his own household retainers, the Duke and his son were arrested for treason; at the trial, his wife, daughter, and even his mistress Elizabeth Holland, testified against him. Both the Duke and the Earl were sentenced to death, but the Duke was saved from execution by the timely death of Henry VIII. He remained a prisoner during the reign of Edward VI, but was released by Queen Mary and restored to his lands and titles. In 1553 he presided at the trial of the Duke of Northumberland. The following year he failed to subdue the rebels of Watt's rebellion, and retired to Kenninghall, where he died. He was buried at his seat at Framlingham.

Henry Howard, Earl of Surrey (1517–47)

Family
I. Son of Thomas, third Duke of Norfolk and Elizabeth Stafford, daughter of Edward, third Duke of Buckingham.
II. Married Frances de Vere, daughter of John, fifteenth Earl of Oxford.
III. Children by Frances: Thomas, fourth Duke of Norfolk; Henry, Earl of Northampton; Jane, married Charles Neville, Earl of Westmorland; Catherine, married Henry Lord Berkeley; Margaret, married Henry Lord Scrope.

Titles
1524   Earl of Surrey
1541   Knight of the Garter, Steward of Cambridge
1543   Cupbearer
1544   Marshal of the Army
1545   Lieutenant-General of the King

Seats
Kenninghall; Mount Surrey

Character
Surrey was one of the first English aristocrats to earn a lasting reputation in literary history as the poet who experimented with the Petrarcan sonnet and introduced blank verse. During his lifetime, he was known as a soldier and courtier whose vanity and hot temper led him into reckless exploits.

In his youth, Surrey divided his time between the households of his father at Stoke Hall, Suffolk, and that of his grandfather at Hunsdon, Hertfordshire. He was carefully educated, perhaps by Leland, who was his brother's tutor in 1525, and by John Clerk, who dedicated his 'Treatise of Nobility' to the Duke of Norfolk. From an early age, Surrey showed a facility for languages and for poetry.

A childhood companion of Henry Fitzroy, the son of Henry VIII, Surrey was early considered as a husband for Princess Mary. However, he married the Earl of Oxford's daughter in 1531, and continued to involve himself at the royal court. With his father, he took part as Earl Marshal in the trial of Anne Boleyn, his cousin. He fought for the King during the Pilgrimage of Grace and in the north, jousted at the 1540 tournament for Anne of Cleves, and participated in Cromwell's fall.

By 1537, however, Surrey's temper was already leading him into difficulties. He served a five-month term of confinement at Windsor for striking a courtier, John a Leigh, who accused the Earl of being sympathetic to the Pilgrimage of Grace rebels. In 1543, he found himself in the Fleet, charged with eating meat in Lent and the malicious mischief of throwing stones at windows in London. He was soon released, for he fought in France the same year and entertained the Duke de Najera in 1544. At about this time, the Earl's household included the poets Hadrianus Junius, tutor to Surrey's son, and Thomas Churchyard, then a page.

Surrey's recklessness continued to haunt him, first as a brave but impetuous soldier in France in 1544–6, then as an intriguer at court, for as Henry VIII grew closer to death, Surrey and Somerset found themselves bitter rivals for power over the young prince Edward. Unfortunately for Surrey, Somerset was the cleverer of the two, and the Earl found himself, in 1547, on trial for his life. The principal accusation against him was that he had assumed the arms of Edward I although the College of Arms had denied him permission to do so. Somerset accused the Earl of treason and of trying to take the throne from Edward, of pandering his sister Mary to Henry VIII, of foreign dress, manners, and retainers, and of strident Catholicism. Surrey eloquently denied the charges, but was nevertheless found guilty and beheaded.

Thomas Howard III, Earl of Surrey and Fourth Duke of Norfolk (1536–72)

Family

I. Son of Henry, Earl of Surrey and Frances de Vere.
II. Married (1) Margaret Audley; (2) Mary Fitzalan, daughter of the Twelfth Earl of Arundel.
III. Children by Mary Fitzalan: Philip, Earl of Arundel.

Titles

1553	Earl of Surrey, Knight of the Bath
1554	Duke of Norfolk, Earl Marshal
1558	Lord-Lieutenant of Norfolk and Suffolk
1559	Knight of the Garter, Lieutenant-General of North
1562–72	Privy Councillor

Seats

Kenninghall; Tendring Hall; Framlingham

Character

After his father's execution, young Howard was removed to the wardship of his aunt, Mary Fitzroy, Duchess of Richmond and wife to the natural son of Henry VIII. Stridently Protestant, the Duchess engaged John Foxe to teach the young Earl. When his grandfather was released from prison, he promptly removed his heir from protestant influences and placed him in the Catholic care of Bishop White. Young Howard assisted at Mary's coronation, and served as First Gentleman of the Chamber to King Philip, who stood as godfather to Thomas's son Philip. Throughout the reign of Elizabeth, Howard continued to serve as a councillor and general.

MANNERS EARLS OF RUTLAND

Thomas Manners, First Earl of Rutland (?1491–1543)

Family
I. Son of Sir George Manners, twelfth Baron Roos, and Anne St Leger.
II. Married (1) Elizabeth Lovell; (2) Eleanor Paston.
III. Children by Eleanor Paston: Henry, second Earl of Rutland, and Roger of Uffington.

Titles

1513	Baron Roos
1521	Cupbearer
1522	Warden of the East and Middle Marches
1525	Knight, Knight of the Garter, Earl of Rutland
1536	Privy Councillor
1540	Lord Chamberlain to Anne of Cleves and Catherine Howard
1542	Constable of Nottingham Castle, Warden of the Scottish Marches

Seats
Belvoir Castle; Enfield Chase; Holywell, Shoreditch

Character

Manners distinguished himself as a soldier, and was a particular favourite of Henry VIII's throughout his reign. He accompanied the King to the Field of the Cloth of Gold, and served at both the coronation and the trial of Anne Boleyn. The King was generous to his friend, granting him monastic lands including Croxton, Beverley, Warter, and Rievaulx Abbeys at the dissolution. Manners divided his time between the court, where he served as Chamberlain to two of Henry's queens, and the north, where he defended the King's realms against the Scottish threat.

Henry Manners, Second Earl of Rutland (1526–63)

Family

I. Son of Thomas, Earl of Rutland, and Eleanor Paston.
II. Married (1) Margaret Neville, daughter of Ralph, Earl of Westmorland; (2) Bridget, daughter of John Lord Hussey.
III. Children by Margaret Neville: Edward, third Earl of Rutland.

Titles

1543	Lord Roos, Earl of Rutland
1544	Knight
1549	Warden of East and Middle Marches
1559	Knight of the Garter, Lord-Lieutenant of Rutland
1560	President of the Council of the North

Seats

Whittington's College, London; Belvoir Castle; Holywell, Shoreditch

Character

Henry spent much of his early life at court, acting as a page of honour at the wedding of Mary Tudor, as an official mourner at Henry VIII's funeral, and as bearer of the spurs for the coronation of Edward VI. In 1547 he assumed the family position of Constable of Nottingham Castle and Warden of Sherwood Forest. A member of the Protestant Reform party, he was a witness against Thomas Seymour, brother of the Protector, and was imprisoned on Mary's accession for his alliance with the party of Lady Jane Grey. Eventually he was released and put to work as a soldier. With Elizabeth's accession, he quickly became one of the Queen's favourites at court.

PERCY EARLS OF NORTHUMBERLAND

Henry Percy, Fourth Earl of Northumberland (1446–89)

Family

I. Son of Henry, third Earl of Northumberland.
II. Married Maud Herbert, daughter of William, Earl of Pembroke.

Appendix D

III. Children by Maud: Henry; William; Alan; Josceline; Eleanor, married Edward Stafford, Duke of Buckingham; Ann, married William Fitzalan, Earl of Arundel; Elizabeth.

Titles

1469	Earl of Northumberland
1470	Constable of Bamborough Castle, Warden of East and Middle Marches
1474	Privy Councillor, Knight of the Garter, Sheriff of Northumberland
1482	Great Chamberlain
1484	Lord Paynings

Seats
Topcliffe

Character
Loyal to the Lancasters, the third Earl was attainted in 1461 and his son was removed to the custody of Edward IV. Edward granted the earldom to John Neville, Lord Montague, but restored it to the Percys in 1469. Percy tried to remain neutral during the War of the Roses, and in 1472 his father's attainder was reversed, restoring the Percys to their properties. Although he was with Richard III at his coronation, Percy was also negotiating with Henry Tudor, and held his troops back during the Battle of Bosworth. Nevertheless, he was taken prisoner, but was quickly pardoned and restored once again to his position. Thereafter Percy remained a loyal servant to the King, although he was chiefly occupied in the north, where he was slain in the rebellion of John a Chamber. He was buried in the Percy chantry at Beverley Minster.

Henry Algernon Percy, Fifth Earl of Northumberland, 'The Magnificent' (1478–1527)

Family
I. Son of Henry, fourth Earl of Northumberland and Maud Herbert, daughter of William, Earl of Pembroke.
II. Married Catherine Spencer.
III. Children by Catherine: Henry Algernon, sixth Earl of Northumberland; Thomas; Ingelram; Margaret, married Henry Clifford, Earl of Cumberland; Maud, married William Lord Conyers.

Titles

1481	Knight of the Bath
1489	Earl of Northumberland
1495	Knight of the Garter
1503	Warden of the East Marches
1522	Councillor of the North

Seats

Wressle; Leconfield; Topcliffe

Character

Percy spent his youth at the royal court as a ward of Margaret Beaufort, the King's mother, after the murder of his father by northern rebels. He participated in many court occasions, including Arthur's investiture as Prince of Wales and Prince Henry's induction as Knight of the Bath. After Percy received control of his lands in 1498, he divided his time between his responsibilities in the north and at the royal court. Leland's account of Princess Margaret's Wedding Progress to Scotland describes the Earl as a magnificently dressed and attentive host, a display for which Henry VII fined him heavily. Percy served Henry VIII at the French campaign in 1513, and allied himself with his conservative friends and kinsmen Buckingham and Norfolk in their machinations against Cardinal Wolsey. In 1516 Percy found himself in Fleet Prison for his actions against Wolsey, although the Cardinal was instrumental in his release. Unlike his brother-in-law Buckingham, Percy was quick to learn the lessons his sovereigns were trying to teach. After being fined for ostentation by Henry VII, Percy's style grew more subdued. After his brief stay in prison, Percy was far more careful about his political activities, preferring to build his own strong court in the north. In 1520, he served as a judge at the lists at the Field of the Cloth of Gold, then returned to his responsibilities in Northumberland. There he died, and was buried at the Percy chantry in Beverley Minster.

Henry Algernon Percy, Sixth Earl of Northumberland, 'The Unthrifty' (?1502-37)

Family

  I. Son of Henry, fifth Earl of Northumberland and Catherine Spencer.
 II. Married Mary Talbot, daughter of George, fourth Earl of Shrewsbury.
III. No issue.

Appendix D

Titles

1519	Knight
1522	Councillor of the North
1527	Earl of Northumberland, Lord Poynings, Warden of the East and Middle Marches
1531	Knight of the Garter
1532	Privy Councillor, Sheriff of the North
1536	President of the North

Seats

Wressle; Leconfield; Topcliffe

Character

The sixth Earl is best remembered for having had the misfortune to fall in love with Anne Boleyn, an affair that ruined his health, his marriage to Mary Talbot, and his political career. Although his father was no friend to Cardinal Wolsey, the younger Percy spent years at Wolsey's household as a page before assuming his martial responsibilities in the north. Banished to the north after the Cardinal discovered his relationship with the King's new paramour, Percy was thereafter constantly ill, in debt, unwelcome at court, and on bad terms with his family. Although he should have revelled in his charge of arresting the Cardinal, he appears to have taken no joy in the mission. Assigned to the trial of Anne Boleyn, he grew ill and left the court. During the Pilgrimage of Grace, he remained loyal to the Crown, although his family sympathized with the rebels and tried to persuade him to throw his force in with them. His brother, Thomas, was executed for his part in the rebellion, but Thomas's son, Thomas, acceded to the Earldom when Henry died childless in 1537.

Edward Seymour, Duke of Somerset and Lord Protector of England (?1500–52)

Family

I. Son of Sir John Seymour and Margaret Wentworth.
II. Married (1) Catherine Fillol; (2) Anne Stanhope.
III. Children by Catherine Fillol: John (died in the Tower, 1552); Edward, second Duke of Somerset. Children by Anne Stanhope: Edward (died young); Edward, Earl of Hertford; Henry, married Joan Percy; Edward; Anne, married (1) John Dudley, Earl of Warwick, (2) Sir Edward Unton; Margaret; Jane; Mary; Katherine; Elizabeth.

Titles

- 1523   Knight
- 1524   Esquire of the King's Household, Master of the Horse to Henry Fitzroy, son to Henry VIII
- 1529   Esquire of the Body to Henry VIII
- 1535   Gentleman of the Privy Chamber
- 1536   Viscount Beauchamp, Privy Councillor
- 1537   Earl of Hertford
- 1540   Knight of the Garter
- 1542   Warden of the Scottish Marches, Lord Admiral, Lord Chamberlain
- 1545   Lieutenant-General of the North
- 1547   Lord Protector, Lord High Steward, Treasurer, Earl Marshall, Baron Seymour, Duke of Somerset
- 1549   Privy Councillor, Gentleman of the King's Chamber

Seats

Wulfhall; Somerset House (on the Strand); Glastonbury

Character

Seymour was said to have been educated at Oxford and Cambridge, and served in 1514 as a page to Princess Mary at the French marriage. Early a favourite of Henry VIII, Seymour profited tremendously from the dissolution of the monasteries. His fortunes took a huge leap when his sister Jane attracted the romantic attention of Henry VIII, who was no longer captivated by Anne Boleyn and desperate for a male heir. By 1535, Seymour, his wife, and his sister were installed at Greenwich, and after the King's marriage, land grants and titles came flowing to the Earl.

The death of Queen Jane did not mar the career of her brother, who entertained Henry VIII and Cromwell for four days at Wulfhall in 1539. Seymour was sent to meet Anne of Cleves in 1539, and dispatched against Cromwell in 1540. He was also instrumental in the prosecution of the Norfolks, who considered him an upstart and refused to ally their families by proposed marriages. After the death of the Earl of Surrey, Seymour acquired some of the confiscated Howard properties, adding considerably to his already great holdings.

At the time of Henry VIII's death, the most powerful noblemen in the realm were Seymour and the Howards. With Surrey dead and the third Duke safely ensconced in the Tower, it was not difficult for Seymour to effect the major coup of his career, taking control of the young Edward VI and establishing, for the first time, the power of the Calvinist Reform party.

After Seymour became Lord Protector, he attempted to rule fairly and well. He tried to end the troubles between England and Scotland by proposing a marriage between Edward VI and the infant Mary, but this policy failed utterly, strengthening Scotland's alliance with Catholic France. In 1549, Seymour's chief enemy, Warwick, led the subterfuge that culminated in Seymour's deposition that year. Citing the failure of the Scottish policy, the war with France, general economic depression in England, the treason of the Protector's brother Thomas, the increase in enclosures, and the Duke's rapacity in grabbing church lands, Warwick and his party succeeded only briefly in stopping Somerset. He was quickly pardoned and restored to some, but not all, of his property. In 1551 Warwick tried again, and this time was successful in having Seymour arrested and imprisoned in the Tower. Seymour was cleared of the charge of treason, but found guilty of felony and beheaded. When he died, the people supposedly dipped their kerchiefs in his blood.

Seymour was apparently a truly pious Protestant reformer, dedicated to the good of the realm. Unfortunately, he was also extremely ambitious and acquisitive. His family relationships, which had catapulted him into power, also made his life difficult. He was utterly unable to control his brother Thomas, who was equally ambitious but not so clever or well intentioned. Seymour's wife, Anne, and his brother's wife, Queen-dowager Catherine Parr, constantly squabbled for precedence. One of his chief errors in judgement was probably trusting to the affections of his rather cold nephew, King Edward VI, who watched a disguising as his uncle died.

Thomas Seymour, Baron Seymour of Sudeley (1508–49)

Family

I. Son of Sir John Seymour and Margaret Wentworth.
II. Married Catherine Parr, widow of Henry VIII.
III. Child by Catherine: Mary, died young.

Titles

1536	Knight, Gentleman of the Privy Chamber
1542–3	Marshal of the English Army in the Netherlands
1544	Master of the Ordinance
1547	Privy Councillor, Baron Seymour, Knight of the Garter, Lord Admiral

Seats

Sudeley Castle; Holt, Cheshire; Seymour Place (at Temple Bar)

Character

Like his brother Edward, Thomas Seymour's fortunes rose with those of his sister Jane. He distinguished himself in the military, and appeared often at court. In 1539 he met Anne of Cleves as she came to marry the King, and rode as a challenger in the tournament of 1540. During 1540–2 he served in Vienna, reporting on the Turkish wars. At Edward VI's coronation he participated in the jousts, and entertained the court that evening at Seymour Place.

After Edward became Protector, Thomas constantly intrigued for a share of his brother's power, chiefly through trying to arrange powerful marriages for himself. He courted Princess Elizabeth (and, according to the French ambassador, Princess Mary and Anne of Cleves), but was rejected, so he consoled himself by marrying Catherine Parr, widow of Henry VIII. Thomas tried to gain control over his nephew, the young King, by giving him money and attempting to marry him to Lady Jane Grey, who was then living in Seymour's household. All of his machinations failed, but Thomas continued to be proud and acquisitive, making deals with pirates for their mutual profit. After the death of Catherine Parr, Thomas lost no time in renewing his suit to Princess Elizabeth, who later remarked that he was a 'man of much wit and very little judgement'. In 1549 he was arrested for his activities, attainted, and summarily executed.

STAFFORD DUKES OF BUCKINGHAM

Humphrey Stafford, First Duke of Buckingham (1402–60)

Family

I. Son of Edmund, fifth Earl of Stafford, and Anne, daughter of Thomas, Duke of Gloucester, son to Edward III.
II. Married Anne, daughter of Ralph Neville, first Earl of Westmorland.
III. Children by Anne: Humphrey, married Margaret Beaufort; Henry, married Margaret Beaufort (widow of Edmund Tudor and mother of Henry VII); John, Earl of Wiltshire; Anne, married (1) Aubrey de Vere, Earl of Oxford, (2) Sir Thomas Cobham; Joanna, married (1) William, Viscount Beaumont, (2) Sir William Knyvet; Elizabeth; Margaret; Katherine, married John Talbot, third Earl of Shrewsbury.

Appendix D

Titles

1403	Earl of Stafford
1421	Knight
1424	Privy Councillor
1429	Knight of the Garter
1430	Constable of France, Governor of Paris
1431	Count of Perche, Normandy
1438	Earl of Buckingham
1442	Lieutenant of the Marches
1444	Duke of Buckingham
1450	Warden of the Cinque Ports

Seats
Penshurst; Maxstoke Castle; Writtle

Character
One of the greatest landholders in England by the time of his death, Stafford was known as a soldier and politician. By 1445, he was one of the chief noblemen in the realm, and protested when the Duke of Warwick was given precedence over him. By act of Parliament, the dukes were ordered to alternate in precedence, but by 1447 Stafford was granted the special privilege of coming before all the Dukes in the country except those of royal blood as a reward for arresting the Duke of Gloucester at Bury. Stafford also received Gloucester's Kent estates, including Penshurst, which remained in the family until the reign of Elizabeth. During the York–Lancaster rivalry, Stafford kept careful balance between the two factions, although his sympathies seem to have been drawn to the Lancaster cause. After the battle of St Albans, however, he remained loyal to the Yorks, until he was killed by Kentish rebels at the battle of Northampton.

Henry Stafford, Second Duke of Buckingham (1455–83)

Family
I. Son of Humphrey, eldest son of Humphrey, first Duke of Buckingham, and Margaret, daughter of Edmund Beaufort, second Duke of Somerset.
II. Married Catherine Woodville, sister of Queen Elizabeth (Woodville) (Catherine later married Jasper Tudor).
III. Children by Catherine Woodville: Edward, third Duke of Buckingham, married Eleanor Percy, daughter of the fourth Earl of Northumberland; Henry, Earl of Wiltshire; Humphrey;

Elizabeth, married Robert Redcliffe, Earl of Sussex; Anne, married (1) Sir William Herbert, (2) George Hastings, Earl of Huntingdon.

Titles

1460   Duke of Buckingham, Constable of Nottingham Castle
1465   Knight, Knight of the Bath
1474   Knight of the Garter
1478   High Steward
1483   Great Chamberlain at Richard III's coronation, Lord High Constable, Warden of the Cinque Ports

Seats

Penshurst; Maxstoke Castle; Writtle; Brecon

Character

In spite of his marriage to the Queen's sister, Buckingham allied himself with Richard III after the death of Edward IV, for which Richard rewarded him with great power in the central and east shires, as well as with valuable lands there. He was reputed to be 'neither unlearned and of nature marvelously well spoken', and used his eloquence to convince the citizens to support Richard. Stafford figure most prominently in Richard's coronation, and received all the de Bohan estates afterward. Then, for unknown reasons, Stafford revolted and began plotting with his kinsman Henry Tudor, for which he was declared traitor in 1483. By October of that year the Duke was in hiding in Shropshire, where a retainer betrayed him for the £1,000 price on his head. He was tried on 1 November, executed on 2 November, and his heirs forfeited his lands.

Edward Stafford, Third Duke of Buckingham (1478–1521)

Family

I. Son of Henry, second Duke of Buckingham and Catherine Woodville, sister of Queen Elizabeth (Woodville).
II. Married Eleanor, daughter of Henry, fourth Earl of Northumberland.
III. Children by Eleanor: Henry, Baron Stafford; Elizabeth, married Thomas Howard, third Duke of Norfolk; Catherine, married Ralph Neville, fourth Earl of Westmorland; Mary, married George Neville, Baron Abergavenny.

Titles

1485	Knight of the Bath, Duke of Buckingham
1495	Knight of the Garter
1509	Lord High Constable, Lord High Steward for coronation
1510	Privy Councillor

Seats

Thornbury; Penshurst; Brecon; London; Writtle; Newport; Bletchingly; Maxstoke

Character

Stafford spent his early years at court as a ward of Margaret Beaufort, the King's mother. Since his father had demonstrated his loyalty to the Tudor cause by his execution at the hands of Richard III, Stafford quickly regained the titles and properties that his family had lost. Supposedly educated at Cambridge, he was often at court, meeting Katherine of Aragon when she came for her wedding to Prince Arthur, and keeping active in government. In 1519 he entertained Henry VIII at Penshurst, and was with the King for the Field of the Cloth of Gold and during the visit of Charles V in 1521. Unlike his friends and relatives Norfolk and Northumberland, Buckingham was not a clever politician. There is every evidence that Buckingham considered himself equal to the King in lineage, wealth, and power, and the Duke's vanity did not encourage him to temper his ambitions. Buckingham deeply resented the power of Wolsey, whom he considered an upstart, but he was by no means astute enough politically to defy the Cardinal. In 1521 he was arrested for treason, with Norfolk as the president at his trial and his own chancellor, Robert Gilbert, and confessor, Delacourt, giving testimony against him. Buckingham went to his death on Tower Hill unrepentant. Although vain and foolish, Buckingham appears to have been genuinely pious, and was a great patron of art and education.

THE DE VERE EARLS OF OXFORD

John de Vere, Thirteenth Earl of Oxford (1442–1513)

Family

I. Son of John, twelfth Earl of Oxford, and Elizabeth Howard.
II. Married (1) Margaret, daughter of Richard Neville, Earl of Salisbury; (2) Elizabeth Beaumont.
III. Children by Margaret: John, died young.

Titles

1462	Earl of Oxford
1464	Knight of the Bath
1470	High Constable
1485	Hereditary Chamberlain, Privy Councillor, Constable of Rising Castle and the Tower of London, High Steward of Lancaster, Admiral of England
1486	Knight of the Garter

Seats

Earls Colne; Castle Hedingham

Character

De Vere is frequently mentioned in the Paston Letters, one of the chief sources for his biography. The family had long supported the Lancasters, an alliance for which the twelfth Earl and his eldest son were executed in 1462. By 1463 their attainder was reversed in favour of John de Vere, but by 1468 the Earl was imprisoned in the Tower for suspicion of Lancaster leanings. By 1470 he was in France, plotting with Warwick to put Henry VI back in power, and briefly enjoyed favour during the restoration before losing once again to Edward IV at Barnet. Oxford fled to France, and renewed his attack in 1475, but was arrested and attainted once again. Imprisoned at the Castle of Hammes, Calais, he managed to escape in 1484 and joined Henry VII for his invasion, reaping honours and properties when the Tudors emerged victorious. Although he continued to be a trusted general under Henry VII, he was heavily fined by the King for ostentation and maintenance during the King's week-long visit to Castle Hedingham in 1498. Thereafter, he was frequently ill, and retired from court life.

John de Vere, Fourteenth Earl of Oxford (1499–1526)

Family

I. Son of Sir George de Vere, brother of the thirteenth Earl of Oxford, and Margaret, daughter of Sir William Stafford.
II. Married Anne, daughter of Thomas Howard, second Duke of Norfolk, and Agnes Tilney.
III. No issue.

Titles

1513	Lord Plaiz, Hereditary Great Chamberlain, Earl of Oxford

Seats

Earls Colne; Castle Hedingham

Character

The fourteenth Earl led a short and unremarkable life. He was never truly able to establish his own household or reputation, for he spent most of his life in the custody of his father-in-law, the Duke of Norfolk, because the Earl was incapable of managing his properties or finances. He did appear with Henry VIII at the Field of the Cloth of Gold in 1520, but was back in Norfolk's household by 1523. Afterward, he is unremarked in chronicles of court activities. At his death, his body was returned to the family property at Earl's Colne, and his title passed to his second cousin.

John de Vere, Fifteenth Earl of Oxford, 'The Good Earl' (?1499–1540)

Family

I. Son of John de Vere and Alice Kilrington; grandson of Robert de Vere; great-grandson of the eleventh Earl of Oxford.
II. Married Elizabeth Trussell.
III. Children by Elizabeth: John, sixteenth Earl of Oxford; Aubrey; Geoffrey; another son; four daughters.

Title

1510	Esquire of the Body
1513	Knight
1526	Earl of Oxford, Hereditary Great Chamberlain
1527	Knight of the Garter
1530	Privy Councillor

Seats

Earls Colne; Castle Hedingham

Character

Called 'Little John of Campes', de Vere is best known as the first Protestant earl of Oxford and as a friend to Henry VIII. He constantly supported the King against Queen Katherine, against Wolsey, and against Anne Boleyn, although he bore the crown at Anne's coronation. He appeared with Henry during the Field of the Cloth of Gold and during the visit of Charles V in 1522. Oxford was knighted after the Battle of Spurs in 1513, but he does not appear to have been much inclined to warfare. He died at Earls Colne in 1540, and was buried at Hedingham.

John de Vere, Sixteenth Earl of Oxford (?1512–62)

Family
I. Son of John, fifteenth Earl of Oxford, and Elizabeth, daughter of Sir Edward Trussell.
II. Married (1) Dorothy Neville, daughter of Ralph, fourth Earl of Westmorland, (2) Margaret Golding.
III. Children by Dorothy: Katherine, married Edward Lord Windsor. Children by Margaret: Edward, seventeenth Earl of Oxford; Mary, married Peregrine Bertie, Lord Willoughby.

Titles
1526	Lord Bolebec
1540	Earl of Oxford
1547	Knight
1550–8	Joint Lord-Lieutenant of Essex
1553	Privy Councillor

Seats
Earls Colne; Castle Hedingham

Character
De Vere served as a captain in the Boulogne campaign in 1544, and was frequently at court as the Hereditary Great Chamberlain. Politically, he maintained a neutral stand. Although he was a member of Jane Grey's party in 1553, he quickly declared for Mary, and bore the sword during her London progress. Mary, however, doubted his Catholicism, and did not particularly favour him at court. He did become one of Elizabeth's favourites, and entertained the Queen for a week in August 1561 at his Castle in Hedingham. The Earl spent most of his life attending to his various responsibilities in Essex.

Select Bibliography

I. MANUSCRIPTS

Bodleian Library

Bodl. MS Eng. hist. b. 208: Second Northumberland Household Book.

British Library

Additional MS 6113:	Court ceremonials, Edward III–Elizabeth.
7099:	Heron's accounts, 1491–1505.
7100:	Extracts from household accounts of Henry VIII.
18825:	Warrants, 1496–1506.
24459:	Edward I's 'Jocalia', Whitsun Feast.
34213:	Buckingham household accounts.
35182:	Royal household accounts, 1531–2.
38174:	Court ceremonials, 1486–1503.
40859B:	Buckingham household accounts.
59900:	Household accounts, Henry VIII.
Arundel MS 97:	Household accounts, Henry VIII.
Egerton MS 2605:	Richard Gibson's 1527 accounts.
2623:	Dramatic miscellanies.
Harleian MS 69:	Tournaments.
1667:	Buckingham household accounts.
Lansdowne MS 824:	Chaloner accounts.
Sloane MS 1494:	St George's Day Orders.

West Sussex Record Office

Petworth Archives, 3538–47: Plans of Wressle.

II. TEXTS OF PLAYS

Albion Knight: Farmer, *Six Anonymous Plays*.
The Book of Sir Thomas More: Greg (ed.), Malone Society Reprints, 93.
Calisto and Melebea: Axton, *Three Rastell Plays*.
Chester Cycle: Lumiansky and Mills, *The Chester Mystery Cycle*.
Four Elements: Axton, *Three Rastell Plays*.
The Four PP: Boas, *Five Pre-Shakespearean Comedies*.

Fulgens and Lucrece: Nelson, *The Plays of Henry Medwall*.
Gammer Gurton's Needle: Creeth, *Tudor Plays*.
Gentleness and Nobility: Axton, *Three Rastell Plays*.
Godly Queen Hester: Farmer, *Six Anonymous Plays*.
Hick Scorner: Lancashire, *Two Tudor Interludes*.
Jack Juggler: Smith (ed.), Malone Society Reprints, 56.
Jacob and Esau: Crow (ed.), Malone Society Reprints, 94.
Johan Johan: Bevington, *Medieval Drama*.
King Johan: Pafford (ed.), Malone Society Reprints, 66.
Lusty Juventus: Somerset, *Four Tudor Interludes*.
Lydgate Mummings: MacCracken, *The Minor Poems of John Lydgate Part II*.
Magnificence: Neuss, *Magnificence*.
Mankind: Eccles, *The Macro Plays*.
Nature: Nelson, *The Plays of Henry Medwall*.
A Play of Love: Somerset, *Four Tudor Interludes*.
The Play of the Weather: Bevington, *Medieval Drama*.
Pride of Life: Davis, *Non-Cycle Plays*.
Prima Pastorum: Cawley, *Wakefield Pageants*.
Rafe Roister Doister: Creeth, *Tudor Plays*.
Respublica: Greg, *Respublica*.
Secunda Pastorum: Cawley, *Wakefield Paqeants*.
Shakespeare: Harbage, *Complete Works*.
Towneley Cycle (the Wakefield Plays): Rose, *The Wakefield Mystery Plays*.
Wealth and Health: Greg (ed.), Malone Society Reprints, 32.
Wisdom Who is Christ (or *Mind, Will & Understanding*): Eccles, *The Macro Plays*.
Wit and Science: Bevington, *Medieval Drama*.
The World and the Child (*Mundus et Infans*): Manly, *Specimens*.
York Cycle: Smith, *York Plays*.
Youth: Lancashire, *Two Tudor Interludes*.

III. WORKS CONSULTED

ALSOP, J. D., 'Entertainments of the Marquess of Northhampton in 1553', *Notes and Queries*, 222 (Dec. 1977), 500–1.
ANGLO, SYDNEY, 'The Court Festivals of Henry VII', *Bulletin of the John Rylands Library*, 40 (1960–1), 12–45.
—— *Spectacle, Pageantry, and Early Tudor Policy* (Oxford: Clarendon Press, 1969).
—— 'William Cornish in a Play, Pageants, Prison, and Politics', *Review of English Studies*, NS 10, no. 40 (1959), 347–60.
ARLOTT, JOHN (ed.), *John Speed's England: A Coloured Facsimilie*

of the First Edition (London, 1626; repr. 4 vols. London: Phoenix House Ltd., 1953).
ARMIN, ROBERT, *A Nest of Ninnies* (vol. i of *The Collected Works of Robert Armin*, London, 1608; repr. New York: Johnson Reprint Corp., 1972).
BACON, FRANCIS, *History of the Reign of King Henry VII* (vol. vi of *The Collected Works of Francis Bacon*, ed. James Spedding; London: Longman and Co., 1857–74).
BALE, JOHN H., *King Johan*, ed. W. Pafford (Malone Society, 66; London: Oxford University Press, 1931).
BARRY, PATRICIA, *The King in Tudor Drama* (Salzburg: Institut für englische Sprache und Literatur, 1977).
BAUGH, ALBERT C., *Literary History of England*, 2nd edn. (Englewood Cliffs, NJ: Prentice Hall, Inc., 1948).
BEAN, JOHN MALCOLM WILLIAM, *The Estates of the Percy Family* (Oxford: Oxford University Press, 1958).
BENNETT, HENRY STANLEY, *English Books and Readers 1475 to 1557*, 2nd edn. (Cambridge: Cambridge University Press, 1969).
BERGENROTH, GUSTAV ADOLPH, GAVANGOS, DON PASCAUL DE, *et al.*, *Calendar of Letters, Dispatches and State Papers Relating to the Negotiations between England and Spain*, 13 vols. (London: HMSO, 1862–1954).
BERGERON, DAVID M., *Twentieth-Century Criticism of English Masques, Pageants and Entertainments* (San Antonio: Trinity University Press, 1972).
BERNARD, JULES E., *The Prosody of the Tudor Interlude* (New Haven: Yale University Press, 1939).
BEVINGTON, DAVID M., *From 'Mankind' to Marlowe: Growth of Structure in the Popular Drama of Tudor England* (Cambridge, Mass.: Harvard University Press, 1962).
—— *Medieval Drama* (Boston: Houghton Mifflin Co., 1975).
—— *Tudor Drama and Politics: A Critical Approach to Topical Meaning* (Cambridge, Mass.: Harvard University Press, 1968).
BLACKLEY, F. D., and HERMANSEN, GUSTAV (eds.), *The Household Book of Queen Isabella of England for the Fifth Regnal Year of Edward II, 8th July 1311 to 7th July 1312* (Edmonton: University of Alberta Press, 1971).
BLACKSTONE, MARY A., 'Notes towards a Patrons' Calendar', *Records of Early English Drama Newsletter*, 1 (1981), 1–11.
BOAS, FREDERICK S. (ed.), *Five Pre-Shakespearian Comedies* (London: Oxford University Press, 1934).
—— *University Drama in the Tudor Age* (Oxford: Clarendon Press, 1914).

BRADBROOK, MURIEL C., *The Rise of the Common Player* (Cambridge, Mass.: Harvard Univeristy Press, 1962).
BRAITHWAITE, RICHARD, *Some Rules of and Orders for the Government of the House of an Earle* (London: R. Triphook, 1821).
BRAY, ROGER, 'More Light on Early Tudor Pitch', *Early Music*, 8 (1980), 35–42.
BRENAN, GERALD, *A History of the House of Percy from the Earliest Times down to the Present Century*, 2 vols. (London: Freemantle and Co., 1902).
BRETT, GERARD, *Dinner is Served: A Study in Manners* (Hamden, Conn.: Archon Books, 1969).
BREWER, JOHN SHERREN, GAIRDNER, JAMES, and BRODIE, R. H. (eds.), *Letters and Papers, Foreign and Domestic, of the Reign of Henry VIII*, 21 vols. (London: HMSO, 1862–1918); *Addenda*, 2 vols. (1929–32).
BRISTOL, MICHAEL, *Carnival and Theater: Plebeian Culture and the Structure of Authority in Renaissance England* (New York and London: Methuen, 1985).
BROCKETT, OSCAR, *History of the Theatre*, 3rd edn. (Boston: Allyn and Bacon, Inc., 1977).
BROOKE, C. F. TUCKER, *The Tudor Drama* (Boston: Houghton Mifflin, 1911).
BROWN, HOWARD MAYER, 'Choral Music in the Renaissance', *Early Music*, 6 (Apr. 1978) 164–9.
BROWN, RAWDON, and CAVENDISH-BENTINCK, GEORGE (eds.), *State Papers and Manuscripts Relating to English Affairs, Existing in the Archives and Collections of Venice*, 7 vols. (London: HMSO, 1864–90).
BULLOCK-DAVIS, CONSTANCE (ed.), *Menestrellorum Multitudo: Minstrels at a Royal Feast* (Cardiff: University of Wales Press, 1978).
—— (ed.), *Register of Royal and Baronial Domestic Minstrels 1272–1327* (Woodbridge, Suffolk: Boydell Press, 1986).
BURKE, JOHN, *Life in the Castle in Medieval England* (New York: British Heritage Press, 1978).
CAMPBELL, LILY B., *Scenes and Machines on the English Stage During the Renaissance* (Cambridge: Cambridge University Press, 1923).
CAMPBELL, WILLIAM, *Materials for a History of the Reign of Henry VII*, 2 vols. (London: Longman and Co., 1873–7).
CARPENTER, NAN COOKE, *John Skelton* (New York: Twayne Publishers, 1968).
—— 'Music in the *Secunda Pastorum*', *Speculum*, 26 (1951), 696–700.

CAVENDISH, GEORGE, *The Life of Cardinal Wolsey* in *Two Early Tudor Lives*, ed. Richard S. Sylvester (New Haven: Yale University Press, 1962).
CAWLEY, ARTHUR C. (ed.), *The Wakefield Pageants in the Towneley Cycle* (Manchester: Manchester University Press, 1958).
CHAMBERS, ALBERT F., 'The Vicars Choral of York Minster and the Tilemakers' Corpus Christi Pageant', *Records of Early English Drama Newsletter*, 2 (1977), 2–9.
CHAMBERS, EDMUND K., *The Elizabethan Stage*, 4 vols. (Oxford: Clarendon Press, 1923).
—— *The Mediaeval Stage*, 2 vols. (Oxford: Clarendon Press, 1903).
—— *Notes on the History of the Revels Office under the Tudors* (London: A. H. Bullen, 1906).
CHAUCER, GEOFFREY, *The Works of Geoffrey Chaucer*, ed. F. W. Robinson (Boston: Houghton Mifflin, 1957).
CLOPPER, LAWRENCE M. (ed.), *Chester* (Records of Early English Drama; Toronto: University of Toronto Press, 1979).
COKAYNE, GEORGE E. (ed.), *The Complete Peerage*, 13 vols. (London: St Catherine Press, 1910–59).
COLLIER, JOHN PAYNE, *The Household Book of John, Duke of Norfolk and Thomas, Earl of Surrey* (London: Roxburghe Club, 1844).
CRAIK, THOMAS WALLACE, 'The Political Interpretation of Two Tudor Interludes: *Temperance and Humility* and *Wealth and Health*', *Review of English Studies*, NS 4 (1953), 98–108.
—— *The Tudor Interlude* (Leicester: Leicester University Press, 1958).
CRANMER, THOMAS, *The Works of Thomas Cranmer*, ed. John Edmund Cox (Parker Society xv, xvi; Cambridge: Cambridge University Press, 1844–6).
CREETH, EDMUND (ed.), *Tudor Plays: An Anthology of Early English Drama* (New York: W. W. Norton and Co., 1966).
CROW, JOHN (ed.), *Jacob and Esau* (Malone Society Reprints, 94; London: Clarendon Press, 1956).
DAVENPORT, WILLIAM A., *Fifteenth-century English Drama: The Early Moral Plays and their Literary Relations* (Cambridge: D. S. Brewer, 1982).
DAVIS, NORMAN (ed.), *Non-cycle Plays and Fragments* (Early English Text Society; London: Oxford University Press, 1970).
DAWSON, GILES E. (ed.), *Records of Plays and Players in Kent* (Malone Society Collections, 7; London: Clarendon Press, 1965).

DESSEN, ALAN C., *Shakespeare and the Late Moral Plays* (Lincoln and London: University of Nebraska Press, 1986).
DOWNEY, PETER, 'A Renaissance Correspondence Concerning Trumpet Music', *Early Music*, 9/13 (July 1981), 325–9.
DUFF, E. GORDON, PLOMER, H. R., and POLLARD, A. W. (eds.), *Hand-Lists of English Printers*, 4 vols. (London: Blades, East, and Blades, 1913).
DUTKA, JOANNA, *Music in the English Mystery Plays* (Early Drama, Art, and Music Series, 2; Kalamazoo: Medieval Institute Publications, 1980).
—— (ed.), *Proceedings of the First Colloquium* (Records of Early English Drama; Toronto: University of Toronto Press, 1979).
EBERLEIN, HAROLD D., and RICHARDSON, ALBERT EDWARD, *The English Inn Past and Present: A Review of its History and Social Life* (Philadelphia and London: J. B. Lippincott Co., 1926).
ECCLES, MARK (ed.), *The Macro Plays* (Early English Text Society, 262; London: Oxford University Press, 1969).
ELLIS, HENRY (ed.), *The New Chronicle of England and France in Two Parts; by Robert Fabyan* (London: F. C. & J. Rivington, 1811).
—— (ed.), *Original Letters Illustrative of English History*, 4 vols. (2nd series; London: Harding and Lepard, 1827).
EMMISON, FREDERICK G., *Tudor Food and Pastimes* (London: Ernest Benn Ltd., 1964).
EVANS, HERBERT A., *English Masques* (Glasgow: Blackie and Son, Ltd., n.d.).
FAIRFIELD, LESLIE P., *John Bale: Mythmaker for the English Reformation* (West Lafayette, Indiana: Purdue University Press, 1976).
FARMER, JOHN S. (ed.), *Six Anonymous Plays* (2nd series, 1906; repr. New York: Barnes and Noble, 1966).
FEUILLERAT, ALBERT, *Documents Relating to the Revels at Court in the Times of King Edward VI and Queen Mary* (Vaduz: Kraus Reprint Ltd., 1963).
FIRTH, RICHARD GREEN, 'Three Fifteenth-Century Notes', *English Language Notes*, 14 (1976), 14–17.
FITZPATRICK, HORACE, 'The Medieval Recorder', *Early Music*, 3/4 (Oct. 1975), 361–4.
FURNIVALL, FREDERICK JAMES, and POLLARD, ALFRED W. (eds.), *The Macro Plays* (Early English Text Society, 91; London: Kegan Paul, 1904).
GAGE, JOHN, 'Extracts from the Household Book of Edward Stafford, Duke of Buckingham', *Archaeologia*, 25 (1834), 311–41.

GAIRDNER, JAMES (ed.), *Letters and Papers Illustrative of the Reigns of Richard III and Henry VII*, 2 vols. (London: Longman, Green, Longman and Roberts, 1861–3).
—— *The Paston Letters*, 3 vols. (London: A. Constable and Co., Ltd., 1900).
GALLOWAY, DAVID (ed.), *Norwich 1540–1642* (Records of Early English Drama; Toronto: University of Toronto Press, 1984).
GATCH, MILTON M., 'Mysticism and Satire in the Morality of Wisdom', *Philological Quarterly*, 53 (1974), 342–62.
GEISINGER, MARION, *Plays, Players and Playwrights* (New York: Hart Publishing Co., 1971).
GIUSTINIAN, SEBASTIAN, *Four Years at the Court of Henry VIII*, trans. Rawdon Brown, 2 vols. (London: Smith, Elder and Co., 1854).
GRANSDEN, ANTONIA, *The Chronicle of Bury St. Edmunds 1212–1301* (London: Nelson Press, 1964).
GREAT BRITAIN RECORDS COMMISSION, *The Statutes of the Realm*, 11 vols. (London: Dawson of Pall Mall, 1963).
GREEN, ADWIN WIGFALL, *The Inns of Court and Early English Drama* (New Haven: Yale University Press, 1931).
GREENBLATT, STEPHEN, *Renaissance Self-Fashioning: From More to Shakespeare* (Chicago: University of Chicago Press, 1980).
GREG, WALTER WILSON, *A Bibliography of English Printed Drama to the Restoration*, 4 vols. (London: Bibliographical Soc., 1962).
—— (ed.), *The Book of Sir Thomas More* (Malone Society Reprints, 93; London: Oxford University Press, 1911).
—— (ed.), *Respublica* (Early English Text Society, OS 226; London: Oxford University Press, 1952).
GROSE, FRANCIS (comp.), 'The Earl of Northumberland's Household Book' (in vol. iv of *The Antiquarian Repertory*; London: E. Jeffery, 1809).
HALL, EDWARD, *The Vnion of the Two Noble and Illustre Famelies of Lancastre and Yorke* (London: G. Woodfall, 1809).
HAMILTON, WILLIAM D. (ed.), *A Chronicle of England During the Reigns of the Tudors by Charles Wriothesley, Windsor Herald* (London: Camden Society, NS 11 and 20, 1875–7).
HAPPE, PETER (ed.), *Tudor Interludes* (Baltimore: Penguin Books, 1972).
HARBAGE, ALFRED, *Annals of English Drama 975–1700*, 2nd edn., revised by S. Schoenbaum (Philadelphia: University of Pennsylvania Press, 1964).
HARDISON JR., OSBORNE BENNETT (ed.), *The Princeton Encyclopedia of Poetry and Poetics* (Princeton: Princeton University Press, 1990).

HARRIS, JESSE W., *John Bale: A Study in the Minor Literature of the Reformation* (Urbana: University of Illinois Press, 1940).
HARRIS, WILLIAM O., 'Wolsey and Skelton's *Magnyfycence*', *Studies in Philology*, 57 (1960), 99–122.
HARRISON, FRANK L., *Music in Medieval Britain* (New York: Frederick A. Praeger, 1958).
HARTNOLL, PHYLLIS, *A Concise History of the Theatre* (London: Thames and Hudson, 1968).
HILLEBRAND, HAROLD NEWCOMB, *The Child Actors* (New York: Russell and Russell, 1964).
HISTORICAL MANUSCRIPTS COMMISSION, *4th Report: Manuscripts of the Duke of Rutland* (London: HMSO, 1874).
HOPE, WILLIAM, 'The Last Testament and Inventory of John De Veer, Thirteenth Earl of Oxford', *Archaeologia*, 66 (1914), 275–348.
HOPPIN, RICHARD H., *Medieval Music* (New York: W. W. Norton and Co., 1978).
HORROX, ROSEMARY, 'Urban Patronage and Patrons in the Fifteenth Century' in Griffiths, Ralph A. (ed.), *Patronage: The Crown and the Provinces* (Gloucester: Alan Sutton Publishing, Ltd., 1981). 145–66.
HUDSON, ANNE (ed.), *Selections from English Wycliffite Writings* (Cambridge: Cambridge University Press, 1978).
HUGHES, PAUL L., and LARKIN, JAMES (eds.), *Tudor Royal Proclamations*, 3 vols. (New Haven: Yale University Press, 1964).
INGRAM, REGINALD, 'The Use of Music of English Miracle Plays', *Anglia*, 75 (1957), 55–76.
JACKSON, J. E., 'Wulfhall and the Seymours', *The Wiltshire Archaeological and Natural History Magazine*, 15 (1875), 140–207.
JAMES, MERVYN EVANS, *A Tudor Magnate and the Tudor State* (Borthwick Papers, 30; York, University of York Press, 1966).
JANSSEN, CAROLE A., 'The Waytes of Norwich and an Early Lord Mayor's Show', *Research Opportunities in Renaissance Drama*, 22 (1979), 57–64.
JOHNSON, SAMUEL, *Selected Writings*, ed. R. T. Davies (London: Faber and Faber, 1965).
JOHNSTON, ALEXANDRA, and ROGERSON, MARGARET, *York*, 2 vols. (Records of Early English Drama; Toronto: University of Toronto Press, 1979).
JONES, GWEN ANN, 'The Political Significance of the Play of *Albion Knight*', *Journal of English and German Philology*, 17 (1918), 267–80.

JORDAN, WILBUR KITCHENER, *Edward VI and the Threshold of Power* (Cambridge, Mass.: Harvard University Press, 1970).
—— *Edward VI: The Young King* (Cambridge, Mass.: Harvard University Press, 1968).
KAHRL, STANLEY J. (ed.), *Records of Plays and Players in Lincolnshire 1300–1585* (Malone Society Collections, 8; London: Clarendon Press, 1974).
—— *Traditions of Medieval English Drama* (London: Hutchinson Press, 1974).
KELLEY, MICHAEL R., *Flamboyant Drama: A Study of 'The Castle of Perseverance', 'Mankind', and 'Wisdom'* (Carbondale and Edwardsville: Southern Illinois University Press, 1979).
KING, EDWARD, 'Sequel to the Observations on Ancient Castles', *Archaeologia*, 6 (1782), 231–374.
KINGSFORD, CHARLES LETHBRIDGE (ed.), *Chronicles of London* (Oxford: Clarendon Press, 1905).
KIPLING, GORDON, 'The Early Tudor Disguising: New Research Opportunities', *Research Opportunities in Renaissance Drama*, 17 (1974), 3–8.
LAFONTAINE, HENRY CART DE, *The King's Musick* (1909; repr. New York: De Capo Press, 1973).
LANCASHIRE, IAN, 'The Auspices of *The World and the Child*', *Renaissance and Reformation*, 12 (1976), 96–105.
—— *A Guide to Dramatic Texts and Records of Britain: A Chronological Topography to 1558* (Toronto and Cambridge: University of Toronto Press and Cambridge University Press, 1983).
—— 'Orders for Twelfth Day and Night *circa* 1515 in the Second Northumberland Household Book', *English Literary Renaissance*, 10 (Winter 1980), 7–45.
—— 'Patrons and the English Moral Play', address given at the Fifth International Congress on Medieval Studies, Kalamazoo, Mich., 1 May 1980.
—— (ed.), *Two Tudor Interludes: 'The Interlude of Youth', 'Hick Scorner'* (Baltimore: Johns Hopkins University Press, 1980).
LASOCKI, DAVID, 'Professional Recorder Playing in England 1500–1740', *Early Music*, 10/1 (Jan. 1982) 23–8; 10/2 (Apr. 1982), 183–91.
LEE, SYDNEY, and STEPHEN, LESLIE (eds.), *The Dictionary of National Biography*, 66 vols. (New York: Macmillan and Co. 1885–1901).
LELAND, JOHN, *De Rebvs Britannicis Collectanea*, 4 vols. (London: J. Richardson, 1770).
LEMON, ROBERT (ed.), *Calendar of State Papers, Domestic Series*,

of the Reigns of Edward VI, Mary, and Elizabeth 1547–1580 (London: Public Record Office, 1856).
LENNAM, TREVOR, *Sebastian Westcott, the Children of Paul's, and 'The Marriage of Wit and Science'* (Toronto: University of Toronto Press, 1975).
LONG, JOHN H. (ed.), *Music in English Renaissance Drama* (Lexington: University of Kentucky Press, 1968).
LUMIANSKY, ROBERT MAYER, and MILLS, DAVID, *The Chester Mystery Cycle* (Early English Text Society, 2nd Ser., 3, Supplementary; London: Oxford University Press, 1974).
LUPTON, JOSEPH HIRST, *A Life of John Colet, D.D. Dean of St. Paul's and Founder of St. Paul's School* (London: G. Bell and Sons, 1909).
LYDGATE, JOHN, *The Minor Poems of John Lydgate Part II*, ed. Henry N. MacCracken (Early English Text Society, OS 192, 1934; repr. London: Oxford University Press, 1961).
LYTE, HENRY MAXWELL (ed.), *The Manuscripts of his Grace the Duke of Rutland, K. G. Preserved at Belvoir Castle* (vol. iv of the *Reports of the Historical Manuscripts Commission*; London: HMSO, 1905).
MCFARLANE, KENNETH BRUCE, *The Nobility of Later Medieval England* (London: Clarendon Press, 1973).
MACKIE, JOHN DUNCAN, *The Earlier Tudors 1485–1558* (Oxford: Clarendon Press, 1957).
MALORY, THOMAS, *The Works of Thomas Malory*, 2nd. edn., 3 vols., ed. Eugene Vinaver (Oxford: Clarendon Press, 1967).
MANLY, JOHN MATTHEWS (ed.), *Specimens of the Pre-Shakespearean Drama* (vol. i; New York: Ginn and Co., 1897).
MEDWALL, HENRY, *The Plays of Henry Medwall*, ed. Alan H. Nelson (Cambridge: D. S Brewer, 1980).
—— *The Plays of Henry Medwall: A Critical Edition*, ed. M. Moeslein (New York and London: Garland Publishing, Inc., 1981).
MILL, ANNA J., *Mediaeval Plays in Scotland* (St Andrews University Publications, 24, 1927; repr. New York: B. Blom, 1969).
MOLINS, MARQUÉS DE, *Chronicle of King Henry VIII of England*, trans. M. A. S. Hume (London: G. Bell and Sons, 1889).
MONTAGU, GWEN and JEREMY, 'Beverley Minster Reconsidered', *Early Music*, 6/3 (July 1978), 401–15.
MOORE, SAMUEL, 'General Aspects of Literary Patronage in the Middle Ages', *The Library*, 3rd series, 4 (1913), 369–92.
MORDEN, ROBERT (ed.), *The County Maps from William Camden's 'Brittania', 1695* (London, 1695; repr. Devon: David and Charles Reprints, 1972).

MORE, SIR THOMAS, *The History of Richard III* (vol. ii of *The Complete Works of Sir Thomas More*, ed. Richard Sylvester; New Haven: Yale University Press, 1963).
MORRIS, RICHARD (ed.), *Specimens of Early English*, 2 vols. (Oxford: Clarendon Press, 1882).
MOTTER, T. H. VAIL, *The School Drama in England* (London: Longmans, Green and Co., 1929).
MURRAY, JOHN TUCKER, *English Dramatic Companies 1558–1642*, 2 vols. (New York: Houghton Mifflin, 1910).
MYERS, ALEC REGINALD, *The Household Book of Edward IV: The Black Book and the Ordinance of 1478* (Manchester: Manchester University Press, 1959).
—— 'The Household of Queen Margaret of Anjou 1452–53', *Bulletin of the John Rylands Library*, 40 (1957–8), 79–113; 391–431.
NAGLER, ALOIS MARIA, *The Medieval Religious Stage* (New Haven: Yale University Press, 1976).
NEALE, JOHN ERNEST, *Queen Elizabeth I* (New York: Harcourt Brace Jovanovich, 1934).
NELSON, WILLIAM (ed.), *A Fifteenth-Century School Book, from a Manuscript in the British Museum (Ms. Arundel 249)* (Oxford: Clarendon Press, 1956).
—— 'Skelton's Quarrel with Wolsey', *Publications of the Modern Language Association*, 51 (1936), 377–98.
NICHOLAS, NICHOLAS H. (ed.), *Privy Purse Expenses of Elizabeth of York: Wardrobe Accounts of Edward IV* (London: William Pickering, 1830).
NICHOLS, JOHN G. (ed.), *The Chronicle of Calais* (London: Camden Society, 1846).
—— *Illustrations of the Manners and Expenses of Antient Times in England, in the Fifteenth, Sixteenth, and Seventeenth Centuries* (London: J. Nichols, 1797: repr. New York: AMS Press, 1973).
—— (ed.), *Literary Remains of King Edward the Sixth*, 2 vols. (London: Roxburghe Club, 1857).
NICOLL, ALLARDYCE, *The Development of the Theatre*, 5th edn. (New York: Harcourt, Brace, World, 1966).
NOTT, GEORGE F. (ed.), *The Works of Henry Howard, Earl of Surrey and of Thomas Wyatt the Elder*, 2 vols. (London: T. Bensley, 1815).
OVEREND, G. H., 'On the Dispute between George Maller, Glazier, and Trainer of Players to Henry VIII, and Thomas Arthur, Tailor, his Pupil', *Transactions of the New Shakespeare Society*, 1st Ser., no. 7, pt. iii (1877–9), 425–9.
OWEN, JOHN (comp.), *Britannia Depicta: or, Ogilby Improved:*

Being an Actual Survey of All the Direct and Principal Cross Roads of England and Wales (London: Carington Bowles, 1764).

PAGE, CHRISTOPHER, 'The Fifteenth-century Lute: New and Neglected Sources', *Early Music*, 9/1 (Jan. 1981), 11–21.

PEARSALL, DEREK, *John Lydgate* (Charlottesville: University of Virginia Press, 1970).

POLLARD, ALBERT FREDERICK, *England Under Protector Somerset* (New York: Russell and Russell, 1966).

—— (ed.), *The Reign of Henry VII from Contemporary Sources* (University of London Historical Series, 1; London: University of London, 1913).

POLLARD, ALFRED W. (ed.), *An English Garner: Fifteenth-Century Prose and Verse* (Westminster: Archibald Constable and Co. Ltd., 1903).

POLLET, MAURICE, *John Skelton*, trans. John Warrington (London: Dent and Sons, 1971).

POTTER, ROBERT, *The English Morality Play: Origins, History, and Influence of a Dramatic Tradition* (Boston: Routledge and Kegan Paul, 1975).

PRICE, DAVID C., *Patrons and Musicians of the English Renaissance* (Cambridge: Cambridge University Press, 1981).

RASTALL, RICHARD, 'Minstrels and Minstrelsy in Household Account Books', in *Proceedings of the First Colloquium*, ed. JoAnna Dutka (Records of Early English Drama; Toronto: Toronto University Press, 1979), 3–25.

RASTELL, JOHN, *Three Rastell Plays*, ed. Richard Axton (Cambridge: D. S. Brewer, 1979).

RAWCLIFFE, CAROLE, *The Staffords, Earls of Stafford and Dukes of Buckingham* (Cambridge: Cambridge University Press, 1978).

REED, ARTHUR WILLIAM, *Early Tudor Drama* (London: Methuen and Co. Ltd., 1926).

REMNANT, MARY, *Musical Instruments of the West* (New York: St Martin's Press, 1978).

RIGHTER, ANNE, *Shakespeare and the Idea of the Play* (London: Chatto and Windus, 1962).

ROPER, WILLIAM, *The Life of Sir Thomas Moore, Knighte*, ed. Elsie Vaughn Hitchcock (Early English Text Society, OS 197; London: Oxford University Press, 1935).

ROSE, MARTIAL (ed.), *The Wakefield Mystery Plays* (New York: W. W. Norton and Co. Inc., 1961).

ROSSITER, ARTHUR P., *English Drama from Early Times to the Elizabethans* (London, 1950; repr. New York: Barnes and Noble, 1967).

RUSSELL, JOYCELYNE GLEDHILL, *The Field of Cloth of Gold: Men and Manners in 1520* (London: Routledge and Kegan Paul, 1969).

SALGADO, GAMINI (ed.), *Three Jacobean Tragedies* (Harmondsworth: Penguin Books, 1965).

SAUNDERS, NORMAN, SOUTHERN, RICHARD, CRAIK, THOMAS WALLACE, and POTTER, LOIS (eds.), *The Revels History of Drama in English: Volume II 1500–1576* (New York: Methuen, 1980).

SELFRIDGE-FIELD, ELEANOR, 'Venetian Instrumentalists in England: A Bassano Chronicle (1538–1660)', *Studii Musicali*, 8 (1979), 173–221.

SERLIO, SEBASTIANO, *Architettura* in Bernard Hewitt (ed.), *The Renaissance Stage: Documents of Serlio, Sabbattini, and Furtenbach* (Coral Gables: University of Miami Press, 1958).

SHAKESPEARE, WILLIAM, *Complete Works*, ed. Alfred Harbage (Baltimore: Penguin Books, 1969).

SHAPIRO, MICHAEL, *Children of the Revels: The Boy Companies of Shakespeare's Time and their Plays* (New York: Columbia University Press, 1977).

SIMMS, R. (comp.), *Bibliotheca Staffordiensis* (Lichfield: A. C. Lomax, 1894).

SKELTON, JOHN, *Magnificence*, ed. Paula Neuss (Baltimore: Johns Hopkins University Press, 1980).

—— *Magnyfycence*, ed. Robert Lee Ramsey (Early English Text Society, 98; London: Oxford University Press, 1908).

SMITH, LUCY Toulmin (ed.), *York Plays* (New York: Russell and Russell, 1885).

SMOLDEN, WILLIAM L., *The Music of the Medieval Church Dramas* (Oxford: Clarendon Press, 1980).

SNEYD, CHARLOTTE AUGUSTA (tr. and ed.), *A Relation or rather A True Account of the Island of England* (Camden Society, 37; London: J. B. Nichols and Son, 1847).

SOMERSET, J. A. B. (ed.), *Four Tudor Interludes* (London: University of London, The Athlone Press, 1974).

SOUTHERN, RICHARD, *The Staging of Plays before Shakespeare* (London: Faber and Faber, 1973).

STEVENS, JOHN, *Music and Poetry in the Early Tudor Court* (London: Methuen, 1961).

STONE, LAWRENCE, *The Crisis of the Aristocracy, 1558–1641* (Oxford: Clarendon Press, 1965).

STOPES, CHARLOTTE C., *Shakespeare's Environment*, 2nd edn. (London: G. Bell and Sons, 1918).

—— *William Hunnis and the Revels of the Chapel Royal*, vol. 29 of

Materialien zur Kunde des alteren englischen Dramas, ed. W. Bang (Louvain: A. Uystpruyst, 1910).

STRATMAN, CARL J. (ed.), *Bibliography of Medieval Drama*, vol. i, 2nd edn. (New York: Frederick Ungar Publishing Co., 1972).

STREITBERGER, W. R., 'Renaissance Revels Documents, 1485–1642', *Research Opportunities in Renaissance Drama*, 21 (1978), 11–16.

TAYLOR, JEROME, and NELSON, ALAN H. (eds.), *Medieval English Drama* (Chicago: University of Chicago Press, 1972).

THOMAS, ARTHUR HERMANN, and THORNLEY, ISOBEL DOROTHY (eds.), *The Great Chronicle of London* (London: G. W. Jones, 1938).

TIPPING, H. AVRAY, *English Homes*, 4 vols. (New York: Charles Scribner, 1937).

TUCKER, MELVIN J., 'Household Accounts 1490–91 of John de Vere, Earl of Oxford', *English History Review*, 75 (1960), 468–74.

TURNBULL, WILLIAM (ed.), *Compota Domestica: familiarum de Buckingham et d'Angoulême* (Edinburgh: Abbotsford Club, 1836).

TYLER, JAMES, 'The Renaissance Guitar 1500–1650', *Early Music*, 3/4 (Oct. 1975), 341–7.

UDALL, NICHOLAS, *Royster Doyster*, in Edmund Creeth (ed.), *Tudor Plays: An Anthology of Early English Drama* (New York: W. W. Norton and Co., 1966).

VAN BRUN JONES, PAUL, *The Household of a Tudor Nobleman* (Urbana: University of Illinois Press, 1918).

WALLACE, CHARLES W., *Children of the Chapel at Blackfriars* (Lincoln: University of Nebraska Press, 1908).

—— *The Evolution of Drama up to Shakespeare* (1912; repr. Port Washington, NY: Kennikat Press, Inc., 1968).

WARD, JOHN M., 'The maner of dauncying', *Early Music*, 4/2 (Apr. 1976), 127–42.

WARTON, THOMAS, *History of English Poetry from the Twelfth Century to the Close of the Sixteenth Century*, ed. W. Carew Hazlitt, 4 vols. (London: Reeves and Turner, 1871).

WATERHOUSE, OSBORNE (ed.), *The Non-Cycle Mystery Plays* (Early English Text Society, 104; London: 1909.

WELSFORD, ENID, *The Court Masque* (New York: Russell and Russell, 1962).

WICKHAM, GLYNNE, *Early English Stages 1300–1660*, 3 vols. (London: Routledge and Kegan Paul, 159–81).

—— *English Moral Interludes* (London: J. M. Dent and Sons, Ltd., 1976).

—— *Shakespeare's Dramatic Heritage: Collected Studies in Medieval, Tudor and Shakespearean Drama* (London: Routledge and Kegan Paul, 1969).
WILKINSON, FREDERICK, *The Castles of England* (London: George Philip, 1973).
WILLIAMS, NEVILLE, *Thomas Howard, Fourth Duke of Norfolk* (London: Barrie and Rockliff, 1964).
WILSON, FRANK P., *The English Drama 1485–1642* (Oxford: Clarendon Press, 1969).
WITHINGTON, ROBERT, *English Pageantry*, 2 vols. (1918; repr. New York: B. Blom, Inc., 1963).
—— 'Thre Brefes to a Long: Technical musical Terms in the *Secunda Pastorum*', *Modern Language Notes*, 58 (Feb. 1943), 115–16.
WOLFFE, BERTRAM, *Henry VI* (London: Methuen, 1981).
WOOD, MARGARET, *The English Medieval House* (London: Phoenix House, 1965).
WOODFILL, WALTER L., *Musicians in English Society* (Princeton: Princeton University Press, 1953).

Index

Abbot of Misrule 47
Agecroft Hall 23–4
Albion Knight 196
aristocracy
 old v. new 166–76, 180–99
 in transition 11–12, 66, 176
 see also patrons; individual noblemen
Armin, Robert
 Fool Upon Fool 133–4
Arthur, Prince
 wedding pageants 18, 38–9
Arthur, Thomas (player) 149–50
audience 3, 109, 116, 133–4, 152, 155–8, 161, 164, 167–8, 198, 200–2, 205–6

Bale, John 110, 117–19
 Anglorum Heliades 118–19
 Christ's Temptation in the Wilderness 118
 Contra Corruptores Verbi Dei 118
 De Sectis Papisticis 118
 De Traditionibus Papistorum 118
 De Traditione Thomae Becketi 118
 God's Promises 103, 118
 King Johan 103, 119, 168, 172, 175, 179–80, 196–7
 Super Vtrogue Regis Coniugio 118
 Three Laws 119
Bassano family (recorder consort) 71, 87–8
Battle betwixt the Spirit, the Soul and the flesh 110
Beaufort, Margaret 120–2, 128
Bernard (fool) 91
Birch, George (player) 139
Blackfriars, Children of 16 n.
Boleyn, Anne 56, 75–6, 117
The Book of Sir Thomas More 111–12, 131, 133
Boy Bishop 17, 47, 50 n.
Brabant, John de (vielle player) 81
Brandon, Charles (Duke of Suffolk) 110, 115, 220–1
 players 141–2, 216
Buck, John (playwright) 100

Callisto and Melebea 104, 183–4
carnival 158, 174
The Castle of Perseverance 101, 154, 160, 189
ceremony, as structural motif 177–80
Chaloner, Sir Thomas 110
Chapel 4, 13–62, 202
 advantages over players 17–18
 Christmas performances 27–8, 41, 50 n.
 in Civic Pageantry 32–4
 concerts 31, 73
 in Corpus Christi cycles 30
 in disguisings 32–48, 57
 duties 4, 16 n.
 ecclesiastical opposition to 32
 facilities 18–27
 Gentlemen 41–3
 and household 4, 14, 14 n., 15–27, 31–2, 62
 performance style 16–18, 38, 44, 46–7, 53–4, 62
 plays 28, 42–3, 49–62, 73
 playwrights in 18
 privileges 17 n.
 protection of 32, 62
 rewards 41–3
 size of 15–17
 status 31–2, 62
 training 17–18, 62
Charles V (Holy Roman Emperor) 45
Cheney, Sir Thomas 143, 216
Civic pageantry
 and Chapel 32–4
 music in 71–2
Clinton, Lord
 and boys of Maxstoke Priory 15
Colet, John (Dean of St. Paul's) 32
Colet, John (harper) 77
Cornish, William (Sr.; Gentleman of Chapel Royal)
 Christmas rewards 42
 disguisings of 37–41, 117
 Troilus and Pandar 41
 wedding pageants for Prince Arthur 18, 38–9

Cornish, William (Jr.; Gentleman of Chapel Royal)
  disguisings 44–5
Corpus Christi cycles
  and household Chapels 30
  music in 71–2, 101
  royal audience 134
costumes
  as character indicants 159–61, 167–8
  for minstrels 72–4, 99–100
  in plays 36, 53, 168
  regulation 138
  source and value 138–40
Coton, John de (Lombard minstrel) 91
Cowper, James de (King of Heralds and harper) 97
Cranmer, Archbishop 119
Cressy, John de (minstrel) 97
Cromwell, Thomas
  and Bale 110, 118–19

de Vere, see Vere
disguising
  for Ambassadors from Spain 98–9
  Betrothal of Princess Mary 44
  for birth of Henry VIII's son (1511) 73
  Chapel in 32–48
  critical neglect 4
  Dangerous Fortress 40, 99
  defined 33 n.
  Friendship, Prudence and Might 45
  Golldyn Arber in the Archeyrd of Plesyer 39–40, 98
  at Howard's 47
  Knights of the Mount of Love 39
  minstrels in 5, 39
  in modern theatre 201–2
  at the Pastons's 48
  Paul's Boys in 15 n.
  Pavillion in the Place Perilous 40, 99, 102
  popularity of 48
  for Queen Margaret 48
  in Rastell's Four Elements 57, 102
  The Rich Mount 99
  Riches and Love 43
  St George 37–8
  at Staffords 48
  Twelfth Night at Percys 94–7
  de Vere's Chapel at Royal Court 47
  see also Cornish, Lydgate, Chapel, minstrels

Dorset, Marquis of 110
Dudley, John (Lord Lisle) 121
Dudley, Robert (Lord Leicester) 209
Dunstable, choir boys's play 110

Edward I
  minstrels 65, 75, 81, 97
Edward IV
  Chapel 15, 31
  minstrels 65–7, 83, 85, 88–9
  players 124, 138
Edward VI
  boys' companies 58
  players 144, 217–18
Elizabeth I 156, 208–9
Elizabeth of York 83
English, John (player) 124, 127, 145
Everyman 154, 178
Exeter, Duke of 123

Fartere, Roland le (minstrel) 91
Ferrers, Sir Humphrey 134
Field of the Cloth of Gold 177

Gammer Gurton's Needle 158
Gentleness and Nobility 175, 183–4
Gibson, Richard 126–7
Godly Queen Hester 22, 55, 122, 168, 171–2, 193–5
Grantham, choristers of 46

Haddon House (seat of Earl of Rutland) 23–6
Hall, Anthony (player) 127
hierarchy, as structural motif 174–7, 203
Henry V
  1415 Pageant 33
Henry VI
  Coronation Pageants 33
  Mumming at Windsor 35–7
  players 41, 123
  progress (1470) 169
Henry VII
  Chapel 31, 41–3
  disguising 43 n.
  minstrels 65–6, 72, 83–4
  players 38, 41, 124–6
Henry VIII
  Chapel 16
  disguisings 43, 57
  minstrels 66, 75, 83–4
  players 144, 218–19

and Skelton 5
Hert, Walter (minstrel) 68
Heywood, John (virginals player) 97
  and Chapel 18
  The Four PP 117, 158, 175, 197–8
  Johan Johan 117, 158, 197–8
  and More 121
  The Pardoner and the Friar 117, 197–8
  The Play of Love 117
  The Play of the Weather 22, 56 n., 117, 158, 167–8, 175, 178, 197–8
  Witty and Witless 117, 197–8
Hick Scorner 49, 115, 122
Horestes 102
Household, Great
  accounts 7
  administration of performers 48, 128–34
  defined 9–10
  personnel 10 and n.
  size of 10
  see also Chapel, minstrels, players, patrons
Household Revels
  as propaganda 11–12
  in Shakespeare 209
  style 3–4, 92–3, 174, 200, 203–8
  see also disguising, Chapel, minstrels, players
Howard, Henry (Earl of Surrey) 226
Howard, John (First Duke of Norfolk) 221–2
Howard, Thomas (Second Duke of Norfolk) 222–4
  Chapel 14, 16, 27–28
  household 9–10
  minstrels 66, 77
  plays 122, 142, 187
  revels 47
  singers 80–1
Howard, Thomas (Third Duke of Norfolk) 216, 224
Howard, Thomas (Fourth Duke of Norfolk) 216–224
Hunnis, William 18

Interludes 5–6
  auspices 153–4
  defined 139
  Henry VII's players 38
  Henry VIII's Chapel 73
  minstrels in 100–7

  structure 6, 170–80
  themes 6
  see also plays
The Interlude of Youth 103, 115, 122, 162, 173, 178, 190
Isabella
  minstrel 67–8

Jack Juggler 158
Jacob and Esau 183–5
James IV (of Scotland) 127–8
Johnson, Samuel 114
Jones, Inigo 2

Katherine (of Aragon)
  wedding pageants 39
  minstrels 83–4
Kent, Earl of 115

Lisle, Lady Honor 110, 134
Lollards 32
London, Sir John de (music teacher) 67
Lovell, Sir Thomas
  Chapel 14–15
Lusty Juventus 190–2
Lydgate, John
  Coronation of Henry VI 33–4
  Henry V's Return from Agincourt 33
  Mumming at Eltham 35
  Mumming at Hertford 33, 35 n., 158, 175
  Mumming at Windsor 35–7

maintenance, as structural motif 170–4, 203
Makejoy, Matilda (minstrel) 91
Mallor, George (player) 127, 139, 149–50
Mankinde 54–5, 103, 154
Manners, Henry (Second Earl of Rutland) 229
Manners, Thomas (First Earl of Rutland) 46, 228
  Chapel 15
  Haddon House chapel 23–6
Manners, Lady Frances 85
Margaret (of Anjou) 48
Margaret, Princess
  wedding progress 127–8, 145, 160 n.
The Market of Mischief 110
The Marriage of Wit and Wisdom 131
Martinet (minstrel) 75

Mary (Princess and Queen)
  boys' companies 58
  in disguising 43–4
  Wealth and Health 115
  Respublica 158
mask (masque), *see* disguising
Maxstoke Priory, boys of 15
Mechelson, John (Gentleman of de Vere's Chapel) 16 n.
Medwall, Henry
  Fulgens and Lucrece 56, 102, 104, 108–9, 118, 122, 158, 165, 174–5, 177–8, 180, 182
  and More 122
  and Cardinal Morton 117–18
  Nature 56–7, 118, 122, 159, 161–2, 171, 178
Memo, Dionisius (organist) 75–81
Miller, Jack (fool) 133–4
Milly, William de (singer) 79
minstrels 63–107
  consorts 81–94
  dancers 98–9
  defined 63–5
  in disguisings 39, 73–4, 94–100
  duties and privileges 84–6
  function in Household 4–5, 63–8, 75–6, 80, 84–92, 214–15, 202
  harpers 77–8, 213
  heraldic 64–74
  in interludes 52–4, 100–7
  itinerant v. resident 64, 81–94
  payments to 89–92, 214–15
  singers 79–80
  size of troupes 83–4
  soloists 74–81, 213–15
  status 75–6, 80, 86–8
  in tournaments 72–3
  training 67–70, 77–9
  virginals 214
More, Sir Thomas, 1, 112, 121–2, 169, 173, 183
morris dance 95–6
Morton, John, Archbishop
  and Medwall 56, 108, 117, 161, 167, 182
  patronage 32
mummings
  defined 33 n.
  Lydgate 33–7
  see also disguising
music
  ceremonial 4–5
  dance 74, 96
  heraldic 64–74
  in interludes 36, 49, 53, 101–7
  solo 74–81
  songs 79–80
  see also minstrels

Naunton, Hugh de (harper) 86
Nevill, George (Lord Abergavenny) 143, 217

Old Custome 121
Opiciis, Benet de (organist) 75, 79

Parr, Katherine 83
Pastons 48
patrons
  function of 2–3, 11, 61–2, 66, 114–15, 153, 205
  modern 201
  motivation 109–10, 122, 134–40, 150–1, 207–8
  and propaganda 2, 118–19, 137, 140, 151, 167, 169, 180–99, 207–8
  relationship to retained entertainers 75–6, 134
  source of playtexts 112–13, 120–2
Paul's Boys
  Christmas plays 49
  perform for households 15, 46, 57
  in *Wit and Science* 104–7
Percy
  Eleanor (Duchess of Buckingham) Household size 11
  Henry (Fourth Earl of Northumberland) 120, 229–30
  Henry Algernon (Fifth Earl of Northumberland) 230–1; Chapel 14–15, 18 n., 28; disguisings 94–7; plays 28, 115; Household books 9; minstrels 66, 83–4, 91–3; Princess Margaret's wedding progress 160 n.; players 112, 124–7; and Skelton 119–20; Twelfth Night revels 31, 46–7, 93–7, 177; Wressle (seat) 18–22, 162
  Henry Percy (Sixth Earl of Northumberland) 162, 231–2
Peres (Percy almoner and playwright) 18, 30, 119

Petre, Sir William
 and Paul's Boys 15, 46
Piero, Zuan (luter) 75
Pilke, Elena and Richard (minstrels) 84
Play of Saint Catherine 110
Play of Self-Love 110
plays 152–99
 Chapel 49–62
 characterization 154–69
 heraldic music in 71–2
 ideology 154–6, 169, 180–99, 207–8
 legislation controlling 116, 136
 nativity 49
 as propaganda 118–19, 121, 137, 154, 203
 reflections of social structure 155–6
 scripts 112–16
 structure 170–80, 203
 by waits of Norwich 100
 see also interlude; individual titles
players 5, 108–51
 alternate occupations 126–7
 duties and privileges 135
 and household 45, 48, 109–10, 123–7, 132, 202–3
 ideology 137, 167
 and *Mankinde* 55
 patronage, need for 134–40, 150
 payments to 123, 132
 regulation of 135–6
 repertoire 110–14
 size of troupe 125–6, 210–12
 style 112, 133–4
 touring 109–10, 124, 140–51, 208, 216–19
playwrights 115–22
 see also individual authors
political allegory 2, 45, 55, 114–15, 156, 193
Pride of Life 168, 173
printers 113, 121–2

Rastell, John 118
 lawsuit over costumes 138–40
 and More 121
 The Nature of the Four Elements 57, 102–3, 190–2
 printing 122
Redford, John
 and Chapel 18, 57
 Wit and Science 104–6, 171, 190–1

Rex Diabole 110
Richard II 134
Richard III 124–6
Ruckshaw, William (Percy chaplain) 120

St Nicholas 47, 51 n.
Sautreour, William Le (psaltery player) 81
school plays 5, 13–15, 18, 28, 49, 52, 57–8, 102–4, 106, 114–15, 117, 121
Scrope, Henry
 chapel furnishings 27 n.
Secunda Pastorum 49–52, 173
Sergeant, John (Gentleman of de Vere's Chapel) 16 n.
Serlio
 Architettura, 2
Seymour, Edward (Duke of Somerset and Lord Protector) 15, 46, 143, 217, 232–4
Seymour, Thomas (Lord Admiral) 143, 217, 234–5
Shakespeare, William
 All's Well that Ends Well 167
 Hamlet 109, 129–31, 133
 Henry IV Pt. I, 167
 Henry V 156
 household revels in 209
 King Lear 156
 A Midsummer Night's Dream 109, 112, 130–1, 133, 158
 Richard II 156, 209
 The Taming of the Shrew 130–1, 133, 152
Skelton, John 117–18
 and Henry VIII 5
 Magnificence 103, 120, 163, 171, 174, 187–90
 patrons of 119–21
Smeaton, Mark (luter) 75–6
Smithhills Hall 23–4
Stafford, Edward (Third Duke of Buckingham), 237–8
 Chapel 14
 Field of the Cloth of Gold 177
 household 9, 11
 minstrels 83, 89
Stafford, Henry (Second Duke of Buckingham) 236–7
Stafford, Humphrey (First Duke of Buckingham) 48, 235–6

tournaments 45, 48, 72–3
Troilus and Pandar 41

Udall, Nicholas
  and Chapel 18, 57
  Rafe Roister Doister 102, 104, 117,
    158, 168, 174, 180
  Respublica 117, 158, 168, 172, 175,
    178–9, 180, 185–6, 194–6
  Thersites 117

Vere, John de (Thirteenth Earl of
  Oxford) 238–9
Vere, John de (Fourteenth Earl of
  Oxford) 239–40
  and Bale 118–19
  Chapel 14, 16, 47
  household book 9
  minstrels 83–4
  players 111, 137
Vere, John de (Fifteenth Earl of Oxford)
  240–1
Vere, John de (Sixteenth Earl of
  Oxford) 241
Veritas Filia Temporis 100
*The vniust suprimacie of the bisshop of
  rome* 121

waits 53, 64–5 n., 83–4, 100–1
Walton, Henry 138–40
Wastell, William (harper) 77
Wealth and Health 115
Wentworth, Lord 118
Wiltshire, Earl of 122
Wisdom Who is Christ 52–4, 102,
  168
Wolsey, Thomas Cardinal
  disguising 74, 122
  Field of the Cloth of Gold 177
  and *Magnificence* 163, 187
  patronage 32
  and Percy's Chapel books 18 n.
Woodlands Manor 23–4
Woodstock, Thomas of
  chapel furnishings 27 n.
*World and the Child (Mundus et
  Infans)* 49, 115, 122, 162, 172,
  180, 190–1
Wressle, seat of Northumberland
  rooms 18–23

Young, John (player) 127, 145

Zacheus 110